THE VANISHING OF
KATHERINE SULLIVAN

THE VANISHING OF
KATHERINE SULLIVAN

Christina Weaver

Library of Congress Control Number: 2022914708

HARDBACK: 978-1-957575-95-7
PAPERBACK: 978-1-957575-94-0
EBOOK: 978-1-957575-96-4

Ordering Information:

For orders and inquiries, please contact:
1-888-404-1388
www.goldtouchpress.com
book.orders@goldtouchpress.com

Printed in the United States of America

CONTENTS

Sullivan Family Tree
Millerton, West Virginia

Samuel Orin Sullivan married Katherine Mae Collins
Martha May Sullivan married David Kincaid
Craig
Sara
Katrina
Robert

Emma Kate married Thomas Conrad
Sandra
Caroline
Stephen
Gregory
Richard

Lucas Samuel –Not married
Henry Orin married Francis Smyth-Danner –no children
Joseph Daniel married Betty McCabe
Matthew Joseph
Kathy Beth
Samuel Orin

CHAPTER 1

COLUMBUS, OH

July 2000

"I'M ON MY WAY, UNCLE LUCAS. HANG IN THERE." Matt swiped his keys off the hall table and slammed the door behind him. He spoke into his flip phone as he jogged to his car. "Thank goodness you called nine-one-one. I'm sure they're on their way. Do you hear any sirens?"

Uncle Lucas' voice whispered, "No."

"I'll be there in twenty minutes. I wish you would've called me when you first felt bad."

"I have these all the time. I'd be calling you every day." Even in pain, his uncle's dry humor made Matt smile.

"Don't talk, Uncle. Just keep the phone close, and tell me when you hear sirens."

He heard a grunt of assent from his uncle. "Are you almost here?"

"I'm pulling out of my driveway now. I have to put you on speaker because I need both hands to drive."

"Okay." Uncle Lucas's voice sounded hollow on the speaker.

Matt continued to talk to his uncle while his car barreled down the streets as fast as he could. Part of him hoped to see blue lights behind him as he might be able to negotiate an escort. Right now, he felt grateful the streets were clear.

He took every shortcut he knew to the rural Columbus, Ohio area. He made the trip twice a month to check on Uncle Lucas but called the older man at least once a week. They both knew Matt called to check upon him, and the older man accepted the attention. Matt suspected his uncle tried to disguise his loneliness. The rest of his family believed him to be more than a little unhinged.

Matt gripped the steering wheel of the car as he turned another corner. The wheels squealed in protest as the vehicle slid across the road.

His thoughts about his uncle's condition wandered to his father and mother's role with Uncle Lucas.

Betty, his mother, tolerated Uncle Lucas at family functions. He hardly ever bathed, and his clothes rarely washed. For Lucas to be allowed in her home, Joseph had to gather what clothes he could find and bring them to their house along with Uncle Lucas. The moment the two walked in the door, Betty pointed to the washer with one finger and upstairs with the other. Uncle Lucas grumbled the whole way up the stairs to the bathroom. Not too much of a grumble. As a boy, he understood not wanting to take a bath. Uncle Lucas seemed to do the chore with a wink at his young nephew.

As Matt turned the car onto the two-lane road that led to his uncle's farm, the wail of a siren sounded in the distance. Down the road, he could see police and emergency vehicles lining the sides of the road, lights flashing. Matt slowed the car to a stop as an officer waved to him.

"Sir, you're not allowed in here." The officer leaned down to speak through the window.

"I'm Lucas's nephew, Matt Sullivan." He inched the car forward.

The officer pressed a button on the radio at his shoulder and spoke into it before nodding. "Go on through." He pointed ahead.

Matt continued down the road, minding the ruts and emergency vehicles.

He pulled the car to a stop in the grass.

An officer met him as he approached the porch and pointed to the back of the house. "Sir, your uncle is stable. The sergeant is right around back and would like a word."

Matt jumped the three steps to the back porch deck and noticed fallen boxes near the door. The mass of newspapers and magazines spewed into the yard in an avalanche of old papers. At the entrance, two men in uniform blocked his way.

"You're Matthew Sullivan, Mister Lucas Sullivan's nephew? He called you?" one of the officers asked. Matt nodded.

The other spoke up, his mouth curled in disgust as he surveyed the backyard rather than looking at Matt. "Your uncle's fine." The officer continued, "They're taking him to the hospital for observation. Go on in and talk to him. He's been asking for you. Then we need to talk." They parted to let him inside.

The screen door banged shut behind him, and Matt walked down the familiar, box-lined hall from the kitchen to the room where his uncle slept, watched TV, and ate.

The pale, gray-haired man lay strapped to a gurney with an oxygen mask over his nose. His watery eyes found Matt's, and he smiled. "Matt."

"Don't talk, Uncle. They're taking you to the hospital to check you out." Matt smiled back, feeling the strain on his muscles.

Uncle Lucas reached out and grabbed Matt's arm. The grip was stronger than Matt expected as his uncle pulled him in close. "Don't let them do anything to my stuff. It's mine, and I need it."

Matt frowned. "What do you mean?"

Uncle Lucas's eyes darted toward the hall with a panicked expression. "Just don't let them do anything to my stuff," he repeated.

Matt nodded and followed as the EMTs wheeled his uncle down the hallway, knocking over more stacks of papers lining the hall. After they'd left, the two officers outside motioned for him to come back to the porch.

Matt winced at the rotted stacks of lumber, logs, and machinery in varying stages of decay. Outdoor furniture and appliances in several shades of rust lay in piles and what he knew Lucas believed to be neat rows. Paths through the heaps eventually led to the barn. Matt met the two men at the bottom of the porch steps, blind to the shock of the mess after years of familiarity.

"Mister Sullivan, I'm Inspector Griffin." He introduced himself and shook Matt's hand. "Did you know we served your uncle with a final clean-up order two weeks ago?"

Matt frowned and rubbed his mustache, then dragged his fingers down to his neatly trimmed beard. "No, my uncle never told me. He's a bit eccentric, as you have no doubt noticed."

The inspector grimaced in a way Matt suspected was intended to be a smile, pulled a folded sheaf of papers out of his pocket, and handed them to Matt.

"This is the order to clean up the property we served last year. It's a fire hazard. I didn't see any rodent infestation, but I'm sure they're here.

The neighbor sold his acreage to a developer. A friendly neighbor next door doesn't want to see this mess." Inspector Griffin shook his head again as he peered around Matt and into the house. "You have two weeks to clean this up." He waved his hand, including the yard.

Matt's eyebrows rose, and he regarded Inspector Griffin with an incredulous expression on his face. "You think I can get this cleaned up in two weeks?" He stepped back and almost tripped over one of the boxes the paramedics had knocked over.

Inspector Griffin grabbed his arm to steady him. "I'll give you a break. If you make a real attempt to get the outside cleaned up in two weeks, I'll give you an extension on the inside." He swept his hand across the clutter-filled yard. "This all has to go. I realize it's a big job, but some places will take this kind of stuff. There might be something salvageable. I can get you the number for a salvage yard that might take the metal off your hands, at least."

"Thanks. I'll get my family to help. We'll have as much of it cleaned out as we can. I can't promise it'll all be gone, but we'll get the trash, and the wood removed."

Matt gave the sergeant his phone number and watched as the two men walked to their cars. At this range, their conversation was inaudible, but their body language told him they believed it a hopeless cause. Matt remained in the yard as the last emergency vehicles, and police cars left the driveway, churning up a dust cloud. He turned back to the house with a sense of dread.

The first order of business was to pick up the fallen papers strewn across the hallway and look for a place to put them. Seeing no piles sturdy enough, Matt walked to the door and set them on the porch.

As he returned inside, Matt glanced into the disused kitchen. Bags of mystery groceries filled every surface, floor to ceiling, except for a narrow path between the door and the refrigerator.

A hose connected to what Matt knew was the sink emerged from between two overstuffed plastic garbage bags. It ended with a leaking sprayer in an overflowing bucket near the door. He unwound the hose and pulled it as far as it would go. It ended across the hall in the grimy bathroom tub.

He shook his head. "This is awful. How can he live like this?"

After beating a hasty retreat from the bathroom, Matt returned to the room where his uncle spent most of his time. A hot plate sat on a table beside a well-used coffeemaker Matt bought Uncle Lucas for Christmas a few years ago. A plate of some dried substance, which Matt had no desire to know its origins, lay discarded on the floor.

The 'never-shows-dirt' brown carpet exhibited a black trail from the hall to the chair, displaying the small rectangle where Lucas Sullivan existed. Matt couldn't, in good conscience, call it "living."

Like the rest of Uncle Lucas's family, Matt avoided coming into his uncle's house if he could. Now he had no choice but to take a hard look at the situation. He had to clean the house and yard in two weeks.

Matt left the stinking mess and locked the back door, pocketing his uncle's key. He almost smiled at the thought. Who would want to steal anything from the old man? If they did want anything, they were welcome to it as far as he was concerned.

At the hospital, Matt asked the plump receptionist for directions to his Uncle's room. The woman snapped her gum at him and directed him to the cardiac ward.

After several wrong turns, Matt found the room and stopped inside to see a doctor and nurse hovering over the bed. Uncle Lucas lay buried under several blankets with a sullen expression on his wrinkled face. The older man's long white hair framed his face in greasy locks that swayed as he shook his head, his jaw set in a stubborn glare. Matt had always thought Lucas was the caricature of Ichabod Crane. Those piercing blue eyes could pin you where you stood and make you feel like a bug on display.

He waited outside the room until the nurse left and the doctor remained.

When Matt stepped in, the doctor turned. "Yes? May I help you?"

"I'm Matthew Sullivan. Hello, Uncle Lucas." He walked to his uncle's bed. "Doctor Walker, this is my nephew, Matt. He can hear anything you have to say." Uncle Lucas's voice was weak but firm. The doctor nodded. "Lucas, you're dehydrated, malnourished, and anemic. You have high blood pressure, and you're pre-diabetic. I'm worried about your kidneys. You say you don't drink, but something is going on with your kidneys or liver. I'm going to run some tests." He looked down at the folder.

Matt looked at his uncle, who glared at the doctor. In an effort to reassure the older man, he laid a hand on Lucas's shoulder and squeezed.

Then Doctor Walker continued, undeterred by Lucas's unblinking stare. "Let's start by getting some good nutritional food in you. That'll get your body feeling right, and you'll feel like getting up and going places."

"I'm fine. I'll just get dressed and go home." Uncle Lucas started to sit up, but Matt pressed him back into the bed.

"Why don't you stay here for a day or so?" asked Matt. "The food's good, so I've heard, and you can rest. I'll take care of everything."

Lucas sputtered for a few minutes longer, and both men stared down at him, booking no excuse. He eventually relaxed into the pillows, closed his eyes, and ignored them.

"I'll write up the order, and we'll start the tests tomorrow." Doctor Walker smiled at Matt and gave him a wink as he left the room.

Matt pulled a chair next to Uncle Lucas. "When you left for the hospital, the county health inspector and sergeant told me about a clean-up notice they sent. How come you didn't tell me about it?"

Lucas stared at his window, ignoring his nephew. His bony arthritic fingers plucked at the sheet, and Matt continued, "I mean it, Uncle Lucas. I have two weeks to get the outside cleaned up, or the city will send out a bulldozer, clear the land, and charge you a bundle for doing it." Matt watched his uncle's face as Lucas' brows drew together, and his eyes took on a haunted expression.

"If you'd told me earlier, I could've helped," Matt added.

"No! That is my stuff. I collected it, and it's useful. I know it's worth something to someone out there. I can fix up the appliances and resell them." Lucas's face grew red, and his eyes hardened.

Matt swallowed a retort and forced his voice to soften as if he were talking to one of his young students. "Uncle Lucas, unless you're healthy, you won't feel well enough to work on even one appliance. If you want to work on anything, there will still be plenty of things to tinker within the barn. Anything in the yard has to go. I'll get someone to start up the tractor, clear out the weeds, and the yard will be fine."

"Boy, there's good money out there! Good machinery, lawnmowers, and a couple of snowmobiles that just need a good tune-up." His uncle straightened, turning to point an imperious finger at Matt's nose.

"Is there room in the barn to put them there until you're up to doing that?" Matt knew the answer, but he needed Lucas to answer it.

"No." Lucas turned his head away and sagged into the bedding in defeat. "Okay. As soon as I have the outside cleaned up, I'll clear out the papers and magazines from the house." Matt threw into the conversation, "The cleanup order included the inside."

Uncle Lucas sat forward again, coughing. He waved his hand, dismissing Matt's movement toward the water. Matt got up anyway and poured water from a pitcher on the bedside table into a plastic glass. He added a straw and held it to his uncle's parched lips. Lucas sipped, and the coughing subsided. He turned his blue eyes to Matt.

"Don't touch anything in the dining room or the dining room. Nothing." He grabbed Matt's wrist with surprising strength, spilling water from the glass. "I mean it! Don't touch anything there. I have important papers I don't want to be moved or messed up."

Matt looked into his uncle's eyes and nodded. "I won't touch anything in those two rooms until you get home. I won't get rid of anything, but I may have to move things around to clean up. I'll be getting rid of anything with four feet and a tail." Uncle Lucas didn't smile at the joke, but he did nod and lay back on the pillows.

"What's in the dining room you don't want to be touched? What's so important?" Matt faced his uncle at the end of the bed.

"Just don't touch anything," Uncle Lucas warned.

Matt nodded as he bid his uncle goodbye and promised to stop by the next day. He left his phone number at the nurse's station if anything changed.

CHAPTER 2
COLUMBUS, OH
July 2000

THE FOLLOWING WEEKEND, MATT, HIS BROTHER Sam, and his teenage nephew, Steve, his sister's son, arrived at Uncle Lucas's farmhouse. Steve jumped out of Matt's 4x4 and ran around the corner of the house to the backyard.

"Hey! Steve, come back here," Matt yelled. The two older men followed the young man at a somewhat slower pace. They met Steve at the back of the house.

"This is cool stuff. Can I take some of it home?" Steve walked around the piles, touching and picking items up. Matt and Sam looked at each other and laughed. "What's so funny?" Steve demanded.

"Nothing. Just a family joke."

The three started with hauling wooden planks and threw them into the dumpster. As they worked, the shadows changed, and eventually, the three decided they needed a break. Hungry, sweaty, and tired, the trio dug into the lunch Sam's wife packed along with some additions by Matt.

Sam cleared the picnic table they'd unearthed from a pile of wood with a couple of broken slats, but it was sturdy enough to hold the three.

"Hurry up; I'm hungry." Steve slid his gangly frame onto the bench.

Matt frowned and handed him a canvas bag. "Make yourself useful. We aren't your servants."

Steve looked up, surprised, as Matt continued to extend the bag to him. "This boy has a lot to learn," Matt muttered to his brother.

Sam nodded and hid a smile.

Steve took the bag and looked inside. He pulled out the plates, plastic utensils, and cups and parceled them out on the table, adding the condiments he found in the bottom of the bag.

"What's for lunch?" he asked.

"Ham sandwiches, potato salad, veggies, and chips. Is that enough?" Matt waited for Steve's answer.

With a sigh, the boy nodded. "I guess so. Is there dessert?"

Sam gave the back of Steve's head a little smack. "Sure, if you clean your plate."

Steve smiled. "I don't think that'll be a problem."

Full and re-energized, they returned to their work. Two dumpsters overflowed with Uncle Lucas's prized junk. It wasn't thoroughly clean, but the yard looked organized. Matt could get someone from town to come over and pick up the rest.

"Uncle Matt, why did Uncle Lucas have all this stuff?"

Matt looked at his young nephew with a teacher's eye for a lesson. "He thinks this stuff is valuable. In your eyes and mine, it might not look like it, but to him, it's like a treasure hunt. He keeps all his treasures close so he can see them."

Steve eyed some of the piles with possibility. Matt knew he was assessing how much he could get for the scrap and various collectibles scattered around.

"Uncle Matt, what do you think this stuff would be worth if we took it to the scrapyard? He sure loves his junk."

"Look around you. If Uncle Lucas had mended the broken things, fixed the engines, and put them up for sale, what would we think of him then?" Matt offered to Steve. It was an old argument the two older men had shared. Despite his eccentricities, Matt loved the strange older man, and it bothered him to hear the rest of the family speak ill of him.

Steve sunk his chin in his hands, elbows resting on bony knees, as he sat on the porch. His face showed the resignation of a teen that had opened himself up for some sort of lesson he didn't know he needed. "I guess he wouldn't have all this junk here and people would be buying the stuff he fixed. Then he would have money to fix his house." Matt could almost see Steve hold his breath.

"That's right. The only difference between a businessman and Uncle Lucas is the businessman fixes and sells his junk. Poor Uncle

Lucas just hangs on to it, promising that someday he'll get around to doing it, but he never does."

"How come he doesn't?" Steve's mouth moved faster than his brain, and a guilty expression crossed his face as soon as the words were out.

Sam spoke up, "That's a question. If anyone knew the answer to it, they'd be the richest person in the world."

Sam and Matt put their arms around the young man, and the three walked to the truck.

When they arrived at Steve's house, the boy sat quietly in the back seat. "I think Uncle Lucas is sick. Who would think any of that stuff is a treasure when all of it is junk?" His voice was determined as if he were trying to convince himself.

"You think so?" Matt left the car and walked to the door; Sam followed behind with a smirk on his face. Once inside, Matt turned to the stairs and took them as if he were on a mission.

"Hey! Where are you going?" Steve repeated as he followed Matt up the stairs, down the hall, and stopped at his door. Steve clamped his lips closed.

"You think it's stupid for someone to have so much junk lying around? Let's just take a look at what's behind this door." Matt waited a moment, and when he got no response from Steve, he turned the handle and pushed on the door. It only opened a fourth of the way. There wasn't any surprise at what they saw. Clothes lay thick on the floor, the sheets were off the bed, and a blanket rolled into a ball. A foul smell hit their noses, and the two men looked at their nephew.

Matt, who had come prepared, pulled a big black plastic bag from under his arm and shook it out. He gathered all the clothing lying on the floor, stuffing them in the bag. Steve started to say something in protest, and Matt looked at him. Steve closed his mouth and waited.

They heard the front door open, and Matt's sister, Kathy, yelled, "Where is everyone? I see Matt's car outside." Her voice had a cheerful lilt, and Matt could hear the rattle of keys as she hung them on the hook by the door.

Matt stopped, looked at Steve, and jerked his head toward the hall.

"Up here, Mom!" Steve hollered. His tone was a cry for help to arrive and save him from this injustice. His mother's steps climbed the stairs and stormed down the hallway.

"What's going on here?" Kathy demanded as she stared back and forth between her brothers. Kathy's mahogany hair was tied up in a ponytail and swished around her shoulders. Her perfectly arched eyebrows practically disappeared beneath her bangs as she waited for an answer.

"Steve's been helping us clean up at Uncle Lucas's place," Sam offered. "I know that, but what are you doing here?"

Matt sighed and spoke as he continued to stuff clothes from the floor into the bag. "Steve thinks Uncle Lucas is sick for having all that junk just lying around."

"He is," Kathy snapped, and Steve moved closer to his mother's side.

"I'm showing Steve that he isn't any different than his great uncle. When I opened the door to his room, I saw the same scene as I saw at Uncle Lucas's house. He thinks Uncle Lucas's stuff is junk and should be thrown away. The way he treats his own things means they should be thrown away, too." Matt raised his eyebrows at his nephew.

"You are not throwing his clothes away!" Kathy started into the room, her eyes threatening bodily harm.

Matt held up his palm to stop her. "I'm not throwing them away. He'll get them back when he learns to respect his things. If all this is important to him, he needs to learn to take care of them and not leave them on the floor." Matt put the rest of the clothes in the bag. When he finished, he dragged it out to the hall.

"What am I going to do for clothes?" Steve whined, looking around his much emptier room with a panicked expression mirroring the one on Uncle Lucas's face when Matt confronted him with the clean-up order.

"What do you do now?" Matt asked.

"I… ah… just… pick them up off the floor." Steve hung his head.

"That's too bad. Whatever you have in your drawers and what didn't fit in the bag is yours. You wash them. Kathy, show him how to wash his clothes." Matt looked at his sister, who nodded, then turned back to his nephew. "Steve, when you feel you've learned to take care of what you have in here, I'll bring this bag back." He faced Kathy, waiting for her support or interference. She stepped back and held up her palms in surrender.

"I've been trying to get him to clean his room for a long time. He says there's nothing wrong with it." She eyed her son. "I guess I should've done this a long time ago, but I was hoping he would learn on his own." She turned to her brother and gave him a weak smile. "Thanks, Matt."

"Steve is no different than his uncle. We all have these tendencies. We got it from our parents."

Kathy stepped back and shook her head. "I do not have packrat tendencies." She held her hands out in defiance. "Does my house look like Uncle Lucas's place?"

Matt shrugged and motioned for Sam to help him take the plastic bag down the stairs. At the front door, Matt left the bag and walked down the hall to the kitchen. Bewildered, Kathy and Sam followed him, exchanging glances. He stopped at the refrigerator and opened the door.

"Look inside." He pointed as Kathy looked in. "You have packages in here that, I'll bet, has green stuff growing on them. You have restaurant boxes of leftovers you bring home and never eat. You can't throw anything away until it's so bad, no one would eat it."

Kathy said nothing, her face reddening.

Matt opened the doors to her pantry and pointed at the shelves. "You line everything up the way Mom did. Food by type, canned or boxed, and I'll bet they're in expiration date order. We aren't packrats; we have Obsessive Compulsive Disorder. We got it from our mother. I'll bet your sewing room is overflowing with bits of fabric, yarn, and craft supplies you just can't throw away because you'll use it sometime." He waited until she nodded again, and he smiled a little.

"You got that from Dad. You aren't sick or anything. We all do this in some form or another. If you go to your friends' houses, you'll see some of the same issues. It's because we were raised by Depression-era parents who had to scrape to get by and use everything they had to make do. We don't have to live like that, but that lifestyle is ingrained in us."

Matt leaned over to her and kissed her cheek. "Call me when Steve has his room cleaned up and has kept it clean." He hugged her and felt her return it. Steve stood next to his mother with his arm around her waist, scowling as Matt and Sam left.

Matt and Sam drove to Matt's house in silence. Sam helped him carry the bag into the house and the laundry room.

"Are you going to do his laundry?" asked Sam.

"This time. I can't let it sit like this for weeks until Steve decides to keep his room clean. I want him to have clean clothes to put away. The threat might give him enough pauses to rethink his ways." Matt waved his hand in front of his nose.

"You aren't coming to my house!" Sam laughed. "I have an office with papers and stuff lying around. There are textbooks I haven't tossed—If you clean my place, my wife will love you. But I definitely won't!" He laughed a little, shaking his head at himself.

"Sam, I'm not perfect, either." Matt flipped the lights on in the kitchen and hung his keys on the hook, placing Uncle Lucas's keys on the next hook. "I pointed them out to Kathy because I do the same things and figured she did, too. You probably don't since Mandy is pretty much more in control of the house." He faced Sam and leaned against the counter. "Our mother, just the opposite of our father, kept him in line much the same way Mandy does for you."

"Yep, but I'm not going there, bro. Maybe you need to find a wife to keep you in line, Matt. I'll see you tomorrow morning to finish." Sam waved and left.

Matt remained still long after Sam left, looking around the kitchen. He was an average cook. Grilled as often as he could and made a mean salad. He cleaned up after himself most of the time and thought he'd make a good husband. It was finding the right wife that gave him pause.

He wandered into the foyer with its striped wallpaper and white enameled wainscoting. On one side sat his father's office, which had been the library when Matt and his siblings were young. On the opposite side of the hall, the living room hadn't changed in years. The same lace doilies covered the backs of the wingback chairs, and an afghan his mother crocheted lay folded on the couch. His father's recliner still faced the TV. Matt had replaced his dad's old tube TV with a slimmer line that just hit the market but had left the rest of the house the way it was. He wasn't ready to remodel.

Heavy drapes covered the windows, preventing sunlight from fading the furniture. Matt grimaced as he remembered his mother's voice relaying the information when asked why the dark drapes. She'd been more worried about the furniture than Matt had ever been able to understand. It was just furniture; it could be replaced.

Matt had also removed boxes of magazines and junk that had begun to line the hallway after his mother died. Matt took them all to the dump despite his father's arguments that they were somehow important or useful. Where had he heard that before?

There wasn't much difference between Joseph and his older brother, Lucas. Matt smiled, thinking of his mother, who pointed to the attic whenever his father entered the house with a box of his "treasures."

Reality faded as a childhood memory came to his mind. The resigned expression as his father made his way up the steps with the box. Matt felt sad for his dad when he was young. Why did he always have to go to the attic? Why couldn't he keep his boxes downstairs?

He heard his father's response to his question. "Your mother has no truck with my junk. It's not all junk, but she won't give it a chance."

On an impulse, Matt climbed the stairs and opened the door to the attic.

After a moment's consideration, he trudged upward.

Matt tugged the string at the top of the attic stairs. In the yellowed light, he understood his mother's orders. He hadn't been up here for years. After his mother died five years ago, his father continued to collect, with no one to stop him, the items stayed downstairs. When his father had been diagnosed with cancer, Matt moved in with his dad and took care of him.

Matt coughed as he yanked a dusty sheet off a piece of furniture: a full-length mirror set into a stand so one could tilt it back or forward for a better view. It was in good shape, and there didn't seem to be any markings on it from some past owner. He held a small flashlight in his teeth and wrote the item name in the notebook paper he attached to a clipboard. He'd have to move a few things from one side of the cluttered room; he paused and rephrased that 'junk-filled attic' to the other.

The attic floor filled the entire footprint of the house, and every bit of space was packed, sometimes to the vaulted ceiling, with boxes. There could be money here in antiques or items fit only for the dumpster. Like Uncle Lucas, Joseph had an eye for a good buy or something free. Betty relegated his finds to the attic, but that action could have saved its value. Matt surveyed the room and thought it might be just as easy to hire someone to come, pick through the stuff, and make him an offer.

To his right, he saw a sheet-covered item that had a familiar shape. This time, he carefully slid the sheet to a resting place on the unfinished wooden floor. Matt felt a smile tugging at his mouth. It was the roll-top desk where his father sat when he wanted to get away from the noise of the kids. As a boy, Matt would crawl up the steps and sit just where he could see his father reading a book, newspaper, or clipping articles from magazines. After a while, Joseph would call to him, "You'll get a cramp sitting there like that. Come up here and sit on the chair proper like."

Matt would jump up as much as his stiff legs allowed and sat in the chair near his father. Together, they would read things from the paper and discuss them. He wiped the moisture from his eyes as a sharp pang of loss pierced him.

Matt sat on the thin, threadbare pad on the wooden rolling chair, running his palms over its smooth arms. He remembered the smell of the attic air: a musty scent and some kind of smoke. He never saw his dad smoke, but there was a smell that he couldn't pin on anything but wet, smoldering wood.

He rolled the top-up in its grooves and stared at the pigeon-holes filled with bits of paper. Matt looked around and saw a metal trash can with a few crumpled papers at the bottom. "Dad, you threw something away?"

He chuckled as he pulled it toward him with one hand while collecting bits of paper out of the little square cubbies with the other. After reading the printed words or his father's writing, Matt either threw it in the can or smoothed it on a clear spot on the desk. The waste bin filled, but the stack on the desk didn't grow much. From a slot, he pulled a rusted spiral notebook. As with everything else, Matt flipped it open to survey the contents and ensure he wouldn't be disposing of anything important. On the faded first page, he saw his father's spidery writing.

There was a date written, '1965', and the word 'Millerton, WV.' at the top along with the names Rose and Lester Jones. No other dates filled that page. He turned to the next one. LUCAS written at the top, and under it were the names of Peter and Mary Garland. Beneath that, in faded pencil, Matt read, 'Found me. Lucas said he knew where Thomas and Emma lived.' Matt turned the page.

HENRY topped the next page. Matt couldn't read the faded pencil writing, but he could tell it was a name. Two first names were illegible, but he could make out the last name of 'McClure' followed by the words, 'Baltimore, MD.' 'Need to find him' was written in pencil, but he must have pressed hard on the paper with the lead because it was a dark spot, and the paper tore.

His elbow bumped a book perched on the edge of the desk, and it fell on the floor. When he bent to pick it up, a paper fell out of the book and slid across the floor, landing near the wall. Grumbling sourly, Matt dropped down on all fours and reached for the paper, pulling it towards him.

It was dark under the desk, and he thought he saw something farther back. He reached his hand up to the desktop, found a flashlight, and hoped the batteries still worked. The weak beam reflected on another slip of paper in addition to the one he was hunting.

Matt reached for it and slid it along the floor towards the chair. Backing up, he banged his head on the bottom of the desk. He rubbed his head, cursing at his stupidity. He felt his head, hoping he hadn't cut himself. His hand came away clean, but it hurt like the dickens.

Curious about what he had hit other than the drawer, he turned the light upward. The beam revealed an edge of wood protruding. It didn't move when he pulled on it. The way it stuck out intrigued Matt since it seemed to have nothing to do with the structural integrity of the desk. He pushed it, and he heard a snick from somewhere in the desk.

Excitement poured through him as he fiddled with the switch again. His fingers pressed the wood to the side, and the wood on the other side of the drawer released, revealing a space. He pulled both pieces toward him to reveal a hidden space with something inside. He felt plastic there and, from its hiding place, he rescued a book. Matt squirmed out from under the desk and reclaimed the chair he'd been using, dragging it back close to the desk. He laid his prize on the desk and pulled the lamp closer. It was an old Bible with the leather cracked and binding broken. He removed the plastic from the Bible and caught a faint odor of smoke. That must have been where the smell had come from all those years!

Matt opened the cover with care and read the title page. 'Presented to Katherine Mae Collins on June 14, 1924.' The following page was titled Marriage. The marriage of Samuel Orin Sullivan and Katherine

Mae Collins. There was a difference in the writing on the marriage page from the front page. Matt flipped to the page titled Births, written in the same script-style writing.

He recognized these names, written in the handwriting as the previous page. They were the names of his aunts and uncles.

He turned the page to Deaths. Only one name occupied that page: Samuel Orin Sullivan died September 1947. No listing for Katherine. Could she have died long after Sam? How come his father never listed his mother's death? None of Matt's aunts were listed, either, and they all had passed in his lifetime.

The next page listed Marriages. Martha married David Kincaid in 1943.

Emma married Thomas Conrad in 1947.

While Matt knew his aunts and uncles, Martha and her husband David Kincaid, Emma and her husband Thomas Conrad died after Matt graduated from college. Uncle Lucas was the closest living relative he had as he had no contact with his remaining uncle, Henry Sullivan.

Henry Sullivan. Matt leaned back in the wooden swivel chair. He laced his fingers together behind his head. What about Henry Sullivan? The man was wealthier than he or any of his cousins would ever be. What he knew about the man could be found in any newspaper.

At present, he is the candidate for President of the United States. None of his cousins that he knew of had ever befriended Henry, nor had Henry and his wife, Francis, ever attended any family gatherings. His cousins, all much older than his siblings, didn't get together with Matt's family.

According to Uncle Lucas, they had nothing to do with him, either.

"I guess if you're running for President, you're above the working man and woman," Matt thought wryly.

None of the names in the little notebook meant anything to him, and the other references made no sense.

Matt picked up the two items, determined to show them to Uncle Lucas and find out what the older man knew about these people. For now, he would tackle Lucas's place; then, in the fall, he resolved to start in this attic.

CHAPTER 3

COLUMBUS, OH

July 2000

MATT TURNED THE CORNER IN THE HOSPITAL hall and came to an abrupt stop in his uncle's room. It was empty. He backed up and looked at the whiteboard beside the door. It was wiped clean, and Matt's heart dropped. He whirled and headed to the nurse's desk down the hall.

He leaned over the high counter and demanded, "Where's Lucas Sullivan?" "Sir, hold it down." The nurse looked up at him and held up her hand with an irritated expression on her face. "Let me look to see where we moved him." The woman tapped some keys and looked at the monitor, frowning, and regarded Matt. She came around the counter and crooked her finger at him to follow her.

"I'm sorry. Your uncle had a relapse and is in intensive care. You can see him from the hall." She led him down a few hallways and stopped in front of a glassed-in room. Inside, he saw his uncle hooked up to machines. His eyes were closed. Matt turned to the nurse. "What happened?"

"We don't know. He went into cardiac arrest, and we had to move him to ICU. The doctor just left and won't be back until later. I can have him call you as soon as he gets in."

"If I stay here, and he wakes up, can I talk to him, Evelyn?" He read her name tag.

"Sorry, not unless the doctor clears him for visitors." She gave him an apologetic expression.

"I guess I'll just go, then. Do you have my cell phone number?" He followed the nurse to the counter again, and her nails clicked on the keyboard for a moment.

"Yes, Matthew, we have your cell number on file." She smiled and winked at him.

Matt realized the woman was his age. He gave her a weak smile and slapped the counter lightly. "Thanks, Nurse Evelyn."

He hurried out the door and to his car.

Sam and Steve were sitting on the porch when Matt pulled to a stop at Uncle Lucas's house. Sam came to meet him, leaving the younger man to play some game on his cell phone.

"Where do you want to start today?"

"Let's tackle the porch and kitchen, and then see what time is left. Thanks, Steve, for helping out."

"Yes, sir." Steve saluted and took the roll of plastic from Matt, and ran to the porch. Kathy had told Matt in the previous week that Steve's attitude changed. He'd begun keeping his room clean and putting his clothes away. He was still on probation.

Matt had called Sam the night before and gave him the latest development with Uncle Lucas.

"I'll have Kathy drop Steve off to spend the night. We'll be there bright and early," Sam answered the unspoken question.

They pitched bags, stacks, and baskets of paper and other junk into the dumpster. The bottom soon disappeared, and the sides diminished as the dumpster filled with garbage.

At last, they cleared the porch and made a path into the kitchen. The three men stared at the room with distaste and trepidation. Matt nodded once and took off for his car.

"Hey! Where do you think you're going?" Sam grabbed his arm, stopping Matt in stride.

Matt grinned at his brother. "Trust me, you want me to get what I'm going for. Just wait here." He left for a few moments and returned with some filter masks and heavy plastic gloves. "I borrowed them from a painter friend who didn't need them this weekend. I think we're going to appreciate these."

He handed one to each of them along with a pair of gloves. Who knew what they'd find in there, and he didn't want anyone getting cut and ending up with an infection.

The masks helped to stop most of the smell after they daubed some aftershave on the filter material. The sight they found under the plastic and paper bags had them all gagging. The smell of rotting food had their eyes watering even through the masks. Beneath the bags, they discovered the carcasses of dead rats, insect larvae, and worse. The men all ripped off their masks and ran for the porch rail more than once. When the mold and maggot-ridden refrigerator was empty, they dragged it out to the back porch, and Steve hosed the thing down.

Empty soup and food cans disappeared into the bags. Any holes allowing animals into the house were boarded or stuffed with caulking. Finally, they soaked the entire room down with bleach. The fumes stung their eyes worse than the smell, but the kitchen was usable when they walked out at the end of the day.

"Yuck! I stink!" Steve moaned.

Sam ruffled the boy's hair. "We all do, son. But at least that's over with, right?"

"I'm going need like six showers," Matt said by way of agreement.

Sam looked at his watch. "Anita's going to have my hide if I don't get home. It's family night. I'll drop Steve off on my way. See you later, bro." He jogged to his car with Steve at his heels.

Now alone, Matt trudged up the steps. He walked down the empty hall, with its faded and stained wallpaper, to the dining room. Dirty white wainscoting lined the wall behind the boxes, which almost reached the ceiling. He turned the old, button-style light switch. Dust and cobwebs coated the chandelier and gave a yellow hue to the room. Once white, sheer curtains hung at the window. He began moving boxes in front of the window, only to have the curtain fall in a dusty heap of thread on the remainder of the boxes.

"How old are these curtains?" he muttered. He remembered them all his life and wondered how long they'd been there before that.

In the living room, where boxes and junk Uncle Lucas collected still accumulated, he could see the upright piano with its lace doilies and the dusty knickknacks still arranged on top. A floor lamp with a blue-patterned shade trimmed in glass beads was almost disguised in the corner—very Victorian. He had a vague recollection of a couple who lived here with Uncle Lucas. He assumed his uncle had inherited the farm. The older woman must have had a hand in it; he didn't see his uncle as a decorator.

The dining room space held newspapers, magazines much like the rest of the house. This room there seemed to have some pattern to the stacks on the table. The boxes dated on the sides went back forty years. He walked as far into the room as he could and ran his fingers through his dark brown, thinning hair. What did his uncle want with all these newspapers?

He picked up a stack and laid them out on a space at the end of the table surrounded by eight chairs. They probably hadn't been moved from their place in more years than the papers stacked around them.

He opened one of the newspapers and saw black ink underlining several names on the page. He turned more pages and found the same names underlined and new names: Barker, McClure, Shelton, Beacon, and Griffin. In one paper, he found a picture of a house circled, and a line to Rose and Lester Mellon listed below. He set that paper aside and picked up the next one. Almost every news had the same names underlined, circled. Sometimes the pen or pencil had pressed too hard, and the paper ripped. Matt discovered a faded, water-damaged notebook and wrote the names most often underlined or circled. Some of the newspapers were damp and practically disintegrated. Matt recognized several names from the faded notebook on his father's desk.

A hutch along the back wall was his next goal. The glass on the back of the cabinet was pitted, and the first drawers that he could pull out any distance contained tarnished silverware and serving dishes.

The next one held folded tablecloths. A mouse ran across the top, looking for a way out. Matt couldn't hold back the scream. His heartbeat was almost out of his chest. He pulled the drawer further out and found a family of rodents nesting in the chewed cloth. He carried the drawer to the back porch and upended it over the side of the railing. Once the little creatures were gone, he decided to throw out the remnants of the tablecloths.

Matt pulled on the lower doors for a moment, finding them stuck. After a few minutes of wrestling, they screeched open, and Matt found a cedar box tucked away in the back. The hinges were brass and sullied. He lifted it out and pushed the papers off the top of the table to clear a space for it. Once settled, he tried to open the lid, but it, too, was rusted. He took a screwdriver from his back pocket and used it to pry the lid open. He frowned at the contents: letters about four inches high in two stacks, one wrapped with a pink ribbon and the other with a leather strip that looked like a shoestring.

Matt stood up, pushed his reading glasses back on his forehead, and pinched the bridge of his nose with his thumb and forefinger. Here was his history, an insight into his grandparents. He stared back down at the wooden box. It wasn't fancy but well crafted. Maybe something his grandfather made for his wife? He decided to take it home to examine.

The rest of the hutch held dishes and glassware, though not the type generally found in a cabinet. It seemed like every day ware. Some of the plates, cups had cracks, chips, and pieces or two of the large platter were stuck together. In a box lay broken pieces of the same pattern as the plates. Why would anyone keep broken pieces of dinnerware?

Matt placed the ribbon-wrapped letters on his lap and slid the top letter from its binder. He couldn't read the date on the envelope, but August 5, 1947, appeared at the top of the letter. He began to read.

Dear Sam. I miss you terribly…

The writing was labored and scratchy at times. The spelling and sentences lacked proper construction as if the person writing had no education at all. Matt knew these letters were from his grandmother to his grandfather, but where was he? If he were somewhere else, why wasn't the rest of the family with him? He picked through the letters and read bits here and there. Most were just common day-to-day happenings.

Then, halfway through the pile, the tone in the letters changed. Matt found the last one, still in its envelope, addressed to Samuel Sullivan, Pine crest Sanitarium, Clarksburg, and West Virginia. What was his grandfather doing there?

He set aside the mystery and returned the letters to the box. He'd be more comfortable reading them at home.

He checked the rest of the drawers to see if there were any other family memorabilia. They held more household items, probably from the couple who had lived with Uncle Lucas all those years ago.

"Who were they?" he wondered aloud.

Matt made his way down the hallway looking for an empty box to carry the things he'd found. The bead board paneled door under the stairs squeaked as he walked by, and it opened a little. Matt stopped and pulled the door towards him. A musty smell assaulted his nose.

Inside the hall cardboard, boxes with split seams, and some items had fallen out. Matt sighed at the discovery. More for him to go through. Wonderful. He shoved several boxes aside, taking a look at the contents of the cubby. On the floor, Matt discovered a wooden box with oval handholds carved into the two ends. A matching lid fits over the top. He picked it up and tugged it out to the hallway before prying the lid off.

The box held rusty-colored newspapers. With a finger, Matt dug into the papers to see how far down they went. The paper disintegrated at his touch.

He stood and walked back to other rooms, looking for paper or something to put on the floor when he upended the box, with Uncle Lucas's frame of mind, who knew what he'd find at the bottom.

Matt found a tarp folded between a stack of boxes in the closet and laid it on the floor. When he upended the box, papers fell out in chunks onto the tarp. On top of the pile sat a rectangular object wrapped in oilcloth and tied with twine. Matt picked up the box and shook it. Two more bundles fell out. He found seven more piles, just like the first three, stuck to the bottom. Ten identical bundles in all were wrapped in oilcloth and tied with twine. Matt's mind reeled with possibilities. He took the closest bundle, one of the last he had pulled out of the bottom, and cut the twine with his pocketknife. With his luck, they'd probably be Confederate script. Even that might be worth something to a collector if they were in good condition.

Matt unfolded the oilcloth to reveal another white fabric similar to flour sack material. He peeled back the cloth, and the contents took his breath for a moment. The air returned in a gush. The bundles held twenty-dollar bills stacked about a quarter-inch high. The wrapper around the top read Bank of Kentucky. Matt lifted one, a second, and the third packet of the twenties lay beneath.

The date on the bill read Series 1948. Matt knew this bill was updated. This newly designed bill for that year included renovations of the White House, namely the Truman Balcony and the growth of the trees. Were these counterfeit? They looked like newly issued bills, not yet folded or handled. How did they come to be here? He sat back and took a few deep breaths as he tried to wrap his mind around what he'd discovered.

Then he opened the following two bundles, which proved to be the same as the first. Looking at the serial numbers, they seemed to be in order. He tore open the third and held it in his trembling hands. These were different.

These were two bundles of fifty-dollar denominations dated 1950. They, too, were banded by the Bank of West Virginia. Under the fifties, Matt found a folded piece of plain paper. He pulled it out and opened it. Typed in the middle of the half sheet of paper were the words, *Make sure the boys never come back.*

What boys? Matt wondered.

The last bundle was like the one before, the fifties and another plain white paper folded underneath. Matt opened it and read, *this is the last one. We don't want to see any of them around Millerton ever again.*

Matt looked at the name, something clicking in his head. It was the same town as all those newspapers stacked in the dining room.

He scrounged through the bits of brown paper that hid the money in the box and managed to find one piece still together with the title of Louisville Gazette, Louisville, Kentucky. How close was Louisville to Millerton, West Virginia? He'd better take this entire pile home and see what he could dig up. Matt found another box pushed back against the steps. With care, he moved the boxes until he could free the matching box.

One of the cardboard boxes split, and the bottom opened. Metal pots clanged to the floor. With a sigh, Matt bent to pick up the mess. It was camping gear: pots, pans, metal plates—a whole stack of them—and metal utensils. The next box held a rusty Dutch oven with another smaller pot and lid inside. Matt pulled open the other boxes to reveal an enamel coffee pot and a couple of iron skillets. It looked like what a cook might have in his cook wagon, not something a family would take camping.

It took a fair amount of effort to wrest the wooden crate from its place under the step and set it in the hall. This box was narrower than the first, only about five inches tall, and the lid overlapped the side a few inches. Again, old paper covered the contents about three inches thick. These came off a little better than the others and were also from the Louisville Gazette. Unlike the other box, however, this one was lined with oilcloth under the paper. He lifted the flaps of the oiled cloth and the white flour sack liner.

There stacked in bank-wrapped packets were the twenties, tens, and fives. Matt took a metal fork from a nearby box and lifted the packets to see how many layers were deep in the box. He sat back against the hallway wall. There had to be a few hundred thousand dollars. If they were all real, how did they get there? He replaced the lid moved the box with the letters. He placed a few of the newspapers from Millerton in the larger wooden box and hauled both to his car.

Matt, too numb with shock to do anything else in the house, closed and locked the hallway door. He slid some of the overstuffed boxes to hide the opening.

At home, Matt settled in his father's office. The wood-paneled walls reflected the soft light around him and helped to soothe his nerves. A cup of stone-cold coffee was inches from his elbow, forgotten, as Matt buried himself in the things he'd rescued from Lucas's house.

The letters revealed his grandfather had left the homestead and went to work somewhere near Aunt Martha and Uncle David in Bowersville, WV. One envelope from his grandmother to his grandfather had gone unopened. Matt pulled the Bible across the desk and opened the front cover, turning the pages until he reached the one titled Deaths. The postmark on the envelope was the day before the written death of Samuel Orin Sullivan.

Matt relaxed, leaned back, and reached for his coffee. He had so many questions. Uncle Lucas was too ill to talk; his father had passed, as had his two aunts. That left his Uncle Henry. He lifted the cup to his lips and made a face. Had he been there that long? He sighed and set the cup of cold coffee down.

Matt knew there was no chance he would get to speak to this uncle. The man was running for President of the United States and didn't talk to anyone in the family. Matt had no idea how to contact Uncle Henry unless his dad had left a number tucked away somewhere.

That question was nothing compared to what he had discovered in the two wooden boxes. Where did he begin to find information like that? Was his uncle a thief? He just couldn't see that. The bundles hidden in the camping gear were suspect. The old couple who had taken Uncle Lucas in, who were they? How had they met Uncle Lucas? What about the note, and what boys did it refer to? His uncles, father?

Matt shook his head. No, that sounded like a sappy movie. He had to break down and confront Uncle Lucas.

CHAPTER 4
MILLERTON, WV
March 1947

KATHERINE PERKED UP WHEN SHE HEARD THE boys holler as they charged down the driveway to meet their father. "Emma, pull the stew to the center of the stove and set the table." She stopped at the small, cracked mirror, tucked in the stray strands of hair, bit her lips to plump them, and smiled as she headed to the front porch to meet her man.

Samuel took long strides up the driveway toward his boys. His dark, wavy hair bounced as he braced himself for the bombardment of his two youngest sons. The farm and his full-time job at the furniture factory kept his body lean and hard. Katherine's eyes softened as she watched him.

I have a perfect life: a handsome husband, five children, one of them married, and a home. What more could a woman want?

Sam played rough-and-tumble with Henry and Joseph, their two youngest boys. Katherine leaned against the porch post and watched their antics until a movement caught her eye. Lucas, his face dark with the first stubble of a beard he was very proud of, stood by the edge of the woods and watched the raucous laughter with an amused expression on his face. It hadn't been all that long ago when he tumbled on the grass with his father. Now, he'd taken over some of the farming duties and went to school while Sam worked. Behind Lucas, the Allegheny Mountains towered over the valley.

Katherine's kinfolk lived up that mountain, deep in the woods.

"Enough now. Go call Lucas and wash up for supper." Sam's voice interrupted her thoughts as he took the porch steps two at a time and pulled Katherine tight in his arms.

She knew something was wrong the moment he kissed her. Katherine wrapped her arms around him and accepted the hard kiss before Sam buried his face in her shoulder.

"I love you, babe," she whispered and kissed his ear.

A pink slip of paper dangled in his fingers as he raised his hand to eye level. Her heart almost stopped. Times were hard with all the soldiers looking for work. They'd be even more complicated now that Sam's was gone.

"We have the farm. We'll grow more produce and sell it in town. I'll raise more chickens for eggs and make butter from the extra milk. Maybe the restaurant in town will buy some of my pies and cakes." Katherine swallowed the panic that clawed at her throat and ran a hand through her husband's soft hair.

Sam squeezed her so tight; she could barely get the words out. "I don't want you to work."

She forced herself to laugh. "It's not working. You know I love to bake and sew. It's the chance to do more of what I love and less of what I hate, like cleaning the stalls."

"You know I love ya. I did from the first minute I saw ya 'cross the dance floor. We're meant for each other. I promised I'd take care of ya, give you a home and children."

"You have, honey. You've done all that and more. I'm blessed." She smoothed the lock of hair that fell on his forehead and cupped the back of his neck. "Don't worry. We will make it."

"Are ya'll goin' to jus' stand there smoochin' while we just starve to death?" Henry's plaintive voice echoed from the house.

"I guess we know what's important to the boys." Katherine grinned and took his hand to lead him to the kitchen.

Four pairs of eyes trained on their every move as they took their places. Will the table be this packed in the months to come? We'll have to start cooking a little less. Katherine wondered that as she sat opposite Samuel and reached for Emma and Joseph's hands on either side of her.

Sam said grace, and the boys dug in like pigs at the trough, arguing over who got the biggest potato until Sam raised his voice. "Stop it!

There's plenty to eat, so fill your traps 'stead of flappin' 'em." The only sound heard after that was utensils as they slid against plates.

"Can we be excused?" Henry asked for himself and Joseph when they had eaten their fill. The boys stared at their parents with large, chocolate-colored eyes wide with hope.

Katherine nodded, indulging them.

The boys took their plates to the cast iron sink and then scrambled out the back door. The screen door banged behind them.

Sam laid his hand on Lucas's arm to keep him at the table as the young man rose to take his dishes to the sink. Sam cleared his throat. "Things are going to be a little tight around here from now on." He laid the pink slip of paper on the table. It might as well have been an elephant for the impact it made on Emma and Lucas.

Lucas swore.

"Now, Lucas, none of that kind of language," Katherine cautioned.

Emma's eyes teared up, and she blotted them with her apron. Unlike her brother, she said nothing and seemed to sink into herself.

"It'll be tough, but we'll make it," Sam continued. "Lucas, when ya get home from school, we'll work in the fields, turning the fallow ground into a larger garden. What we don't use for ourselves, we'll sell in town." His finger scratched the red-checkered oil tablecloth in an anxious gesture as he spoke.

"Good luck with that idea," Lucas muttered. "Why not?" Sam frowned.

"Every Saturday, there's a farmer's market in Barker's parking lot. Everyone brings their produce in to sell. There isn't enough people in town to buy all the stuff that's brought in."

"Isn't," Katherine corrected. "I know, but—" she paused and held up her finger— "we have better produce. I don't know what you do, Lucas, or what magic you perform on the seeds, but everything I take to Barker's during the week sells before I get there. I come in the back door, and Mr. Barker says, 'Finally, you're here! I've got people complaining and asking for the good stuff.' He takes my baskets and writes me a credit slip, and I leave. I see all those women trotting out the front door with what I brought in the back." She giggled, but it faded when she saw Sam's expression.

"You've been selling stuff to Barker? You didn't tell me." Sam leaned forward, his eyes drilled into hers.

"Sam, not now," her soft voice warned.

Lucas tools his dishes to the sink. The screen door banged against the frame as he escaped off the back porch. He never asked to be excused.

Katherine watched him go, her heart aching for her oldest son. It wasn't fair to lay all this on him at his age, but there was nothing else they could do.

Sam took a deep breath and leaned back, balancing his chair on the back of two legs. Katherine recognized the expression on his face. A slight wrinkle formed between his brows when he was deep in thought, and he stuck out his lower lip.

Emma stood and took the rest of the plates to the sink, her head low as she tried to control the flow of tears down her face.

Sam's voice filled the void. "I had a visitor at the factory today. It was odd and sure got a lot of attention."

Katherine frowned. "Who was it?"

"Thomas Conrad." He looked at Emma, now stopped dead in the middle of the kitchen. "Is there something you should've told your mother and me?"

Katherine spoke up. "Sam, don't tease. We talked about this. We figger'd… figured," she corrected herself, "he might talk to you before he officially asked Emma." She waved her hand at her daughter to continue to the sink.

Emma scraped the dishes, and then rinsed them in the enamel dishpan.

"What did he have to say?" Katherine asked her eyes on Emma's back as she turned the water to a slow stream to avoid missing anything said at the table.

"We had a good talk. It seems his children love Emma and she loves them." Sam leaned his elbows on the table and winked at Katherine. "He loves her. That's a sure fact. He'll be here in a half-hour, I'd say. I told him we eat early. He said he'd come over. He has something to give Emma."

Emma shrieked and whirled to face her parents. Her hands flew to her wild auburn hair, which had escaped the ponytail. "What? He's coming here in half an hour? I'm not ready, Mom!" she wailed, all worries about the family forgotten.

"Go on, girl. Get gussied up for your man. I think I can handle the rest of the dishes." Katherine shook her head at the thumping of the girl's shoes on the wood steps and down the hall. "That girl is going to have to learn some decorum."

"Some what?" Sam asked as he covered his cough with a hand.

"Decorum. It's a new word I learned from Cassie. It means to act lady-like." Katherine rinsed the last of the dishes. She picked up the flour sack towel she'd edged in pretty blue flowers to dry them and then put them away. "I'm glad she's marrying him. He's a bit older, but he seems to want to take care of her." Sam took a sip of coffee after another bout of coughing.

It was the sawdust at the mill that did it. Blessing in disguise, Katherine thought. Maybe it'll clear up now with him being out of that place.

"He gave her complete control over his household this last year as his children's nanny." Katherine poured water into the coffee pot. "He's often away from home for his job. She orders his food, cooks it for him and the children, and talks to their teacher when he can't make it. Thomas has come to rely on her for everything since his wife died. I'd say they act like a married couple without the advantages." She hummed as she measured coffee into the speckled pot and set it on the stove to boil.

"Are you sure they haven't had the 'advantages'?" Sam gave her a look, his mouth tugging down in a scowl.

"Yes. Emma says he's a gentleman. She told me, as she blushed the whole time, he'd kissed her. I didn't press for details. It isn't any of my business, but she said that was all they did. I believe her."

Katherine felt Sam's arms wrap around her waist, and he laid his chin on her shoulder. "When he's gone, and we go to bed, let's try out those 'advantages of marriage' you was talkin' 'bout." His breath tickled her ear.

She turned her head and kissed his cheek with a grin. "That could be arranged as long as you don't give the boy too hard a time when he gets here."

"He's no boy, but we had our talk already. He's free to marry my girl, and I'm comfortable he'll take good care of her. I don't think he's going to be given a pink sheet anytime soon." He spoke with a bit of rancor.

A week later, Katherine, Emma, and Cassie Lundgren, their nearest neighbor, drove into Millerton to find a pattern and order material for Emma's wedding dress.

Katherine looked back at her daughter, who had her left hand stretched out in front of her. She turned her hand back and forth to see the stone sparkle in a different light. Katherine caught Cassie's brown eyes and shook her head. "You'd think she was the only one with a ring."

"One likes that, for sure." Cassie smiled and waved her left hand with its diamond sparkling.

Katherine looked at her gold band. Size and price didn't matter. It was still the symbol of all the love she and Sam shared since the moment he slipped it on at the registrar's office.

Her mind wandered to that particular day. She'd worn a borrowed silk dress and a cute birdcage hat. She'd rolled her hair perfectly and felt as if she were wearing a hundred-dollar dress and ring. It didn't matter that they'd changed at his friend's house and put their regular clothes back on after the ceremony. They returned the dress and hat with hugs of appreciation and rode to his rooming house in the backseat of his friend's car. The kind woman who had run the rooming house made a cake and insisted they cut and serve it to each other. Someone had taken their picture and later gave them copies. One framed, sat on a shelf in the living room. The other tucked into the back of the family Bible she'd been given by the minister in town.

The memory faded as the car wove its way along the curves of the two-lane road to Millerton. The houses sat closer to the street in town while the farm homesteads were sometimes a mile up their driveways. Katherine sometimes wished to live in a town with a house surrounded by a white picket fence and the front walk to the porch lined with flowers in every color. She sighed, lost in her daydreams when Cassie turned the corner that led to Barker's Market.

"What was that for?" Cassie asked as she stopped the car and pulled the handle to set the brake.

"Just wishin' on the wind… Some things are just not meant to be."

"That's for sure. If wishes were horses, every beggar could ride." Cassie laughed. "Well, it goes something like that. You get the idea."

They climbed out and walked around the corner of the parking lot to the front of the store. Katherine grimaced at the line of men sprawled on the porch and steps. Their ages ranged from eighteen to eighty, and some of the oldest reclined in rocking chairs and the Adirondack chairs lined against the wall. Their ragged, faded clothing smelled of unwashed bodies, stale tobacco, and too much whiskey. The men laughed, whistled, catcalled, and made rude suggestive remarks.

One hulking young man straightened from his seat on the porch rail and sidled toward Emma. "Now whatcha goin' on an' gettin' hitched to that fancy dude for? You know you ain't worth him. You ain't better than us. You need a real man to fatten you up with kids." A cigarette, mostly ash, dangled from his lips; he flicked it off and smiled. The yellowish-green teeth did nothing to enhance the twisted nose and cracked lips. Puffy, yellow skin under one eye and a large bruise on the other cheek offered no additional enticement.

He reached out his hand to touch Emma, but Katherine stepped between them. Her hand clamped down on his wrist, her delicate fingers barely closing around it.

"She hasn't had to deal with trash like you, but I have. I'm always carryin'." Katherine stared into his eyes, but he didn't move. "Buddy, iffen ya don't want to be orderin' yer next kids from the Wards Catalog, ah suggest ya step back and join yer lazy friends an' leave us alone." Katherine lapsed back to the dialect of her roots.

Buddy lowered his arm and glared at Katherine.

Katherine didn't back up, but her hand went to the purse strap slung across her full breasts. His eyes widened at the sight of the knife sheath attached to the strap. Narrow, but long and lethal.

"Jus' jokin', little woman. Jus' jokin'." He took a few steps back to the rail. "The Momma bear isn't one to be messin' with, boys." He tried to dismiss her.

Katherine took Emma's arm and followed Cassie into the store.

Inside, they heard a scramble of footsteps as those who must have come to the window moved away. Cassie marched up to Robert Barker and slammed her palm on the counter. "When are you going to run those lazy no-goods off your porch? Are they buying anything? They're trying to intimidate your customers. I'm filing a complaint with the sheriff if they aren't gone when we're finished shopping. One of those sloths tried to accost us!"

Mr. Barker drew himself up and looked down at the five-foot-three Cassie. "Ma'am, who are you to be tellin' me what to do?" His hand pulled at his salt and pepper beard as his mouth turned downward in a scowl.

Cassie leaned forward and narrowed her eyes at the man. "If I stop buying from your store and go over to Conner's, how is that going to affect your profit?" she whispered.

"Ma'am, I'll have them gone. Don' cha worry none at all." He turned, the sound of his leather heels pounding on the wood floor as he stormed to the door.

Cassie whirled and faced several women peeking from behind the shelves. "Well? What are you staring at? Can't you stand up for yourselves? Shame on you." Cassie then followed Katherine and Emma to the small section with pattern books stacked on shelves. They looked through them for a wedding dress.

"How about this one?" Emma pointed to a picture with a low-cut lace bodice.

"I think this one is more appropriate for the church." Katherine pointed to the high-necked gown pictured in her book.

Emma made a face at her mother.

"Keep making that face, and it will stay that way."

"Mother, I'm a little old for that." She turned the page. "I don't want one as frilly as Martha's," Emma cautioned.

"You're nothing like her." Katherine smiled at her second daughter. Martha, her oldest girl, and her husband lived three hours away in Bowersville. "I'm glad you're going to live close."

Cassie thumbed through the material offerings they could order. They laughed at mixing the patterns to make a regal-looking and sexy dress.

The front screen door slammed, and heels clicked across the floor. The steps didn't stop at the counter but approached the three women. The Mayor of Millerton's wife, Miranda McGuire, marched around the racks of cloth and table of patterns. She stopped at the end of the table and waited expectantly, her made-up eyes narrowing.

Katherine lifted her head and stared at the woman, as did the other two.

"I asked you at least two weeks ago to make my Angie a dress for the prom. I haven't heard from you." The woman held her chin even with the floor, her pocketbook firmly anchored to her arm. The other hand was closed over the handle as if someone might yank it from her.

Katherine turned away to look through the pages of the book in front of her. "I told you I needed a pattern so I could see exactly what it is she wants. I'm not sure I can do it right now." She opened her hand to the page of wedding dress patterns. "I'm going to be pretty busy for a while."

There was a loud harrumph from Miranda, and she even gave a small, irritated stomp of her shoe. Behind her were two other ladies—Cynthia Shelton, the sheriff's wife; and Clarinda Beacon, the bank president's wife— who stood as her backup.

Katherine took in their similar shirtwaist dresses and short jackets. They wore hats, one broad-rimmed while the other two were birdcage hats with netting. It was as if they all shopped from the same catalog.

"We heard Thomas was at the mill the other day and talked to Sam. Then Thomas's car was seen turning into your driveway later on that night." Her voice grated in the silence.

Katherine and Cassie looked at each other, eyebrows raised.

"What?" Miranda demanded. Her purse hand now moved to her ample hips, curled, and rested there.

"Oh, nothing." Cassie dramatically turned the large page of the book. "I'm surprised you listened to all that gossip."

"I do not listen to gossip!" Miranda huffed. "It's a fact." She tilted her head to see Emma's left hand under the pattern book.

Katherine lifted the appendage to let the woman and those gawking from behind shelves see the large diamond set into the white gold band.

"So it is true," Cynthia spoke between clenched teeth. "I don't understand why he picked you."

Her expression changed, and her eyes narrowed into ugly little slits. "Are you expecting? Is that why he's getting married to you? You seduced him when he was weak and then told him you were—" Her voice choked as Katherine stood, stepped around the table, and ignored everyone but Cynthia. The woman backed away but bumped into the shelving. "Help me," she gasped, but no one moved.

Katherine stopped a foot away from her. "You dare to speak something like that when we all know that's exactly how you and the sheriff got hitched. Funny how there have been no babies after the marriage. That was what? Ten years ago? Are you infertile now? Or maybe he didn't want to touch you anymore."

Cynthia's face went beet red. She let out a filthy cuss word that made the others gasp as she stomped out the door. The sound of her heavy footsteps rang in the room.

Katherine turned to Miranda. "I'll sew your daughter's dress, but you'll have to choose the pattern in the right size and order the material."

"I can't do that. I know nothing about sewing or ordering. What if I don't order enough?" Miranda whined then quickly bit her lip.

"Okay, you pick the pattern. My guess is she's a size eighteen. Have her get a swatch of the material she wants, and I'll have Mr. Barker or Mrs. Barker order the right amount."

Miranda nodded, turned on her heel, and walked off. The silent Clarinda waddled after her with appropriately scandalized expressions on both their pudgy faces.

Katherine sank into the chair and fanned her face with a pattern package. "Lawd, why do they act like that?"

Cassie patted her arm. "Let's forget that and get back to the important things." She nodded her head at the onlookers that slowly moved away.

When they completed the order for Emma's pattern, material, and all the trim, Katherine picked up a few items from the grocery.

Before she could push the screen door open, Sheriff Beau Shelton opened it, holding it for them to walk through. When Katherine stepped onto the porch, the catcalls and rude gestures began again until the sheriff turned and grabbed the first offender by the neck of his shirt, which ripped.

"I hear one noise or remark like those in the presence of these ladies ever again, and I'll have you hoeing my back forty for the rest of the summer." He gave the offender he held a push, which landed him in the middle of the men; they fell like dominoes.

Katherine held her composure at the sight.

"Ma'am, I'm sorry for that. Let me carry that bag for you." He spoke to Katherine as if she were the only one carrying anything. Reluctantly, she handed him the paper sack rather than have a tug of war. When she reached the steps, he held out his elbow for her to hang on to.

"I can make it down the steps on my own." Katherine stepped on the first step. The sheriff quickly switched the bag to the other arm and took her elbow until she reached the sidewalk. She stepped away from him and walked ahead of him to Cassie's car.

"What was that all about?" Cassie asked as they pulled away.

"I have no idea, but it sure wasn't a good thing. At least the Sheriff was acting nice. There's something about him that makes me nervous." Katherine didn't share the fact that when she was younger, Beau followed her at a distance.

He was a 'towney,' and she was a hillbilly. Once, he had come up the mountain, and her brothers ran him off, threatening him if he ever came back. She was surprised to see him as the sheriff when she and Sam moved to Millerton.

Emma spoke up from the back seat. "He always gives me the shivers. He stands at the window of his office and watches me when I walk to Tom's house."

"You never said anything about it." Katherine turned to her daughter, who shrugged.

"You can't fault a guy for lookin'."

CHAPTER 5
COLUMBUS, OH
July 2000

MATT PULLED INTO THE PUBLIC LIBRARY parking lot an hour or two later and mounted the steps. As he reached the door, he paused for a moment, wrestling with himself. He had no idea where to look for family history books other than the Dewey Decimal System and wanted nothing to do with that nightmare. After a few seconds of indecision, he shouldered open the door and made a beeline for the information desk. After all, that's what they are paid for: help people.

"I'm starting some research on my family history. Where would I find books or other materials that would tell me where to start?" he asked the young woman, dressed in goth style, behind the desk.

"You've come to the right place. Miss Davenport teaches beginning genealogy for adults." The young woman waved to an older woman who pushed away from her desk. With a smile, she moved to stand in front of him. Ms. Davenport, an older woman by a good twenty years, was doing her best to fight it. Her false eyelashes fluttered at him a few times, and she smiled a slow, welcoming smile that made Matt want to back up and leave. He steeled himself; he'd come here for information, and he wasn't leaving just yet.

A young man stood beside him at the desk. "Help him first." Matt stepped back. "Sorry."

"Hi. I'm Tim." He leaned on the desk as if he were part of the information staff.

The younger woman reached out her hand for the slip of paper Tim held. Her nails painted black matched her black hair that looked as if she cut it herself. When the girl walked away, Tim looked at Matt and winked. "She has an IQ Mensa would die to have. I love women with a great mind."

The older woman crooked her long, red nail at Matt to follow her. Once Matt had circled to her desk, she pulled a packet from a drawer. "I teach beginning genealogy, and this is my handout. I'm Livonia Davenport." She held out her hand to him.

"I'm Matthew Sullivan. I teach World History at the High School." He shook her hand and, after a moment, extracted his mangled fingers from her firm grasp.

Ms. Davenport grinned and leaned toward him, so the V in her wrap dress allowed for a view far into the cavity between her breasts. Matt picked up the packet, opened it, and stared at the pages. Anything was better than the view he had down her dress.

"Are you, by any chance, related to Senator Henry Sullivan?"

Matt frowned and backed away. "Why do you ask?"

"You have the same last name."

"So do many other people." He returned his eyes to the pages in the folder.

Some were forms and included a list of Internet search sites.

"I heard he might have relations around here. I work in his local election office. I could find out if you are." There was almost a challenge in her voice. She tapped her red nails against a rouged cheek.

"If you must know, yes, we are related," Matt conceded with an irritated sigh.

"I thought so. You look like a younger version of the candidate. I had a crush on him when he first ran for senator, but he was married, and so was I. Not anymore, though." She ran the red nails up along her cheek, then through the dyed red and brown-streaked hair. It was a short crop moussed into spikes. The style might have worked if she were a little younger, but she was trying too hard, and the effect was sickening rather than enticing.

"Could you explain a little about what these pages are? Where would I find the information to fill them out?" Matt tossed the folder on the desk a little too hard, and it slid across to her. Ms. Davenport didn't stop it, and it fell on the floor, spewing pages across the carpet. She eyed him for a moment, her lips pursed and gaze sharp.

"Sorry, I've had a rough day." It was more of an excuse than an apology. Matt picked up the pages still on the desk.

Ms. Davenport bent over, picked up the folder, and slapped it on the desk.

"You fill out what you know about each family member." She pointed to the lines at the top. "You put your name, wife's name, and important dates, then fill in the kids' names down here."

"I'm not married." He looked at the tags beside the lines.

"I can see why," she muttered, her tone acerbic. "What do you know right now about your family?"

"Not much. I know my aunts' and uncles' and cousins' names. What I want to know is what happened to my grandparents."

"You don't know?" She hiked a well-proportioned hip on the edge of the desk and covered part of the folder.

"No. I have some old letters, but my Uncle Lucas won't talk about his parents. I found their names in an old Bible, and the letters said my grandfather died."

"Interesting. So you don't know anything about your ancestors? How about hiring me to do your research?" Ms. Davenport lay her hand on the desk and leaned toward him, her eyes smoldering. At least that's what he thought she was trying to portray; all Matt could see was desperation. "We could work well together. I would love to have a reason to call the Senator." Her voice dropped into a purr.

Matt recoiled and picked up the folder, pulling it from her posterior anchor. "Thanks, I want to do this on my own and quietly. I doubt this would make the national news, but who knows. I just need to know where to start."

"Is there something suspect about your family that you want to keep hidden?" She stood up again, running her tongue hungrily along her lower lip.

"Other than I'm related to a senator who's running for president? No, I just wondered what happened to my ancestors and where they came from."

"Go on over and find a table. I'll bring you some examples of what others have done." She reaccessed him. "It's usually women about your age who get the genealogy bug. Men, that takes longer. I'm glad you're starting young enough that some of the family is around to talk."

Matt retreated, the folder pinned under his arm. He walked around the shelving and spotted the young man who had stood next to him at the desk.

"Hi. Tim, isn't it?" Matt set the folder down across from the young man. "May I sit here?"

"Tim Pelton. Sure, you can sit there if you want." Tim shuffled some papers aside to clear a little more space for Matt.

"I'm Matt." He deliberately left off the last name. He didn't know if Tim had heard the conversation between him and Miss Davenport, but he didn't want to rehash it.

Tim's dark hair, cut short and a fake earring had Matt at odds with the boy's brain. He was doing calculus and had a stack of psychology books half spilling out of his backpack. The young man looked like he belonged in a rock band, not sitting in a library on the weekend working on mathematics.

"I think you got under her skin a little." Tim grinned, revealing even white teeth. "Ms. Davenport comes on to almost all the new guys who walk into this library." He grimaced and looked back at his laptop.

"You, too?" Matt opened the folder with the forms and pulled one out.

"She used to. I come in to study for classes a couple of times a week, and she's known as the 'Welcome Wagon.'"

Before they could say anything more, Ms. Davenport strode over, carrying a small stack of books. "Look at the way these people set up their family trees and went about printing them." She set them on the table beside him and flounced off without further comment.

Matt slid the first book off the stack and read a few pages before opening the next book. When he had looked at almost all of them and got the idea of what he needed to do, Tim cleared his throat a few times. Matt looked up at him.

"I think someone squealed on you." Tim's eyes were on something across the room, but his head stayed low.

"What?" Matt's eyes remained on the family tree he was studying.

"I think the lovely Ms. Davenport wants to be on the news with you. She's called someone, and it seems like they are all waiting for them to arrive. She has Maid Marian on watch at the door. Do you want to be interviewed?"

Matt's head jerked up and then looked around. "What?"

"The Goth girl, Marian, is at the door. Miss Davenport is grinning and looking at you as if you're her ticket to the red carpet. She's probably called the TV station, and they're going to interview the nephew of the Senator."

"How did you know that?" Matt rubbed his neck.

"I was standing right behind you when she asked if you and the Senator were related. Do you want to be on TV?" Matt shook his head. Tim glanced over his shoulder before continuing. "We don't have much time. The back door has an emergency alarm on it, but we can outsmart them if we have a plan. What did you drive?"

"Why?" Confused by the young man's questions, Matt kept his eyes on the women gathered around the front desk. The ladies were shooting him furtive glances and trying to look inconspicuous, though they were doing a lousy job of it.

"I'll give you my keys. You drive my car, and I'll drive yours. They'll follow you to get the plates of the car you're driving and then 'your' address." He laughed as he slid his laptop and notebook into the backpack. "But they'll end up with mine instead. Do you know the Tick Tock Diner?"

"Doesn't everyone?" Matt retorted his head spinning as he gathered his materials in a rush.

Tim slid his keys, palmed in his hand, across to Matt. "Now follow me and give me your keys. I hope you can drive a stick." Tim stood, stretched, and pulled his backpack over his shoulder. "Meet me at the emergency door in thirty seconds." He nodded his head toward the back wall and walked away with long, purposeful strides.

Matt closed up the books and checked the clock. Counting the seconds, he moved around the shelves, and then hustled to the emergency door when he was out of sight of the front desk occupants.

At the door, he handed Tim his keys and prayed this wasn't a setup. "It's the red Mustang at the back of the lot."

"All right! Mine's the Jeep, black, right by the back driveway. Are you ready? They're looking for you."

"Let's do it."

Matt's heart raced in fear and excitement. Tim leaned into the bar, and the alarm sounded. The two men spilled into the parking lot as the door slammed behind them. Tim pointed to his Jeep, and

Matt pointed to his mustang. A TV van and a car right on its bumper pulled into the parking lot as he scrambled into the Jeep's front seat.

Matt jammed the key into the ignition and turned it. The ignition ground angrily. He tried again, and this time it caught. It took all of his self-control not to let out a whoop of relief at the sound of the engine growling to life. He looked over his shoulder at the library's front doors and saw the goth girl run outside. She pointed at the Mustang to the driver of the van. The Jeep slid into the street as the other car pulled out behind him; he grinned. Matt learned to drive a stick shift from a friend whose father was a race car driver. Those lessons came in handy now as he sped down the street in a squeal of rubber. In a few short blocks, he outdistanced the car. He let the guy move in just close enough to get the Jeep's license number then sped off. Matt took several turns, leaving the other driver at a red light, and in a few moments, he was alone. A ridiculous grin covered his face as he glanced in the mirror one final time and headed to the diner.

Matt scoured the diner's parking lot for the Mustang. At first, he didn't see it, and a cold sick feeling sat in his stomach. As he drove around the back of the lot, he found it between two delivery vans. His smile returned at Tim's camouflage, and Matt pulled in behind it.

In the diner, he found Tim with his hands cupped around a chipped white porcelain cup of coffee. The ripped vinyl covers were the same as they had been during the late nights of his college days. A quick look around told him not much had changed. Derelicts, college kids, and a few truckers graced the counter and booths.

"You made it." Tim nodded in approval, showing that same cocky grin he'd had on his face in the library.

"How did you know she called the TV station?" Matt slid into the booth.

"I wasn't sure, but it was the way Miss Davenport was prancing and preening. Then Maid Marian stood guard at the door. I suspected Miss Davenport had called someone important. With her, it's always TV. She's desperate for her ten seconds or more on camera. The reporters aren't going to let it go. They'll question her and then follow up to see if the Senator has family here."

"Yeah, well, there are a few left. Not that any of us are going to be talking to the media about Henry. He doesn't talk to us or have anything to do with us, so I don't think there's much love lost there." Matt held up a finger for the waitress to bring him a cup of coffee. The woman walked past and set a mug before him, and he grimaced when he saw the black liquid. It didn't do any good to ask for decaf in this place.

"I'm guessing there was some fall out in the family?" Tim slurped the hot beverage.

"No. The mighty Henry never came to family gatherings. I guess we were too common for him. We're all middle working class, and he lives in New York with as much money as the Rockefellers." Uncle Lucas had told him he kept in contact with his brother, but Matt doubted Henry had any more contact with Matt's cousins than he did Matt and his siblings.

"What do you think of his politics?" Tim asked.

"I don't talk about politics. I vote privately, and I expect others to do the same. I don't get why people want to know who I'll vote for; it's not any of their business."

Tim nodded. "So you're doing a genealogy. What made you start that? You aren't an old lady looking up her ROOTS." He emphasized the last word.

"I came across a bunch of letters between my grandfather and grandmother. I guess my grandfather was sick and died in a hospital. I didn't find anything about my grandmother. My Uncle Lucas hasn't talked about her, nor did my dad when he was alive. I wondered what happened to her and why no one will talk about it."

"Have you signed up online for 'Genroots'?" Tim took another swig from his mug.

"What's that?"

"It's a website that people searching for their family trees sign onto and post what they know already. Any others who might have similar family members connect and share information, like your cousins on either your mother's or father's side."

"I know all my aunts, uncles, and cousins on my dad's side. I need to find more information about his parents."

"One more thing: you need to look at census records. The best place to do that is the Mormon Library." Tim pulled out a notebook from his backpack, wrote the address down, ripped off the page, and pushed Matt. "I'm a Mormon. Here's where you can find the closest library. Would you like some help navigating the place?"

Matt grinned and folded the paper. "Sure, when?"

"I have classes tomorrow, but how about Thursday?"

Matt nodded. They agreed on a time and went their separate ways.

The hospital corridors were quiet as Matt made his way to his uncle's room. He had received a call from the doctor stating Uncle Lucas was stable and could have visitors again. Matt lingered in the doorway, watching his uncle for a moment before he knocked on the door. The older man slurped his soup around a mouthful of some kind of sandwich. Lucas's eyes followed the program on TV, and most of the soup landed on his gown rather than in his mouth.

When he saw Matt, he grinned. "Matty-boy!" He must've been in good spirits to call him by that boyhood nickname. "Sit, boy, the food here isn't bad at all. Do you want some?" He shoved the tray towards Matt, presenting him with a half-eaten sandwich, a cup of soup, and an untouched apple.

Matt shook his head and closed his eyes against his uncle's open maw as he chewed his food. "No, thanks." Matt sat in a chair next to his uncle but faced the TV mounted on the wall. "You look better than the last time I saw you, Uncle Lucas." Matt set the box he brought on the floor beside the bed. "Can you turn off the TV? We need to talk."

At the seriousness of his expression, Lucas fumbled for the remote and pressed the mute button. "Did you throw anything out of the dining room or my den?" Lucas fixed a sharp, blue stare at Matt.

"Funny you should ask. We cleaned outside the back porch and part of the front porch. I went into the house and removed all the bags and boxes in the back hallway and mudroom. Then we hit the kitchen. That took us most of the day. The kitchen was the worst, I think. I don't know how it got that way, but we ended up having to go outside for air more than once." Matt tried to settle his stomach at the memory of the maggot-infested takeout boxes. "After Sam and Steve left, I went into the dining room you told me to leave alone. I saw what you meant about important things." Matt leaned his arms on his knees.

"What?" His uncle tried to sit up but began to cough.

"There isn't anything to make you upset. It was just a bunch of newspapers."

"Those newspapers—" Lucas coughed— "are important." He coughed again and waved his bony hand at the plastic cup with the bent straw. Matt held it to his uncle's lips and waited while Lucas took a couple of pulls from it and sunk into the pillows.

Matt heard machines beep and the whisper of soft-soled shoes in the silence. He leaned down and pulled a couple of newspapers out of the box. "Uncle Lucas, who are the McGuires, the Sheltons, and the Bacons?" Matt opened the newspaper and laid it on the blanket covering his uncle's lap.

Lucas looked at the paper and the underlined names. He turned his head away soundlessly. The documents varied yellow depending on their age, but the names were consistent.

"Why are they circled? Who were these people?"

"No one, you need to know," Lucas muttered.

"Uncle, I'm trying to be sensitive. You told me everything in that room is important. If you think they're important enough to keep, I want to know why. If it all went up in flames for some reason, how upset would you be?" He watched Lucas wince and clench his teeth.

"Not fire. Never fire," Matt heard Lucas say whisper a response. An expression of pain and fear painted his tired face.

Matt, encouraged by a response, continued. "Please, tell me what you remember about your mother and father. How did Samuel die? What happened to Katherine?"

At the direct question, Lucas turned his back to Matt and stared at the wall. "I don't want to talk about it. It's all in the past. Those things need to be forgotten."

"Forgotten?" Matt walked around the bed to face his uncle. "Forgotten?" His voice rose, and he clamped his teeth together. "Forgotten like all those papers with the names of families and people circled? Letters to and from Sam and Katherine, kept in a box for someone to read but not to understand? Is this what you call forgotten?" Matt tapped the newspaper on the bed. "I'm going to be upfront right now and tell you I'm going to find out what happened to Grandma Katherine. I can probably find Grandpa Samuel's burial records somewhere near Millerton. The letters stopped in 1947 when he died. I found the family Bible in Dad's stuff. It lists all your birth dates and Samuel's death date, but not where he's buried. There isn't any mention of Grandma Katherine dying. Finding what happened to her would be a whole lot easier if you'd just tell me."

He waited, but Lucas's eyes closed. Matt was silent a little longer, his frustration ready to boil over.

"Was she killed or murdered? What happened to her? Why won't you tell me?" Matt's lowered his voice to a softer pleading tone as he leaned closer to his uncle.

"Because I don't know." Matt heard Lucas's voice as he spaced the words out in a whisper.

Matt picked up the box and strode to the door. "I'm going to find out what happened to her and why you and Dad never talked about her." He left Uncle Lucas's room, strode out of the hospital, and sat in his car for a good ten minutes before he turned the key. "I'm going to find her."

Matt tapped the steering wheel, waiting for Tim to join him in the Mormon Library parking lot. He looked at his watch for the twenty-fifth time. Where is he?

Matt watched Tim's Jeep squeal around the corner in his rear-view mirror and screech to a stop in the spot beside him. Matt slung his bag over his shoulder and pressed the automatic lock as he came around Tim's car.

As Tim climbed out of the Jeep, Matt noticed he didn't have his regular messenger bag. Instead, he carried his laptop under his arm and had a tired expression on his young face.

"What's up?" asked Matt.

"I had a break-in." Tim pointed the way to the back of the building. "I got to my apartment and found it ransacked, really trashed. They took my computer tower, monitor, and my bag. They even tipped over my filing cabinet. I don't know what they were looking for."

"I'm sorry. Did you call the police?" Matt frowned as Tim spoke, worry bubbling up in his chest.

"Sure, but the police said it was probably someone looking for drugs or something to sell for drugs. Matt, I'm not so sure about that. Yeah, the bedroom was a mess, but I had cash in my file cabinet. If someone had been looking for money, they would've found it. I think they wanted my computer."

"What for? You're a student." Matt opened the library door and followed Tim inside.

"That's it. I do some freelance writing, but nothing more than an editorial here and there."

"That's too bad. I hope you get it back." He followed Tim to a bank of microfilm machines.

A half an hour later, Matt stared at the census from 1920. The pages were a mass of names, some of which he remembered seeing underlined in his uncle's newspapers. He found the name Sullivan, Samuel, but he wasn't married. At the time, he was living with someone named Crestwell. He must have been living with another family. There was another boy in that family the same age, probably his friend.

Silence reigned between the two men as they continued to search the records, but a little while later, Tim asked Matt from the other side of the cube, "Hey, what was your grandmother's maiden name?"

"Collins," Matt told him.

"Timothy, this is a library! SHHH!" The woman in charge of ordering the census records put her finger to her lips, scowling at Tim in a motherly fashion.

"Sorry," Tim whispered loud enough for her to hear, and then leaned over to Matt. "She was my teacher for too long. Come and look at this; I think I've found something."

Matt leaned over and saw where Tim was pointing. "There's something weird here. A Katherine Collins lived in a small community with her father and a number of people with the same last name. Some were born a year apart, and some the same year." He frowned and pressed the print button and turned the button to the next set of names and pressed the print button again. "It looks as if this family was huge. Let's find out where they lived." Tim looked at a set of maps he pulled up on his computer, but no Miller Hollow, WV showed up.

Tim scrolled forward and back, trying to find some city name or area that would tell him where Katherine lived. Finally, he shook his head. "I can't find any reference to where they lived. From what I can tell, they must have lived up in the mountains. I wonder how the census taker ever got up there to take the census?" Tim shook his head and went to collect the pages he printed and handed them to Matt. "If this is your Katherine Collins, you might have an interesting history."

Matt looked at the census pages. The name Lucas showed up multiple times. One Henry, one Joseph, and one Elijah. Most were Biblical names. He shook his head. "Where can we find the next census to see if they were still there?"

"Sorry, that's the last census. There aren't more available to the public after 1920." Tim returned to his monitor.

The two men stayed a few more hours, gathered what they found, and headed out. "I have plans tomorrow, so I won't be able to meet you until Thursday," Tim told Matt.

Tim stopped at his car and turned to Matt. "Is there someone who might not want you to find your roots?"

Matt gave him a grimace. "What kind of a question is that? I don't know anyone who would have any interest in what I'm doing. I'm just a guy wondering what happened to his grandmother. Does that sound sinister?" He gave a little laugh to dismiss the question.

"I'm not so sure. You are, after all, related to Senator Sullivan. If your Uncle Lucas won't talk about his mother, do you think your Uncle Henry might?"

Matt mulled over the question as he drove home. He would look for Henry's phone number in his dad's old address book. What would his Uncle have to say about what he was doing?

At home, he pulled out the map of West Virginia. Going over the mountainous areas, he still couldn't find where Katherine Collins and her family lived. He looked at the Bible again, but there were no names of any other family besides Sam and Katherine's children written anywhere or on any paper tucked between the pages.

CHAPTER 6

MILLERTON, WV

March–May 1947

KATHERINE AND EMMA SAT IN THE DINING room, hunched over Emma's wedding dress. Each wore gloves as they sewed on the details of the dress. The harsh soap and hot water took its toll on their skin, and the gloves prevented the soft satin fabric from snagging on their worn hands as they worked.

"Mom, I don't want a wedding like Martha." Emma looked down at the dress for a moment, then up at her mother. "I know her wedding was hard on you and Dad. I don't have all that many friends in Millerton. Tom's parents aren't coming, so if we get married at the church and have a small dinner at Tom's house, that will be just fine for me." Her mouth curled up at the corners, and her eyes were soft.

Katherine reached her hand to Emma's and patted it affectionately. "If that's what you want. You have a wonderful man. The fact that he finds you as wonderful as we do shows me he will be a great husband to you. I want you to have the most wonderful day that you will remember with pride."

"Mother, I understand." Emma blushed. "I don't need a lot of fluff. Simple is better."

Katherine squeezed her daughter's hand, then returned to the minute stitches on the lace.

Martha's wedding had been a big affair, just as she had wanted. She was the leader of her group of friends, and when David had met her at a dance, Martha manipulated an introduction to him. The rest was history.

She had planned a big wedding in the Millerton Church right down to the last flower arrangement and table setting. They hadn't been able to afford much, but they had enjoyed cake and homemade ice cream. The reception was held in the school gym, which she and her friends had decorated.

Katherine needed some air and stripped off her gloves. "I'll be right back." She headed outside and leaned against the back porch railing.

Before her, the great Allegheny Mountains reached up towards the sky. Their dense green forest hid the remnants of a society of miners, immigrants, and a way of life so different than what she wanted for her family.

Her mind returned to the day she and Samuel made their way up the mountain to confront her family with a demand. It had been early summer, and the trail was almost overgrown. Samuel had to get off his horse several times and use a machete to clear the way so the horse would be safe from brambles. Katherine knew her family was already aware of their every move up the trail; they had scouts and lookouts to warn them of visitors.

Four clapboard shacks and a log house sat on each side of the natural ravine. Chickens scratched at the dry, bare dirt, trying to find food, and men lounged on the porches with long-barreled shotguns across their arms or laps.

Katherine stopped her horse in front of one of the houses. Samuel rode up beside her, his rifle on his arm.

"Well, little girl, you came home." A skinny older man with long, straggly white hair stepped out on the porch. A stained leather vest covered his faded plaid shirt. A rope held up threadbare, broadcloth pants that barely met the tops of black mountain boots.

"I didn't come home to stay. I came to talk." Katherine remained on the horse.

"Get down, girl. Show some respect for your pappy." Another man, older than her father, roared from his rocking chair on the porch. She didn't respond, nor did she get down.

"Millie! Get out here and bring your granpappy sumthin' to drink." The older man banged a cane on the porch as he returned to his seat. Katherine stiffened.

The door opened, and Katherine held her breath. Millie stepped onto the porch, and her gaze never left the ground. Katherine recognized the faded calico dress she'd made her aunt some years ago. A lump rose in her throat as she slid from the horse, tossing the reins to Samuel. He tried to protest, but she ignored him.

Katherine walked toward the porch. Her father stepped in front of her, stopping her with the barrel of his rifle.

"Y'are pretty, girl. You come back here to find out what a real man is? Not some mamby pamby citified boy like the one sittin' there?" His voice was low enough for only Katherine to hear.

"Lander, you're one sick fool if you think I want anything to do with you or your ilk." She shoved the barrel away and walked up the steps to Millie, no longer afraid.

Katherine watched the woman who had been the only mother she had known. Millie had taken care of her, protecting her from her father and the other men that skulked around the nearby mountains, watching her grow up.

The other women in the commune could've been a sister, aunt, or even mother to any one of the children running around half-dressed and caked with dirt.

"Millie?" she called, but the woman said nothing and turned, walking into the darkness and letting the holey screen door bang between them. Katherine followed, holding her breath at the stench of body odor and a myriad of other smells she was glad to be no longer accustomed to.

"Millie, it's Katherine." She stopped a little ways from the emaciated woman.

Her heart broke when Millie turned to face her. There were bruises in various shades of purple and yellow on her face. Her nose swollen as a result of a recent blow. Katherine reached out her hand, but Millie recoiled, shielding her face and whimpering.

"Oh, Millie, I'm not going to hurt you." Katherine stopped a few feet from her. "Millie, look at me. Do you know who I am?" Tears gathered in her eyes, threatening to spill over her lashes. The pain of the abuse to this woman ripped at every emotion. Katherine lifted her hand out to Millie but didn't touch her.

Millie opened the eye not swollen and tried to focus on the blurry figure in front of her. "Katie girl?" The voice was rough, as if she hadn't used it recently. Her lips looked like a hair lip from repeated beatings.

Katherine moved closer, but Millie stood still as she stared at the other woman. Katherine folded the older woman into her arms and held back the tears that threatened to fall.

"You didn't come. I waited, but you didn't come." There was no animosity or anger, just a statement as dry and barren as the yard where scrawny chickens scratched. It released the hurt in Katherine, and the tears flowed as she hugged the bony figure. There was no response to the hug, but it didn't matter to Katherine.

"I'm so sorry. So sorry." The words repeated over and over as the tears flowed. She felt a movement and a pat on her lower back.

"It's okay, baby girl. I knew you were safe, happy, and word came now and then that you had babies of your own. It made me happy to know you weren't here."

"Millie, will you come with me now?" Katherine sniffed and pulled the hankie from her waist pocket. "I have a place for you, and I can take care of you."

"No. I'm not long for this world now."

Katherine jerked her head up to look at Millie. "What's wrong?"

"There is somethin' inside me, eating me up. I feel it. One of these days, I'm not going to wake up." She touched Katherine's arm. "Will you come and say the words for me? Bring your children so's I kin know sommin' cared?"

"I care! I'll take you to Dr. Mallory; he might have something for you."

Millie took Katherine's hands in her own and squeezed them. "No. I've put up with all this, now they jus' leave me alone. I tol' 'em I have an insect inside me, and it's eatin me. They's all skeered of it, so I stay alone." There was a long pause before Millie spoke again. "Why you here after all this time?"

"My oldest is marryin'." Katherine caught herself. "Martha's getting married. She's having a proper wedding and reception and doesn't want any booze or rough housing. You boys aren't invited. I'm here to ask Paw to keep them home."

"You kin ask, but I don't know it'll do ya any good. They'll come if they wanna." Millie patted Katherine's arm. "Come with me. I have sumpin for ya."

"For me? Oh, Millie, I don't want to take anything from you."

The woman turned to her and got right up in her face. "Don't you be tellin' me nothing, girl! I've been savin' it all this time. You'll take it."

Katherine felt the same shame she had as a child when she had done something wrong. Even then, she never wanted to hurt Millie. She knew her dad and others hurt Millie, and she didn't want to do that or make her cry. Katherine followed the woman into the small room with its boards stuffed with mud and rags to keep the cold out. She had no idea how they stayed warm all those years ago, cuddling up in the twin rope bed with its tick stuffing. Millie made sure there was plenty of lavender dried to stuff in the ticking to "keep them damn bugs away."

Millie knelt on the floor and pushed the bed to one side, aided by Katherine. Millie's bony hands pried a floorboard door up and pulled out a wooden box that smelled like cedar. Millie handed it over to Katherine, then struggled to stand up and motioned for Katherine to put it on the bed. Millie opened the lid and lifted out dresses, pants, and shirts for baby boys and girls. At the bottom lay a quilt. She proudly displayed it for Katherine. "This is your wedding present."

Katherine felt the shame rise past her throat, and she fought the tears that threatened to fall.

"Oh, it's beautiful, Millie." She fingered the material and the fine stitching around the edge. She recognized the material from some of her and Millie's dresses. Katherine put her arms around the only mother she ever knew. "I love you, Millie. I don't know if I ever said those words. I don't think I heard them much growing up around the menfolk, but I knew you loved me. I want you to know that I have always loved you." Emotion broke her voice, and the tears flowed again. "Are you sure you won't come down the mountain with Sam and me?" She whirled to face the door as she realized she'd left him alone out there with a bunch of hostile men. "Sam! I have to get out there; I don't know if Paw's killed him or the other way around." She didn't even correct the slip.

"You go on, girl. I'm goin' ta jus' lay here for a while. I'm a bit tired." She waved Katherine out.

Katherine folded the quilt and the clothes. "Millie, I need to ask you something." Millie turned her back, but Katherine continued, "Who are my mother and father?"

It was a long moment before Millie spoke. "What you wanta go knowin' that fer?" Her voice sounded tired and a little offended.

"I'm old enough for the truth. I hold no blame. I just want to know for my peace of mind."

"You're my own little baby. You're paw, well, I'm not exactly sure. Back then, I was pretty like you. Some just had to have it, even Paw. Did that make you feel any better, baby girl?" Millie still didn't turn around. Her voice was bitter and hurt.

"Why didn't you ever tell me?"

"What do you think of me now?" It was almost a challenge, trying to prove she didn't deserve the kindness.

Katherine stepped around the stiff, almost skeletal form. "Mother, I love you as much as I did then. You were my mother in secret. While you never said so and wouldn't tell me, I dreamed that you were my mother." She wrapped her arms around the other woman. "You will always be my mother. I have no ill thoughts about what happened. I know what goes on up here and all over these hills. That's why I had to get away. When Otis and Luke cornered me, I had to fight to get away. I knew I would end up like the others. I left. I met Sam, and we have a wonderful family. I hope you'll come down and see them."

Katherine gave Millie one last hug and picked up the box. "I'll come again when I can." She qualified the promise.

"You will sweetling'. Bye now." Millie lay back on the bed and closed her eyes. Her hands lay crossed over her waist.

Katherine fought back emotion as she stepped out on the porch. Sam stood by the horses, his face set in stern lines.

"I'm fine, Sam." She walked to him and handed him the box. He strapped it to the back of the saddle.

Two of the men started toward them, their guns leveled at the couple. Katherine turned, and a knife stuck straight up on the ground between one of the men's feet in a flash. "Don't come any closer. I haven't lost my touch. Y'all step back, and I'll take what's mine."

The men scrambled back so fast, one fell and crab-walked out of her way. She bent to pull her knife out of the ground and slid it back into the sheath, hidden in the folds of her riding shirt.

"Listen up! My daughter is gettin' married and you're not invited. She wants none of your shenanigans, no moonshine, fighting, or your sloppy dress. I don't want it, either. We've lived apart all these years except for the few times you've come to town, shot it up, and ended in jail. I don't want to see hide nor hair of you anywhere near that weddin'." She swung into the saddle and nodded to Sam.

"Are you sure we should turn around and ride away?" Sam's voice was tight, and he stared at the men around them with concerned eyes.

"We're safe, Sam. We aren't feuding, so there isn't anything to worry about." She nudged the horse's sides, and they moved faster down the trail until they were out of sight.

Her mother died that night; Shadrack came down to tell her. Sam rode back to the little town on the ridge at her side. She and the other woman washed Millie's body and readied her for burial.

Her name, Millie Collins, and her death date burnt into the coffin's lid. Katherine had no idea how old her mother was, though she looked to be in her fifties.

One of the women spoke with Katherine in a private moment, "She was just a youngin' when she stumbled to our house holding her gut in pain. She didn't know what was wrong. You were born. Millie was probably fourteen or fifteen." The other women nodded. "She loved you from that moment 'til her death. Even when you left, she never spoke again' ya."

No one from the mountain came to Martha's wedding. They wouldn't come for Emma's either.

On the day of Emma's wedding that June, the sun shone bright, and not a cloud floated in the azure sky. The entire town met at the church and watched as Emma Sullivan married Thomas Conrad with his daughters looking on.

"They're tearing up their hankies," Cassie whispered to Katherine as they waited for Thomas and Emma to come outside to the reception.

"What do you mean?" Katherine shot back.

"Those old biddies have to be here to put on a good front for Thomas. He's in high standing here in town. It wouldn't be good if they snubbed him. The fact he chose Emma and not one of their girls is rubbing them like sand in a swimsuit." Cassie waved her fan, disguising their conversation.

Katherine giggled. "Look at them over there, just waiting for the cake and ice cream to be served so they can leave."

Most of the town remained at the reception until Thomas and Emma ran through the rain of rice to Thomas's car. The newlyweds were driving to Columbus, taking Thomas's daughters to stay with their other grandparents while the two went on their honeymoon.

Cassie and Katherine waved them off, then turned to clean up the reception tables.

After school, two weeks later, Katherine heard the water run in the sink. Longer than to fill a glass. Lucas must've been in the kitchen. She hadn't heard the screen door squeak open or slam closed.

She frowned. "Lucas! Come here, please." She eyed him as he slunk into the living room and saw blood on the side of his neck, his head turned away from her. Katherine leaped to her feet and rushed to him, and turned his head to face her. Lucas had a swollen left cheek and a cut on the other.

"What happened?"

"It's nothing. It'll be okay." Lucas pushed at her hands and tried to escape, but she held onto his arm.

"I need to know why you were fighting." She moved to stand in front of him. The young man ducked around her, but Katherine held firm. Lucas was taller and stronger, but she stopped him. "I can take anything you have to say."

Lucas turned to face her, and she saw the pain he tried to hide. "The guys were saying bad things about you, things that men shouldn't say about a guy's mother. I had to stand up for you." He pulled away from her and balled his fists at his sides.

Katherine ached for his hurt, both physical and emotional. "I hope the other guy looks worse than you." The woman smiled and smoothed her thumb over the bruised cheek. "Sit down and let me wash you up." Katherine guided him back toward the kitchen, her hand on his wrist.

Lucas winced when she put the mercurochrome on the cuts, but he waved her away when she held out the adhesive. "That's all right. I don't need it."

"It'll leave a scar. Let me put a couple of little ones over the cut, at least.

No one will see them," she teased.

He turned away, and paper crinkled in his pocket. "Ma, I got the mail. There's a letter for you from Martha."

She stopped and held out her hand. Lucas gave her the letter and escaped the kitchen.

Katherine poured hot coffee into a mug and spooned in a dollop of cream before sitting at the table and placing the envelope on the red-checkered oilcloth. The woman ripped the end off and pulled out the paper. A smile spread across her lips.

"Dear Mother," The letter began. Martha wrote about painting the walls of their apartment and how she had found a job at a hotel helping set up for parties. She was learning how to set a fancy table, fold napkins, and serve properly. Katherine could tell she was excited to know all the things that people in society took for granted. Katherine felt a moment of envy before it passed.

"Mother, David is now the Foreman at the foundry. There's an opening that Father could fill, but it would mean moving here. He can stay with us for a few weeks until he gets paid. Then he can move to the boarding house where other workers live. This isn't a great opportunity, but I know you're concerned about how to keep things together. The pay is good, and after Father pays his room and board, there'll be some left to send to you. There's overtime, too, so he can make enough to put away, and maybe you all can move here."

Katherine stared at the words. Thoughts whirled around her head. Sam would be leaving her for who knew how long? Her chest clenched so tight she couldn't catch her breath. No Sam to snuggle up to on the cold winter nights and put his cold feet on her. No Sam to greet the boys at the door. No Sam to drink all the coffee. He was everything to her. How could she ever get along without seeing him? She could do it if she had to. If it meant moving to the city, having the money to go to one of the fancy dinners that Martha helped serve. She could do it with that goal in mind.

After dinner and the boys left to do their chores, Katherine took Sam's hand and led him to the oversized chair in the living room. It was one they found in the back of a store ready to be thrown out. The owner had laughed and said, "Take it." They loaded it into the back of an old truck and hauled it home. She bought new fabric and recovered it. Now it was their favorite chair.

Sam sat down and pulled Katherine over the large arms and into his lap. His full lips came down on hers, and Katherine clung to him, pressing her lips to his desperation. Sam broke the kiss and frowned down at her. He looked confused and then concerned at the tears that gathered in her eyes. "What's wrong, babe?"

"I got a letter from Martha today."

"That brings tears? What's wrong with her? Is everything okay?"

She patted his cheek and pulled the letter from her apron pocket. "David became the foreman at the factory where he works. He has a job for you."

"He does?" Sam's eyes lit up, and he grinned. Then the realization of what that meant settled in, and the smile faded. "I'd have to go there."

Katherine nodded. "You can live with them until you get paid, and then you can move to the boarding house where other men who work at the plant life." She told him the pay, and Sam's eyes widened in appreciation.

"I know. It's almost too good to turn down." Katherine leaned against his chest, and her husband wrapped his arms around her in a tight hug.

"Let's think about this a little bit before we make a final decision."

CHAPTER 7

COLUMBUS, OH

July 2000

MATT ENTERED HIS UNCLE'S HOSPITAL ROOM later in the week and was pleased to see his Uncle Lucas looking better. He'd been bathed and shaved, and the older man smiled as he watched the latest game show.

"I won the last three games!" He gave Matt a grin as he announced his success.

"I'm not surprised; you're one smart guy." Matt pulled the chair closer. "I finished throwing out the moldy, mice-chewed pillows and junk from the upstairs. Steve, Sam, and I spent the whole of a Saturday and Sunday on the rooms upstairs, going through closets. We threw out anything that was broken and kept anything that looked salvageable or something you could wear or want to use at some time. They're clean, and we hung them up in your closet. We had to throw out the mattress and box springs.

"Do you want me to buy you a new bed, or are you going to keep living in the den when you get home?" Matt kept the judgment and condemnation from his voice as he spoke. It didn't go unnoticed as Lucas sat up straighter in the bed and smoothed the sheet over the bony appendages that poked beneath.

"Thank you." The words lost in a cough, and then he added, "I think I'd like a new bed. One that fits the body and you can move up and down with a button, like this one." He held up the white control. "I saw them on TV."

"You're welcome." Matt ignored the reference to the hospital bed. "Lucas, in one of the bedrooms upstairs, we found a stack of boxes full of dishes and glassware labeled 'Ferris.' How come their dishes are in boxes when there are already plenty in the hutch downstairs?"

"The dishes in the hutch are my family's. I got them from home we lived in." His voice trailed out, and his eyes went distant.

"How did you get your family's dishes? Did your mom give them to you?" The younger man was hungry to hear the truth from his uncle, and his voice was sharper than he intended.

"No. I put it all in boxes and hid them in the woods. I went back later and brought them to my house."

Matt sat back. "Where was your mother?" He got no response. "Are you ready to tell me what happened to Katherine?"

"I don't know what happened to her." Uncle Lucas turned away, but Matt didn't give up.

"Who are these people?" Matt put the box on Lucas's lap. "Where did you get these?" Uncle Lucas demanded.

"In a box partially eaten by a rodent or two. See the teeth marks on the wood? They were trying to get inside, Uncle Lucas; this is what I'm talking about. When you have important things, they need to be taken care of, not left to decompose or become a habitat for the local animals."

Lucas gently lifted the class pictures out of the box. "This is your father's class." He pointed to a face.

Matt leaned close to look at the face of the young man. There was a family resemblance in the jawline and nose. He took the picture and turned it over to write his father's name on the back, row, and place.

"This is nothing." Lucas slipped another picture behind the others, trying to hide it.

"Let me guess: that would be one of your school pictures." Matt waited, but Uncle Lucas ignored him and continued.

"This is another of your father's." He pointed to Joseph, Matt's father, in the picture. Matt wrote the information on the back as he had with the first. The following photo was of Henry as a little boy. There were two of Emma and two or three of Martha and Emma in the same class picture.

Matt took the photos and marked them with the names and places. He would call his cousins later to see if they wanted them. If not, he'd scanned them into his computer, at least, so they wouldn't be misplaced.

"Now, who is this?" Matt held out the pictures of the man in the casket.

Lucas looked at the first photo, closed his eyes, and leaned his head back against the pillows. An expression of sorrow and pain crossed his weathered face, and Matt could see his throat muscles move as he swallowed convulsively.

"It's your dad, isn't it?" Matt whispered.

Uncle Lucas nodded, the photos lying loosely in his trembling hands. Matt took the photographs and looked at the man again, studying his features. Uncle Lucas looked a lot like his father with the same high cheekbones and gaunt appearance.

"He died of TB, didn't he?" Matt asked. Uncle Lucas nodded again. "Did he live with you the whole time?" Matt was pretty sure the answer was no but asked anyway.

"No, he got a job in Bowersville where Martha and David lived. He had a cough for a long time. Doc Mallory gave him syrup." A smile pulled at Lucas's lips. "It was that stuff you can't get nowadays; illegal, they say. Dad said it made him feel like he did when he sipped the moonshine from his dad's jug as a kid. He'd only take a sip if the coughing got real bad.

"When he went to work in the foundry, it got worse, and the doctor there said he had tuberculosis. They sent Dad to the hospital, but they didn't have a bed for him. They sent him to Clarksburg General Hospital. We didn't see him again until they brought him home for burial." Uncle Lucas's voice dropped to a broken whisper. He turned his head away. Matt reached out and squeezed his uncle's arm with a gentle touch.

"You forget, Uncle, I lost my dad, too. Not quite as young as you, but I miss him just as much." The loss of his father and friend rose in his throat. "I know how you feel."

Uncle Lucas pulled his arm away. "You don't have any idea what I'm feeling. Don't get all mushy with me, boy. There's a lot you don't know."

Matt ignored the curt response. It was a response he expected. He pondered what Lucas said and pulled a few more photos out. Uncle Lucas named the couple in one picture as Ben and Cassie Lundgren, their neighbors. Each name wrenched from his mouth as if someone pulled them from some dark corner of his mind, and he was fighting to hold them in. Finally, Matt showed him a picture of two women.

One Matt knew one was Cassie from a previous photo. The other, he guessed, was his grandmother. He could see Aunt Emma's features on her face.

"It's Cassie and my mother, Katherine. A man came by with a pony in a trailer. He went around taking pictures of the kids. He saw Mother and Cassie standin' there, laughin' at the horses' antics and the kids. He just turned his camera on them, and he took a picture. They just laughed even harder, so he took another. They're both there." He waved at the box. Matt found the second picture, automatically smiling as he saw the two women holding each other in uncontrolled laughter.

"What happened to her?" The words just slipped out of his mouth. Matt regretted them as soon as he'd said them.

"Is that what you want to know? Do you still want to know what happened to her? Look, boy, it's in the past. Most of the people are long gone and forgotten. She's gone. I have no idea what happened to her, but she's dead— dead to all of us."

Matt didn't speak for a moment, then took the pictures and put them back in the small box. He started to close the lid when a claw hand clamped over his wrist.

"Leave it," Uncle Lucas choked out.

Matt nodded. "I'll take them back later." He sat the box next to his uncle. "Tell me about the Ferrises. How did you come to live with them?"

Uncle Lucas opened one eye and stared. Matt returned his look with unconcerned interest. "I'm just curious."

Uncle Lucas leaned back again and closed his eyes. "We found them one night, Joseph and I, as we were making our way to Martha's house. They were campin'. They had food they shared with us. They traveled in a beat-up old van but were willin' to take us to Martha's."

Matt started to interject with a comment when his uncle paused longer than to take a breath.

Uncle Lucas continued, "We stayed outside of Millerton for a few days. I was worried the sheriff would find us, but Mr. Ferris picked us up one day, and we were off.

"When we got to Martha's, she wouldn't let 'em in the house. She called 'em 'dirty gypsies.' I didn't understand what she meant. I got angry and yelled at her. I told her these nice people took us in and fed us and then drove out of their way to bring us to her." Uncle Lucas lay stiff as he recounted the story. The anger he felt back then rose in his face, turning him red.

He turned to look at Matt. "She said, 'I wish you would've stayed in Millerton. What am I going to do with you two?' Then she looked at me the way I had seen others look at shit on their shoes." He fell back and stared at the ceiling. "I took Joseph by the hand and pulled him away. He began crying and yelling for Martha to take him. She finally called me back and agreed to take Joseph but not me."

Matt felt the pain in his uncle's voice. Anger rose at his Aunt Martha, and a rock the size of Alcatraz lodged his chest and throat. He tried to clear it up. "What did you do?"

"George and Iris Ferris took me with them. We traveled around for a while. I saw the way people treated them and the names they were called. After a couple of years passed traveling around the United States—I've been in every one—they came to Ohio and bought the farm." He chuckled. "Not literally. That came later; they were old."

"Uncle Lucas, what do you know about this couple before they took you in?"

"Not much." He turned his head to look at Matt. "They were gypsies, or 'Romany,' as they preferred to be called."

"I'm not against them. I didn't even know them." Matt protested. "Matt, you were very young when they died."

"I remember them when Dad brought me with him to visit you. I remember them sitting in that big room in the front with the woodstove. It was hot outside, but they had a fire in the stove."

Uncle Lucas gave a dry sound that was his version of a laugh. "That's right, boyo. They kept that house so hot, I was sure one night I'd come in from the fields, and the heat would explode the house when I opened the door!"

Matt rubbed his palms over his thighs. The smooth jean material seemed rough against his palms. "How did they live? How did they afford to travel around and then buy all that land for the farm?"

Lucas shrugged. "I don't know. They had cash. They paid for everything with cash. I figured they were rich when they came over from Europe and changed their money into U.S. money. I never asked what they had, and they never told me. When they got old and couldn't care for themselves, I had to put them in a county home. I wasn't happy about that, but they were happy to be fed three squares. I wasn't much of a cook." He took on a faraway expression.

"They didn't have a bank account? How did you get the farm?"

"Joseph helped me get them into a home, and Henry made sure a lawyer drew up papers signing everything to my name. After they died, I paid for their funeral, but no one came. There was just me and your dad and you. Do you remember that?"

Matt searched his memory and came up with a vague recollection of when he got dressed in his church clothes but didn't go to church. Matt's father, Joseph, picked up Uncle Lucas, and the three of them went to a big park without jungle gyms or slides. They walked a long way to a hole in the ground where a priest was standing.

"I remember that," he said at last. "I thought we were at a park to play."

"Yeah, you kept askin' 'Where's the swings?' Finally, Joseph told you to be quiet; this wasn't a park to play at." He gave a dry rasp that might have passed for a laugh.

"I don't remember much of what came next. I remember stepping on all the stones until you yelled at me, telling me to stop, that I was stepping on dead people's heads. That scared me to death, especially when Dad agreed with you. I had horrible dreams for months that the stones popped up and dead people yelled at me not to step on their heads." Matt's lips spread to a broad smile at the memory.

"Your mother wasn't happy your dad took you to their funeral." Uncle Lucas's voice was weak and sad, and he closed his eyes.

"One last thing. Did you ever look through their camping gear after they were gone? Used any of it to go out camping?" Matt stood at the end of the bed as if his question were an afterthought.

The bushy white brows crawled together on Uncle Lucas's face. "Nope. I didn't see any need to go under the stairs. It was their stuff, and I wasn't doin' any campin'. Do you camp?"

"Not much. Sometimes, I go with my friends, but they have a big trailer, so it isn't roughing it as you did."

"If there's anything you find that you can use under there, have at it."

Matt froze for a moment. Should he tell his uncle about the money? Matt shook his head at himself, making a quick decision. He'd do some more checking before he revealed what he found, just in case the money came from some heist or something.

"We'll talk later about the Ferrises. You should rest awhile."

Matt walked to the door, nearly running into Nurse Evelyn, who came from the opposite way. She laughed as they did a little dance around each other and bustled around, fiddling with the blanket and pillow.

"Are you going to take this?" She motioned to the box as her eyes moved toward Matt.

"Not this time; he wants to look at it some more."

"I'll put it in the bottom drawer here. You can let my uncle know it's there, or I can if he asks." She walked up beside Matt as he walked to the door. "I'm sure he'll be getting better. He's made a remarkable recovery since the heart attack. It's good he has you to visit him." She smiled up at Matt, her eyes twinkling. "It's much easier to recover when you have people who love you coming by."

He didn't look at her but nodded. "I'm all he has. The rest of the family doesn't understand him and thinks he's a freak." This time he gave her a slight smile and lifted his hand in parting as he headed down the hall to the elevator.

At home, Matt called his Uncle Henry's local campaign office and, after some runaround, obtained Henry's campaign manager's name and number. Matt felt a little nervous and awkward as he dialed the number, unsure what exactly to say.

"Kenneth Mullins here." The man who answered had an abrupt voice and all business.

"Sir, I need to talk to Henry Sullivan. How can he be reached?"

"Who are you?" The abruptness intensified, becoming almost combative.

"His nephew."

"Which one?"

"Does it matter?"

After a pause, the man took a deep breath. "What do you want to talk to the Senator about?" The voice sounded both weary and irritated.

"I'm not asking for a handout if that's what you're implying. I need to talk to him. It's a family matter."

"He doesn't have anything to do with his family." Kenneth's tone turned clipped and terse.

"Look, Kenneth. You can have him call me, or I'll have his family tree spread across every paper in the United States." Matt felt the heat rise in his face as his temper threatened to overwhelm his better judgment. "Here's the number where he can reach me. Tell him it's Matt Sullivan." He rattled off his phone number and hung up.

After a moment, Matt slumped in his chair. *That was a stupid thing to do. I don't need to alienate the guy or Henry. I just need some information. Oh well. I can't cry over spilled milk now.* He stood and went to the kitchen to fix a sandwich.

Matt had just finished his coffee when the phone rang. He glanced up at the clock. It was about twenty-five minutes since he talked to Kenneth, so he picked up. "Hello?"

"Is this Matthew Sullivan?"

"Yes." Matt sat heavily in the office chair.

"This is Henry Sullivan. I hear you want to talk to me about the family." His tone was firm but not impolite.

"First, sir, I apologize for what I said earlier. I'd been given the runaround and was at the end of my rope."

"Understandable. What can I do for you?" Uncle Henry's tone remained impersonal, and the sound of shuffling papers came over the line.

"I want to let you know Uncle Lucas is in the hospital." He gave the address of the hospital. "He's doing fine, but I received a clean-up order for his house."

"At last!" There was a sound like a laugh.

"So you know how he lives?" Matt countered.

"Yes, and I've tried over the years to get him to let me have someone clean it up for him. But Lucas is Lucas, and there's nothing I could do. What's the problem? Is he not letting you throw out his 'treasures'?" The last word was heavy with familiar sarcasm.

"Nothing for him. I just wanted you to know he was in the hospital."

"I knew." The statement surprised Matt, and he didn't respond.

Henry continued. "I'm listed as his emergency contact with his primary care doctor. When he went to the hospital, they called his doctor, who, in turn, called me."

"Okay. So I don't need to worry; you have him covered and have taken care of everything." Matt felt the dismissal in Henry's voice and resented it.

There was a sigh on the other end. "Don't get your hackles up, son. I mean, Lucas and I have an understanding. I know you've been keeping a close eye on Lucas over the years. He appreciates it, and so do I. I didn't see any need for us to double up on the job, so I haven't called you."

"I see. So you know about me and what I do to help, but I know nothing about your role in his life." Matt bit off the words as he spoke.

"Matt, is it?" He didn't wait for a confirmation. "Years ago, Lucas gave me a sizable bit of money to invest. I make him money and pay the taxes. Or, rather, my accountant does. Lucas told me you're the only one who truly cares about him, and he appreciates it. That's all I know; he and I don't talk much."

"Thank you." Despite the compliment, Matt couldn't make himself sound anything but deadpan. "Can you tell me where he got the money to invest?"

"Why do you ask?" The voice at the other end became guarded almost immediately, though it wasn't unfriendly.

"I got the impression the old couple he lived with had money. Did they leave him something other than the farm?"

"Are you hoping to inherit it?" The question wasn't friendly anymore.

"No, I don't want the farm, nor am I after his money. I found some money when I was cleaning. I wondered if he was saving it. What do you know about Ferris' background?"

There was a pause. "Can we talk about this some other time?" Henry's voice was pleasant but distant.

"What I called to talk to you about is your mother." Matt dropped the bomb. There was silence at the other end of the phone. "I did some digging and discovered your father passed away from tuberculosis and is buried somewhere in Millerton, West Virginia. I have his death certificate. What I want to know is, where is your mother buried?"

"I don't know."

"You don't know, or you don't want to know?"

"Both."

"Why is everyone acting like this? I want to know what happened to my grandmother, and no one wants to talk. You and Uncle Lucas are the only ones alive who remember her. What was she like? What happened that split you all up?" Matt's voice raised a little as he pressed for an answer.

"My mother went her own way, or maybe she decided she was better without us. For whatever reason, she never contacted us. She disappeared, and that was that." Henry's voice left Matt no question of his feelings.

"Everyone leaves a trail somewhere." Matt tried to speak the words gently, but frustration with his family's attitude toward the situation had him clenching his teeth.

"Good luck. I tried years ago and met with a stone wall I couldn't climb over, dig under, or walk around." A bit of low mumbling came across the line as if he were talking to someone else; then, he spoke into the phone again. "All I ask is that you keep what you're doing to yourself. I don't want the media following you around, looking over your shoulder, and reporting on everything."

"That's no problem. I don't know any reporters. I'm doing this for my own information. You tell me it can't be done, and I have a purpose. I'll find a way. Since you're not going to do anything to help me, I guess what I find is for me to know." He didn't finish the childish taunt that slipped out.

"Fair enough. Goodbye and good luck." The line disconnected with a dial tone. Matt slammed the phone down in a fit of pique.

It wasn't more than fifteen minutes later when his phone rang again. "Hello?"

Instead of Henry, what greeted him was Kenneth's cold, brusque tone. "I just have one thing to add to that conversation: you make sure you send a copy of everything to me."

Matt was surprised but said nothing. "Do you hear me? I want a copy of everything you have."

"Unless you're paying me to do the research, you don't get a thing from me." Matt pressed the disconnect button with no small amount of satisfaction.

CHAPTER 8

COLUMBUS, OH

July 2000

MATT PULLED INTO A PARKING SPACE AT THE Mormon Library three days after his conversation with his Uncle and Kenneth. He had big news to share with Tim: he'd found his grandfather's death certificate and an obituary.

Since the official cause of death was tuberculosis, Matt called a friend to find the protocol for TB. He returned to the library and went straight to the reference section. Matt discovered the antibiotic hadn't been developed as an effective treatment until 1946-1947. By then, it was too late for Samuel, his grandfather. All they could have done at the time was to keep him away from other people.

After the conversation with Uncle Henry, Matt was hungry to do more research, maybe even more so. He still had to figure out the story behind the money he now hid in the attic.

He sat in the Mormon Church parking lot and waited for Tim to arrive and share all he had found. Matt looked at his watch for the tenth time. Tim was scheduled to meet him at 3:30, and he was late.

Time slid on as Matt watched older patrons come and go, still no Tim. Frustrated, he grabbed his briefcase and went into the library. Matt spent his time searching more census records and printed every one that had a Collins or a Sullivan name from 1910 to 1920. The two older women who monitored the patrons asked him about Tim, but he shrugged. "He was supposed to meet me."

Closing time at the library forced Matt out of the archives, and he drove in the direction Tim had vaguely mentioned. He drove up and down streets, peering into carports and around apartment parking lots until he found Tim's car.

He pulled next to the car parked in a numbered space. Matt climbed the steps to the upper level of the nearest building two at a time and found the apartment with the corresponding number.

Matt knocked and pounded and called Tim's name with no answer. Something's wrong. He tried again, rattling the door and calling Tim's name louder this time.

A door opened down the hall behind him. Afraid someone would call the cops: Matt abandoned his attempts to rouse his friend and walked back to his car. He drove to the nearest police station.

At the desk, a weary officer regarded him with tired eyes and a blank, uninterested expression. Matt took a breath and pleaded his case.

"Sir, I think there's something wrong with my friend. His car is in its parking space, but he didn't answer his door." He leaned forward on the corner of the desk to emphasize his point. "I knocked and knocked but got no answer. I'm worried something's happened to him."

"I'm sorry. We can't just break into this man's apartment on your say so." The officer continued typing information into the computer.

"So what you're saying is, until he starts stinking and someone complains, there isn't anything you are going to do." Matt pressed.

The officer stopped and turned to him. "Technically, that's correct. What if you forgot about a meeting or went to spend the day at a friend's house, only to come home and find the police have broken into your house? Now, you might be a real good friend, or you might be a criminal. What makes you think there's something wrong just because he isn't at his apartment?" He narrowed his eyes.

Matt stuffed his hands in his pockets and slouched. "I know you're right, but I just... I feel there's something wrong. I want to file a missing person's report. If he doesn't turn up in twenty-four hours, then you can break down the door. Let's hope he isn't in there."

"Are you sure you want to do this?" The man's tired voice continued. "He's probably with friends."

"Tim told me a few days ago someone had broken into his apartment. His computer, along with some files, was stolen."

"Did he report it?" The officer looked up with a little more interest.

"I don't know. I'd just met Tim. He's been helping me with some genealogy research at the Mormon Library."

At that, the officer pulled some papers out of a file cabinet and pushed them across to Matt. "If he's an older gentleman, he may have had an accident. Does he have family that can check on him?"

Matt debated whether he should explain that Tim was a younger man but didn't. Instead, he filled out the report and left.

Matt felt an odd prickle, like an itch, at the back of his neck the entire way home. Needing to talk to someone, Matt dialed his brother's number on his cell phone.

"Hey, whatcha doin'?"At Sam's familiar voice and response, Matt sighed in relief.

"You got a minute?" Matt asked.

"Sure. What's up?"

"Are you alone?" Matt persisted.

"Uh, you do know who you're calling?"

"Come off it, Sam, I'm serious. I don't want Anita overhearing this."

His tone connected must've connected with Sam because he became serious. "Yes, I'm alone. Anita's gone grocery shopping."

Sam's voice sobered. "I told you I was going to make our family history."

"Yes. You said you found an old Bible, and there was nothing on Grandma Katherine."

"Right." He relayed what happened at the library where he met Tim and their escape from the media.

"Matt! You've got to be kidding. Why would the TV station want to interview you?"

"Not just me. My guess is they'll start bugging you and Anita along with Kathy. We need to be on the offensive. No comment! Or look incredulous and say, 'Wow, I would love to be invited to the Senator's house.'"

"You're the actor; I'm not." Sam laughed. "Seriously, is this what the cloak and dagger are about?"

"No, there's more." Matt leaned back in his father's office chair and rubbed his hand up and down the back of his head to his neck. "The young man who helped me escape also showed me how to use the Mormon Library."

"What do the Mormons got to do with this?" Sam shot back. "We aren't Mormon."

"Nothing. The Mormon religion is all about finding your roots and family tree. Something about getting them into heaven: they let anyone use their research materials if you give them a copy of what you find. You don't have to, but they charge so little that—"

Sam interrupted, sounding annoyed. "What does this have to do with the cloak and dagger stuff?"

"Yeah, Tim was helping me, and he didn't show up for our meeting today."

"That sounds menacing." Sam's tone was dry and condescending.

"Listen!" Matt shot forward. "I was worried since he hadn't called about missing our meeting." He told Sam about Tim's break-in. "He was excited about doing this research and called me a couple of times to change the time we'd meet due to his schedule. It isn't like him to miss an appointment, so I drove around until I found his car in a parking lot."

"Wait a minute, Matt." Sam drew the words out. "You drove all over Columbus looking for this guy's car? That sounds a little like being a stalker."

"It's not like that. Tim told me where he lived, just not the actual address or apartment number. I found his car parked out front and figured out which apartment was his. No matter how much noise I made at the door, he didn't answer."

"He might have gone to visit his family for the night."

Matt ignored the obvious. "If he comes home tomorrow, all is well, but if something happened to him, I don't want to put off another twenty-four hours to have his apartment opened."

"Matt, is there something you aren't telling me? Why the deep concern about a stranger?" Sam put the pressure on.

Matt rested his head in his hand, leaning on the desk. "I called Uncle Henry."

"You've got to be kidding me. How did you get his number?" Sam sounded surprised.

"I called his local campaign headquarters. They gave me the campaign manager's number. I had to go through Kenneth, his manager, to get to Uncle Henry, but I did talk to him." Matt relayed the conversation to Sam. "Kenneth warned me I was to send him a copy of anything I found out about Katherine."

Sam frowned. "Who's Katherine?"

"Our grandmother, stupid." The little dig came out just like old times.

"No, you're stupid," Sam shot back.

"This is too weird. With Tim missing and Uncle Henry's manager telling me to stop what I'm doing. I wonder if someone did something to Tim?"

"I can see why you're worried, but don't you think you're overreacting?" Sam's sounded conciliatory.

"Maybe you're right. I'll wait until tomorrow and see if Tim calls. Thanks for being the voice of reason, Sam."

"You're welcome." They rang off.

The following day, Matt drove to Tim's house. He climbed the steps to the apartment and knocked on the door repeatedly but still received no answer.

Matt heard a door open down the hall and turned to see who it was. An eyeball behind glasses peered at him through the crack of the door. Matt stopped and watched the door open wider.

An older man with nappy gray hair crooked a finger for Matt to come to him. A little afraid, Matt looked around to see if he meant to call someone else, but there was no one else in the hall. Matt walked toward the doorway and stopped just at the side of the door hinges.

"You lookin' for Tim?" the wheezing voice asked.

Matt nodded, and the man opened the door wider and stuck his head out. Pale gray eyes squinted up and down the hall, and then the man motioned for him to come in.

Matt made a quick decision and hoped it wasn't his last one. He stepped into the apartment, and the man closed and locked the door, which didn't make Matt feel any more relaxed. He didn't move as the man hobbled past him and around a small stub wall to the eating area.

"You want a cup of coffee?" A wizened old handheld out a stained mug as he poured coffee into his mug and sat at the table.

Matt shook his head. "No, thanks. Do you know where Tim is?"

"No. But I saw three other men knock at his door beside you. When he opened the door, they just pushed him aside and shut the door behind them."

Matt took a few steps into the living area. It was dark, and only one lamp next to a chair shed light into the shuttered room. A sagging couch covered with a faded quiltlined the long dividing wall. The man nursed his coffee at a round table with three mismatched chairs.

Matt pulled one chair out and gingerly sat down: unsure the aged wood would hold him. "Did you get a good look at the men?"

"They were Feds like, you know, like the ones you see on TV. All of them had dark hair, close-cut and military-like, and they had those things in their ears as the secret service wears—and, in this weather, they wore coats! Short, not like the long ones that those other guys wear. I wondered if ol' Tim had written something against the president, and now they came and got him." He slurped the coffee.

What would Tim have that the Secret Service would want? Or was it someone in the presidential election ring? Kenneth Mullins? Would he have something to do with Tim missing?

"Did you see them leave?" Matt leaned his elbows on the table.

"I heard the door open and shut, but I was afraid to peek out just in case they caught me. When I looked out the window—" a boney finger pointed to one facing the parking lot— "I saw the men get into a black SUV with tinted windows. The last man shut the back passenger door, and he looked around at the building to see if anyone was watchin'. Then they drove away."

"Did you see Tim get into the SUV?"

"Not actually. I heard Tim give a yell inside his apartment. Then it was silent. It wasn't too long after they left."

"Which way did they go?"

"They went out the driveway and turned left. I don't know what good that'll do you. I don't know nothin' else."

Matt frowned a moment and rubbed his hand around the back of his neck. "You didn't see Tim leave with them?"

The man shook his head.

"How come you told me all this?"

"I saw you come the first time, and it looked like you cared about Tim. He's a good boy. He's polite to me and even brought me a Thanksgiving and Christmas dinner when I couldn't. He brought me a little Christmas tree with some lights, blankets, and clothes. The boy is good. I want to make sure nothing bad happened to him."

Matt stood and patted the older man's shoulder. "Tim was helping me on a research project. I didn't know him real well, but he was a good kid. I'll do my best to find out what happened to him."

"Tim told me the other day he was working on a story that might finally give him the break he needed to be an investigative reporter." The man's watery eyes stared into Matt's. The younger man backed up a step. "He was a reporter?"

"Not yet. He was still in school studying to be a reporter. He said he just needed a good story to get his big break. Tim told me he thought he had it."

Matt fished an old school business card from his wallet. "Call me if you see anyone else hanging around the apartment. If anyone goes in, call the cops."

The older man nodded and locked the door when Matt left.

Had Tim played him? Was Tim helping him, or was he using him as an easy way to write a story he could sell? Matt put the car into gear and checked his watch. By the time he got to the station, the twenty-four hours would be up.

When he arrived at the police station, Matt waited almost an hour for an officer to agree to check out Tim's apartment. He followed the patrol car to the complex and waited while the officer talked to the complex manager.

"I don't know what this man's talking about. Tim's gone. He came by two days ago and told me he was leaving. He said it was an emergency and to store his things."

"How could he tell you that? Two days ago, he called me, and we set a time to meet yesterday," Matt insisted as they stopped in front of the apartment.

The landlord opened the door. "I haven't moved anything." He stepped aside and let the police and Matt enter first.

"No. You stay here." The officer held out his arm to stop Matt. Matt stepped back but stood in the doorway. The landlord moved to follow, but the officer stopped him.

After five or ten minutes, the officer came back, shaking his head. "No one's here. All his possessions are packed." The officer motioned for Matt and the landlord to enter. "Don't touch anything. Is there anything missing?"

Matt went to a stack of boxes against the wall in the living room. He peeked inside and saw Tim's possessions were thrown in, not packed. He looked in the bedroom—empty, except for a bed and dresser.

"You've been around here all day?" Matt asked the manager, "Yes."

"Then, you packed all this?" The officer was writing in his book.

"No! I just opened the door for you all." The landlord held his hands out in a defensive gesture.

"Then how did you know Timothy was gone? Why didn't you come in before this and remove his stuff? Were you told to leave it alone?" the officer pressed.

The manager looked at his feet and everywhere but at the officer. "They paid me to leave the stuff alone."

"Who?"

"The men that came. They said Tim moved, and they were helping him. They paid the rent and a little extra for me not to move his stuff until the end of the month." He shrugged and stuffed his hands into faded pockets.

The motion drew Matt's eyes downward. The ripped sneakers revealed no socks. Matt wondered what he did with all the money he was taking under the table—snorting it most likely.

"What did they look like? Who did they say they were with?" The officer poised his pen over his pad. The manager moved from one foot to the other. "I didn't ask."

The officer shook his head. "I'll bet greenbacks were their ID." He made a call to the station.

Matt held off telling the officer what the man down the hall told him. The police hadn't ruled him missing yet, and he'd wait to see what they did.

Matt couldn't do anything, and that fact frustrated him. He wanted to ask Tim if it were true that he'd just been a meal ticket. Knowing there was nothing else he could do at the apartment, he left.

At home, he wandered house aimlessly, lost in thought. Where is he? What happened to the boy? Matt thought about the boxes he had seen and frowned. Where was the computer? Tim had told him he had a tower and monitor stolen, but he had his laptop. Where is Tim's laptop? It hadn't been on the table, or anywhere Matt had looked. He picked up his house phone and started to dial the number Kenneth Mullins had given him, but then thought better and disconnected the call. Snagging his keys, and drove to the Tick Tock Diner. Inside, he slipped into the back hall and dropped change into the payphone.

"Mullins," said the voice on the other end.

Matt cut right to the chase. "Why did you do it?"

"Who is this?" Kenneth demanded.

"You should know who it is. What did you do with Tim? Was he going to sell a story about Henry's family?"

"I have no idea what you're talking about." Kenneth's voice was a little too easygoing. He didn't bother to ask who it was again.

"If anything happens to him, I will put you down as a person of interest."

"What for? I've nothing to do with whatever you're asking. Who is this, Tim?"

"You know who he is. You had your goons haul him off. You have his computer." Matt accused.

"Again, in case you didn't hear me, I don't know who or what you're talking about. If you know what's good for you, you'll end this little game before anything serious happens."

"So, you do know what happened to Tim."

"I have no idea who this Tim is or what happened to him. I assure you, the only one I know doing any research is you. It won't go well with you if you try to sell any story to the press."

"Sell a story to the press? I'm looking to find out what happened to my grandmother, not sell some story to the press. Do you know something about her that Uncle Henry and Uncle Lucas won't tell me? If you tell me, then I won't have to do any more searching and digging in public."

"I'm not talking anymore. I'm just warning you that I'll keep an eye on you." Kenneth hung up.

CHAPTER 9

COLUMBUS, OH

July 2000

MATT DIDN'T SLEEP WELL THAT NIGHT AND only managed to doze off around two A.M. He woke as sunshine filled the room and groaned, covering his face with a pillow.

Once he dragged himself downstairs, Matt turned the TV on and stretched. After glancing at the morning commercials, he headed into the bathroom to brush his teeth. The sound of a breaking headline caught his attention, and Matt poked his head out, still brushing his teeth.

"In breaking news, a body was found in the Columbus River this morning by a frightened fisherman. Police are looking for someone to identify the body. The deceased is said to be a young male in his mid-to-late twenties with brown hair. If you have any information, please call."

Matt's eyes bugged out, and he turned to spit hurriedly into the sink before rinsing off his brush and walking over to turn up the TV volume. More commercials flew by before the camera returned to a male reporter standing at the edge of the Columbus River and facing the camera. EMTs and police moved around in the background.

"We are here where the police have removed a body from the river. This man, Robert Colby, was fishing this morning when he felt a tug on his reel that he knew wasn't a fish."

The camera cut to an older man looking grim and uncomfortable. He spoke into a microphone. "I fish out there every morning and have been fishing for as long as I can remember. When I felt that tug at the line, I knew it wasn't a fish. I figger'd I was jus' caught on a log or somethin' and pulled. The kid just popped up to the surface like a wine cork."

The camera returned to the reporter. "Officers say it looked like the body had been tied to something and dumped into the river. We'll bring you more information as the story develops, Tom."

"Do they have any ideas about the identity of the body?" Tom, the anchorman, asked.

"None that the police have released." The man looked at his notebook. "I did have a previous report of a missing person yesterday. It was a young man in his twenties, but with no description of the person, we don't know if this could be that missing young man." The camera panned back to the action. "Police are looking into who filed a missing person report."

Matt watched the EMTs in the background lift the body onto the stretcher. One arm slipped sideways, and Matt saw the color of the shirtsleeve. It was the same shirt Tim had worn when they were at the diner. Matt remembered the boxes in the apartment, particularly the one containing Tim's clothes and how they'd been full of blue denim shirts. He couldn't remember Tim wearing anything but those same shirts.

Matt paced his bedroom floor. Should he contact the police or just wait for the news? The phone rang and interrupted his thoughts.

"Mr. Sullivan, this is Gail Taylor from the Mormon Library. I know you and Tim are working on your family history. I tried calling Tim, but he isn't returning my calls.

"Two gentlemen came looking for information on what you and Tim were working on and what you found. I told them I had no idea what you found; we just supplied the records. They told me they were from the government, but I told them I didn't have to show them anything unless they had a court order. They left."

Matt didn't have an answer. What would the government want with his research? Were these the same men who visited Tim? "When did they come in?"

Gail gave the day and time, which turned out to be from before the men visited Tim, according to the elderly neighbor. "I have a friend who works in Charleston, West Virginia, for the Historical Society. She gave me the name of a woman in Millerton, West Virginia, who works as the part-time librarian and a school teacher there and does genealogy. Her name is Selma Greeley. Here's her phone number." She rattled off a number while Matt fumbled for a pen and paper. "Call her and talk to her; she might be able to help. Have you talked to Tim lately?"

Matt took a breath, then spoke. "No. Does he have family around here?" "No. Tim is an orphan. His last foster home was one of our members, so he found himself here and became part of our Ward. He's so faithful. We all think he's priest-ready. We love that boy."

Matt was careful with what he was about to ask. "So, he has a foster family?"

"Gary and Nancy, his foster parents, passed on a few years ago."

"I called his cell and left a message. If I hear from him, I'll call you," Matt responded, though he was pretty sure Tim wouldn't be returning her call. Or his.

Did this have anything to do with the news reporter he and Tim ran from that first night they met? Did the fact he was a nephew to the Presidential candidate have anything to do with Tim's disappearance? It was a far-fetched idea, but it was the only one he had.

The two said their farewells and disconnected the call, leaving Matt with a heavy heart.

After eating a quick breakfast, Matt drove to the police station. Inside, he found the same surly officer he'd told about Tim's apartment the first time behind the desk. The officer looked up and recognized him. "You again. Did you find your friend? Probably sobering up at some friend's pad, right?"

Matt narrowed his eyes, "No. I think he's your dead body. I want to talk to one of the officers on that case." He spoke with quiet authority.

The officer didn't respond but punched some numbers on the phone and spoke to someone. A couple of minutes later, two officers approached from the back of the station.

"You think you know who we have at the morgue?" one of them asked.

"I'm not sure, but I have a missing friend who matches the description I saw on the news."

The two men motioned for Matt to follow them back to an office cube. "Can I get you something to drink, coffee, soda?" The tall, thin officer asked.

"No, thanks." Matt sat in the chair across the desk from one officer while the other sat on the corner, his arm crossed over his knee.

After taking Matt's personal information, one officer asked, "I'm Detective Roby; this is Detective Reese. How do you know this man you reported missing?"

"Who?" Matt asked, distracted by the sudden question.

"The one you think is our dead body," Detective Reese clarified from his seat on the desk. His short-cropped grey hair made him look almost bald while his partner sported a deep farmer's tan.

"I reported Tim missing a couple of days ago. An officer went to his apartment, and the landlord told us that Tim had left town. That sounded odd to me because he showed no signs of leaving the area. He's in school. Why would he leave in the middle of the semester?" Matt waited for one of the two men to speak.

"You didn't answer the question, Mr. Sullivan." The officer narrowed his eyes at Matt, jotting something down on a pad of paper on his desk.

"We're working on a research project of mine at the Mormon Library.

Sorry, it's a shock to think that he's died, you know?"

"What made you think that the body was your friend?" the other officer asked.

Matt frowned. "Look, can I see the body or not? If not, I'll go home. Matt extended his six-foot-two-inch frame.

"What's your hurry? Sit down; we have more questions." He waited for Matt to retake his seat.

"Did you see your friend wearing a shirt similar to the one you say you saw on the body?" the other officer asked.

"Yes." Matt decided he would not offer any information and only answer what he had to. He didn't want to end up a suspect; it would only draw media attention he didn't want right now.

"When was the last time you saw your friend, and what did you say his name was?"Matt answered the last question. "Tim."

"Oh, yeah, Tim. Tim, what?"

"Pelton."

"Where does he live?"

"You go down Magnolia, turn at the 7-11, and about a half a block down is an apartment complex. You turn in there—"

"What's his address?" Roby interrupted.

"I don't know. The apartment number is 26." Matt wanted to snap, he wanted to yell, but neither of those things would help him right now.

"What's his phone number?"

Matt reached for his cell in a pocket.

The two men jumped up. "What are you doing?" They both had their hands on their guns, and the officers around them were watching.

"You asked for his phone number, and I'm going to give it to you." Matt pulled out his phone and showed it. The men relaxed and sat down again.

"I'm through here. I don't know what your problem is. I offered to help out, and it seems I'm now a person of interest. You can use your own damn devices to find his phone number." Matt stood and held his hand out. "Don't get up. If you aren't going to arrest me for something, we're through."

He walked toward the exit when another officer stopped him. "You're the person here to identify our body?"

Matt looked at him and then back at the two men who looked everywhere but at Matt.

"I was, but I ended up questioned like a criminal. I'm leaving. You can figure out who he is on your own."

Matt walked around the officer and almost made it to the door.

"Sir." The officer at the front desk called out. "Sir, Sergeant Bolton would like to talk to you. Would you mind waiting a moment?"

"Who's he?"

"I'm Sergeant Bolton."

It was the man who had stopped him as he left the cube. "I'm sorry for the runaround. We don't have any other leads. Would you follow me to the morgue?"

Matt curbed his anger, nodded, and walked beside him to an elevator. They didn't speak as the box moved downward and jerked to a stop. The sergeant led the way down the chilly, narrow hall to a metal door and opened it.

"Doc, I have someone to see our new resident," he said.

The tiled room was sterile, cold, and populated with shiny metal appliances. A slender man with wire-framed glasses looked up as they entered, offering the sergeant a smile. "Sure thing, Sergeant Bolton."

The white-coated doctor walked to a wall with metal doors lined in two rows. He snapped the latch, grabbed the rollout, and pulled. The table slid out with the quiet squeal of bearings that needed greasing. The body, covered by a white sheet, lay about chest high to Matt. He tensed as the doctor tugged the sheet back from over the head.

Matt saw the brown hair and high forehead, then the pale, waxy skin. The features formed in his mind and, as if they were fingerprints in AFIS, he identified the face of Tim Pelton.

"It's him." Matt took another quick look for any telltale signs of how he died. There was nothing above the sheet that indicated the cause of death. "How did he die?"

There was a pause as the coroner and officer exchanged unspoken communication, then the doctor spoke. "It was a through and through."

Matt looked at the doctor then the officer, seeking clarification. "What's a through and through?"

"A gunshot where the bullet goes in one side and out the other. Do you have any idea who would want him dead?"

"I only met with Tim three times: once at the public library and twice at the Mormon Library. We talked a little on the phone in between to set up a meeting. He helped me get in contact with people who could help me with my family tree search. He was Mormon. Gail Taylor, the librarian at the Mormon church, called me with some information and said she had been trying to call him, and he didn't answer."

"What information did she give you?" Sergeant Bolton asked.

"She told me where I could call the Historical Society in Kentucky for help. Oh, about Tim? He was an orphan and lived in foster homes. The last couple he lived with was Mormons, and he converted. She said the couple died a couple of years ago."

"What are you researching for?"

Matt looked at the Sergeant. "My family tree. I wanted to do this to see how easy or hard it was so I can have my students do it for a term project." He smiled.

"Do we have your contact information?" Bolton asked. "I don't know why you'd need it."

"In case there are any questions."

"I don't see any need for more questions. You can verify the body with dental records and Tim's driver's license. As far as I can see, we don't need to speak again." Matt walked toward the front door.

"Do you have some reason why you don't want to leave your information with us?" Bolton asked. He crossed his arms and waited for an answer.

"Yes. I have no idea why they would want to kill Tim. The less I'm involved, the better."

"They? Who are they?" Bolton stopped in the center of the hall so Matt couldn't pass.

"I heard there were two men who came to see him."

"You heard or saw?" The sergeant frowned and leaned a little closer to Matt.

"Heard. One of Tim's neighbors mentioned it when the other officer went to check his apartment." Matt turned and started to walk away.

"We'll call you if we have any further questions." It sounded more like a promise.

Matt walked through the automatic sliding doors and drove directly to his house.

There was so much to do at Uncle Lucas's house before he could come home. Matt didn't have much time to call the referral Gail Taylor gave him.

When he got home Saturday, the message light on his phone blinked, showing ten messages. The first five were clicks with no recording. There were two telemarketers, then a familiar voice.

'This is Kenneth Mullins. Call me as soon as you get this message. It's about your uncle." A phone number followed the command.

There were a few more calls later in the day and another couple of calls with no message. He checked the caller ID, and they all came from the same "private caller" tag.

He dialed the number Kenneth had left and waited for an answer. "Mullins."

"This is Matthew Sullivan."

"Matthew. Hold on a moment. I need to get to a place where we can talk uninterrupted."

There was some static, and Matt heard a lot of voices in the background.

Then there was a thud and no more background voices. "Now we can talk. Matthew, are you there?"

"Yes. What possible reason would you have to want to talk to me?" Matt paced the length of the kitchen. The curling cord twisted around his legs and nearly tripped him before he paused to untangle himself.

"You've been making noise in the media lately. What are you doing down there?"

"What are you talking about?"

"I got word that you called a TV station telling them you were doing a family tree and that they want to interview you."

"If that's your information, verify your facts before you have to eat them. I did not call the TV station; the librarian did. She wanted a few seconds of fame. I ran out the back door. They've tried calling my house a few times, but I didn't answer. I have no reason to broadcast what I'm doing. Besides, what's the big deal?"

"Your uncle doesn't want the media delving into his past and bringing up that he was adopted."

"How could he be adopted? His parents were alive. If he were adopted, he would have a different last name, and this conversation is a moot point." "You know lawyer jargon. Were they alive? Do you have any proof?"

Kenneth's voice rose in a confrontation.

"I know his father died of tuberculosis and is buried somewhere in Millerton, West Virginia. That means Uncle Henry must know what happened to his mother."

"Just stop doing any more research until after the election."

"Why? What I find is my own business and none of yours or Uncle Henry's. He hasn't had a thing to do with us all these years; why would I care what he thinks or does?"

"I take it you aren't voting for him?"

"Whether I do or don't, it isn't any of your concern." Matt wrapped the tangled cord around his hand.

"It is if anything you find leaks to the media and is used against Henry. I'll do whatever it takes to stop any smearing of Henry's name."

"Even killing?" Matt threw in.

"I'm just warning you. Stop what you're doing until after the election."

"I don't know what you think I'm going to find. I don't even know what's so important that you have to threaten me. Why don't you just tell me what I want to know, and we can be done with all this?"

There was some muffled talk as if a hand covered the receiver, and a different voice came on the line. "What do you want to know?"

"Who are you?" Matt's sarcasm rang over the line. "Your uncle. Henry."

"Oh. Are you going to tell me the same thing?" The cord caught on a chair and stopped his travel around the kitchen table. He pulled it free.

"What exactly do you want to know? Why didn't Lucas tell you that you want to know?"

"For the same reason, I'm sure you won't tell me. What happened to my grandmother? Why did all you Sullivan children leave Millerton? When and where did Katherine die?" The silence that followed was long, too long. "Are you there, or did you hang up on me?"

"I'm here. I won't, and can't, answer those questions. One, I don't know what happened to my mother after she left Millerton. Two, what precipitated us leaving is something I don't remember. I told you before: I tried to find out myself and got nowhere."

"Even with Uncle Lucas? You seem to have some rapport with him."

"What I know won't help you, and Lucas is like the good citizens of Millerton with their lips buttoned up."

"Maybe they aren't as tight-lipped as you and are willing to tell me what I want to know," Matt parlayed.

"Don't count on it, boy. They don't want to be reminded of what happened any more than I do."

"You're pretty sure about that." He smiled at the term boy. It sounded just like Lucas talking.

"Yes, I am."

"Then you shouldn't mind me nosing around Millerton. If you think no one will talk, then what are you worried about?" Matt grinned; he was winning.

"I warn you—life there is not like you think, so if you decide to go, be sure you go armed and prepared."

"You think they might want to kill me? Did you have anything to do with Tim's death?" Matt stood still in the dark kitchen. Only the light over the sink lit the small area.

"Who's Tim?"

"He was helping me do this research, and he just turned up dead in the river. They're looking for his murderer now."

"I don't know anything about this man or him dying. Ken, what do you know about some man getting killed in Columbus?" Matt wanted to hear that answer, too, but he couldn't hear Ken's response.

Eventually, Henry spoke into the phone again. "We know nothing about this person."

"Really? When I told Kenneth, he didn't ask who he was or what happened to him."

There was another silence. "Matthew, I'm asking you to stop what you're doing until after the election."

"To do that, Uncle, I ask you to tell me what happened all those years ago."

"I can't. I just can't."

"Then it's on your head." The phone went dead.

Matt sat in the dim light of his living room. His hand curled around a mug of coffee, now lukewarm. The events of the days since he'd started looking into his family history rolled around in his head like dice in a cup. What did he know about his father?

He thought back over the years and remembered his aunt had raised his father. Then why weren't their families close? He recalled a few family picnics when he was little. Aunt Martha was stern and demanded the kids be quiet when they were at her house. There wasn't much of a memory of her, but Matt knew he didn't like her very much. He didn't think his mother did, either. Aunt Emma and Uncle Thomas were different. Her smile was what he remembered. She hugged him and slipped him cookies.

Matt picked up the phone and punched Sam's number. "Hi, Matt. What's up?"

"I hate caller ID," Matt muttered.

Sam laughed. "Get into the times. How's the research going?" "That's what I called about." He filled Sam in on the details of Tim.

"I think you need to drop this whole thing. I don't know what's going on. Is there any connection between Uncle Henry and this Tim? I'm just saying that you don't need to do this now. Wait a few years and then see what you can find." Matt could hear a tapping sound from Sam's phone.

"Are you doing something? I hear an odd noise."

"Sorry, I was tapping my pencil on the mat. It helps me think."

Matt made a face even though Sam couldn't see it. "Sam, I can't let this go. If I have the dates right, and if Grandma Katherine is still alive, she'd be around ninety years old."

"Or dead."

"Yes, that, too. Just in case she's alive and of a sound mind, I want to find her and learn what happened." Matt's voice rose a little.

"You're pretty intense about this. Why? What difference will finding her make in your life?"

Matt thought a minute. The question was a valid one. One he wasn't sure of the answer to. "I was sitting here thinking about Dad, Aunt Martha, and Aunt Emma. I know you were too young and maybe I don't remember going to visit them.

"I remember Dad talking to Aunt Emma and Uncle Thomas. He smiled and laughed while he was there. I think Mom liked Aunt Emma; I don't think she cared much for Aunt Martha and Uncle David."

"I never met them. At least I don't have any memory of them," Sam interjected.

"They were different. Our cousins were older and didn't play games or do stuff. If they were there, they talked with the parents or just put in an appearance. I tried calling them about their memories, but none were helpful, and they weren't interested in talking to me about their mother or their memories of what she might have said. Even when I told them what I was doing."

"I get it. You have this itch to know your history. Not all of us have that interest or care where our parents grew up or lived." Matt could almost see Sam's shrug.

"I get it. I'm alone in this."

"Matt, what do you want to know? Why is it so important to find Grandma?"

"I know you just asked this, and I'm thinking. Did you know Dad whittled?"

"No, but what does that have to do with anything?"

"Sam, I found a trunk full of animals he made. They're collector quality. If I wanted to, I could sell them for quite a bit of money. Don't you think it odd that Dad sat up in that attic and whittled these fantastic creatures and never showed them to us? Never encouraged us or taught us the same thing? What if he had decided to paint or draw? Maybe he was an artist that never did anything with his talent. Sam, you're an architect, an artist of sorts. You may have gotten that eye for buildings that Dad had for his animals. Did he ever say anything to you about it?"

There was a long pause on the other end. "Yes. We sat a few times and talked about my drawings. He liked to see what I had done for my class projects. He even asked if he could have some." Matt heard the catch in Sam's voice as he spoke. "I didn't understand his interest. To me, it was something he did to connect with me. Maybe he was interested in my ability. He never said anything except that he was proud of what I drew. Before he died, he called me to the house and gave me a brand new portfolio with all the artwork I had done in it. I was happy to get the folder, but I didn't connect that this might have been his way of telling me to take pride in my work and that he did." There was a sniff, and Matt wiped his eyes, too.

"That's why I'm doing this. I think Dad and Uncle Lucas might have been different if they had the support of their mother. I'm just guessing since I have no idea what she was like. I want to honor Dad. I'm going to find his mother or at least find out what happened to her."

"Go for it. Keep me posted and watch your back."

Matt set the phone on the table and picked up the small carved bunny. His thumb smoothed the edges of the ears that lay against its back. This time, he didn't bother to brush the tears away. Regret for ignoring or not taking more time to talk to his dad flowed with the tears.

CHAPTER 10
MILLERTON, WV
June 1947

KATHERINE GRIPPED SAM'S HAND IN THE BACK seat of Ben and Cassie's car. Joseph sat on Lucas's lap beside his mother while Henry sat between Ben and Cassie in the front seat. No one spoke during the whole twenty-minute trip.

Ben pulled the '42 Plymouth sedan into the parking lot beside Barker's Market forty-five minutes before the bus was due to arrive. Joseph and Henry jumped out of the car and headed to the school playground.

"Don't go far. You come on back when the bus gets here," Sam hollered out the window at their running figures.

Lucas sat for a few minutes before opening the door. "I'll go keep an eye on 'em."

Sam nodded. There wasn't much to say. Katherine laid her head on Sam's shoulder and stroked his large, callused hand with her small fingers.

"Are Martha and David going to meet you at the bus station?" Ben asked, turning a little in the front seat. Cassie slid across to sit next to him, taking Henry's spot.

"Yes. I get there after David gets off work. He'll pick Martha up and come to the station to get me." Despite how hard Sam was trying to keep his tone even, Katherine heard the hitch in his voice.

"Sam, I want you to know we'll do all we can to help Katherine. I don't want you to worry. Just do what you have to do to bring your family together again." Ben smiled at Sam, trying to ease the tension.

"I appreciate your help. I know the boys are going to need some lookin' after while I'm gone, and I hope you can step in now and then and see to them. I don't know how long it's going to take me to save the money to bring the family from Millerton. If the work is good, we might have a home there in a year or so."

"Let's hope so. I've been to Bowersville, and it's a nice city. I think you'll like it there."

"I'll continue to sell things at Barker's to help," Katherine said, nodding at Sam in encouragement. It took him some time to come to terms with her working, but pragmatism won out in the end.

Sam chuckled. "She might get the men to buy a cake or a pie to take home after a night in jail. It would be a great way for the men to make nice with their wives." Ben agreed with a snort of his own.

There was a long silence as time crawled minute by minute.

"I think we should get going. The bus should be here any time." Sam pulled his arm from around Katherine but not before he captured her lips in one last, deep kiss. "I love you," he whispered and slid out of the car, offering his hand to her to help her out.

Ben lifted a suitcase and a duffle bag from the trunk and set them on the ground. Seeing this, the boys ran from the playground and slid to a stop by their father.

"Hey, Dad! Is the bus coming?" Henry hopped from one foot to another.

Sam ruffled the boy's light brown hair, ran a finger down Henry's nose, and then tapped his chin. "I'm sure it's just around the corner."

The growl of an engine sounded as the bus turned into the parking lot. The hiss of air brakes and the belch of black smoke puffed from the exhaust pipes, filling the air with the stink of diesel. A group of men emerged from Barker's Market and sauntered into the parking lot. They stood in a loose line watching the family group.

The door opened with a soft whoosh, and the driver eased his girth out of the bus and gave Sam's group a nod. "Be right back, and we'll be on our way." He lumbered off around the corner to Barker's Market.

Lucas remained a few feet away from his family, his eyes on the men near the market wall. They were laughing to themselves as though sharing a private joke. Lucas stood with his feet spread apart and his arms crossed.

The driver turned the corner and hitched his belt under his large gut as he walked toward them. The man opened the luggage compartment beneath the bus, hefted Sam's bags in, and pulled the doors shut. Then the driver walked over to Sam, a knowing expression on his face. "Take a moment, but we need to get on the road to stay on schedule." He heaved his heavy body up the steps.

Sam gave Ben a hug and a pat on the back. Cassie hugged him and kissed his cheek. Joseph and Henry stood quietly, holding back tears when their father turned to them.

"You boys help your mother. I don't want to hear that you aren't pullin' your weight or sluffin' off. I'll be back as soon as I can, or I'll at least send for you to come for a visit. Now give me a big hug to last me while I'm gone." The boys rushed Sam and hugged him, tears flowing. After the embrace, Sam put them down and turned to Lucas, who hadn't moved.

"Lucas, I expect you to watch over your mother and brothers. I know that's a lot to put on your shoulders, but you're the oldest, and I have to rely on you to keep me informed of what's happening."

Lucas's eyes remained on the men across the parking lot for a moment longer, then turned to his father. "I will, Dad. I'll take care of Mom and the boys."

Sam squeezed his shoulder and then pulled the boy close for a brief hug. "I love ya, Son." Lucas nodded but didn't speak.

Sam patted his shoulder and turned to Katherine. He hugged her and kissed her hard. When he broke the kiss and looked up, the men began giving wolf whistles and rude sounds.

"I'll keep an eye out, too, Sam." Ben stepped up and stood between him and the men.

Sam nodded and took the basket Katherine packed before they left home. The family's eyes followed his journey as he stepped onto the bus and walked down the aisle to his seat in the half-empty bus.

The door closed, and the driver put the bus in gear. The motor revved and pushed the vehicle forward. The younger boys ran beside the bus, waving at their dad, who kept a smile on his face until the bus gathered speed and left them at the corner.

The pair returned to stand next to their mother. Each held her hand and rested their brown-haired heads against her side.

"Let's go home." Ben motioned for them to get into the car as Lucas brought up the rear.

When the youngest got into the back seat, the men began to holler.

"Hey, Kate, when you get a little hungry, just give me a call. I can take care of you." There was some laughing then.

"Hey, Baby, you know I can take care of you while Sam is gone." Rude sounds followed that.

"Get in, Ma," Lucas ordered. Katherine complied, unable to look at the men. Lucas, meanwhile, fixed his eyes on them.

"Who you lookin' at, boy?" one of the men hollered.

Lucas glared at the gathered group as he climbed into the car. The boy pointed his finger at each man as they passed on their way out of the parking lot.

Ben pulled the car into the Sullivan driveway and stopped at the back of the house. Cassie got out and hugged Katherine. "I'll be over tomorrow."

The boys slid out of the car, and Lucas ushered them into the barn. Katherine waved to her neighbors before walking around the house to the front porch and sitting in the rocker. Tears flowed until she buried her head in her handkerchief and sobbed.

CHAPTER 11

COLUMBUS, OH

August 2000

TWO WEEKS AFTER THEY FOUND TIM'S BODY, Matt spent several afternoons at the police station until they finally ruled him out as a suspect. Other than the fact he was Senator Sullivan's nephew, a question they didn't ask, he had nothing to hide. Matt was careful how he answered and stuck to his story that the genealogical research was for his students' assignments and his only connection to Tim.

After a particularly hectic day, Matt flopped into the creaking chair at his father's desk. His eyes wandered across the papers on his desk. Selma Greeley's name on the notepad jumped out at him. He'd forgotten the woman from the Mormon Library called and referred to her. Like his father, Matt kept all the bits of paper, notes, and receipts he wrote on, just in case. He picked up the phone and dialed the number.

"Millerton Library, Selma speaking." The low, throaty voice spoke into his ear.

"Hi." Matt's tongue glued itself to the roof of his suddenly dry mouth. He cleared his throat. "Sorry about that. I'm Matt Sullivan, and I was given your name by a woman at the Mormon Library here in Columbus, Ohio."

"Yes, I've been waiting for your call. I'm Selma Greeley."

"Sorry, I was detained. I'm looking for information about my grandmother, Katherine Sullivan." Matt relayed to her everything he knew about his grandmother and offered to fax over the pages he copied from the Mormon Library.

Selma provided him the fax number, offered information about the town, and invited him to visit. She gave him the phone number of a local bed-and-breakfast. "It's the only respectable place to stay. We're so far off the main highway there isn't much need for tourist accommodations."

"Thanks. As you can tell, I don't have much to go on. Just a bunch of old newspapers from Millerton and a death certificate that my grandfather's buried somewhere there."

"I'll ask around and see if I can find out anything for you. When do you think you might come?"

"Would next week be too soon? I'll make reservations and call you when I get to town," Matt promised.

"Not at all. Summer is pretty slow at the library. I'll be here," Selma answered.

Matt pulled his car into the small parking lot next to the Dew Drop Inn a week later. The Inn backed to woods, on the edge of town, with a sweeping view of the Allegheny Mountains.

The inn was painted a soft yellow with white trim and shutters. It was a nod to a Victorian-style but didn't have as much gingerbread. The wood creaked beneath his feet as Matt climbed four worn steps to the painted porch. A sign next to the door read "Enter" in a curling script.

The air-conditioned foyer made a welcome contrast against the muggy air outside. The yellow-and-white motif continued inside with sunny wallpaper covered in yellow flowers. A bead-board counter with three angles and a dropped desk behind it disguised a computer.

Matt set his briefcase on the floor next to his suitcase and tapped the bell. From somewhere at the back of the house, he heard shuffling feet move towards the front.

A woman in her seventies, her white hair pulled to a loose bun at the back of her head, and bright green eyes smiled at him. She tugged at the bottom edge of the pink sweater, stretching it over her sagging breasts and the top of grey slacks.

"Hello. Can I help you?" She pushed her rimless glasses up on her forehead.

"I'm Matt Sullivan. I called about a room for a week or so." He smiled. "I'm Josephine Millard. I've been waiting for you!" Her voice was warm and motherly, matching her smile. Josephine pulled a card from under the counter and pushed it across to him. "Please fill this out and then sign the register book." She pointed to the book on a lazy Susan.

Matt signed the register and the card, and Josephine slid a key attached to a metal card with the inn's name engraved on it across the counter.

"I'm the owner. If you need anything, give me a holler. Your room is upstairs at the back. I gave you the larger rooms as you're a friend of Selma's." She winked at him as if it were a special privilege afforded to those equal to a president.

"Thank you, Ma'am. Can you tell me where the library is?"

"It's two blocks to town and across the square. I serve breakfast from seven to eight AM. I'm sure you've had a long day. If you want dinner, there's a diner two blocks down, then turn left and go another two blocks. It's called Randy's Diner."

Matt thanked the woman before retiring to his room. The staircase complained as Matt climbed to the second floor. The hall had two doors on each side and one at the end with the number five nailed to the center. The old house whispered around him much as his own did. It was both familiar and comforting. Pulling the key from his pocket, he unlocked the door and stepped into the room.

Matt set the suitcase on a low table beside the door as he surveyed his room. A king-size bed covered in a yellow-and-white flowered comforter, a huge armoire, and an oversized desk filled the wall space. He peeked into the bathroom. A claw-foot tub dominated one corner, and an old pull-chain toilet sat nearby. Matt smiled. His father would have loved this room.

Through the window, a large garden with rows of corn and vegetables in various stages of growth spilled across the yard. He could see the edge of the parking area to his right with a wide deck with chairs and gliders below for guests to relax. The mountains rose from just past the back fence. A well-worn path led from the parking lot area into the woods, disappearing after a few yards. Matt made a mental note to ask Mrs. Millard where the trail led. Turning from the view, he unpacked his suitcase and slid his clothing into the armoire. Then he left to drive around.

Millerton baked in the afternoon sun, and the heat had most of the folks living there seeking relief in the air-conditioned indoors. A small knot of children played on the grass in the middle of the town square, kicking a ball back and forth between them. Matt absorbed the sights as he drove below the twenty-mile speed limit. A few people stopped to look at him as he passed their expressions curious but not unfriendly. He almost waved but decided to refrain and pulled into a parking slot at the library.

Once inside the glass doors, Matt looked around, but no one sat at the desk. He heard a faint murmur from the back of the room and headed that way. As he turned the corner of a book rack, he collided with another body.

"Oh! I'm so sorry." Matt clung to the soft form he almost knocked over.

The young woman looked up at him with startling blue eyes.

"No, I'm sorry. I thought I heard the door open; I was coming to see who came in." The slender woman stepped away from him and took a deep breath as though steadying herself.

"Are you okay?" Matt asked. He was reluctant to let go of her but forced his arms back to his sides. As he studied her, Matt realized she must be close to his age.

The woman's head came to his chin, and she wore her blond hair pulled back into a braid that disappeared over her shoulder. A bright yellow zippered jacket with a hood and cap sleeves rested open over a white, long-sleeved shirt and topped the ankle-length denim skirt that completed her outfit.

"Can I help you?" She slid past and walked toward the counter he had passed.

"I'm looking for Selma Greeley." Matt followed her and decided he liked the way the skirt cupped her cute behind. He reprimanded himself for the indiscretion, reminding himself he was here for business.

She turned, and Matt almost ran into her again but managed to catch himself in time. "I'm Selma Greeley, and you must be Matthew Sullivan." The newly-announced Selma held out her hand, and Matt took it in his.

The contact left all his nerve endings tingling as if hit by lightning. The sensation caused something to tighten in his stomach, and he let the contact linger almost too long for propriety. Coming back to himself, Matt allowed her fingers to slide from his. He couldn't remember the last time a woman had made him react so strongly, but Matt couldn't make himself regret it.

He lowered his voice. "I'm pleased to meet you, Selma Greeley. I hope you can help me find something about my grandmother, Katherine Sullivan."

"Likewise. Follow me. I have some things to show you." Selma spun on her heel, and her braid swung back and forth behind her, teasing Matt as he followed.

Selma's office held papers in folders that stood in a wire holder and books shelved by size on the bookcase. Colorful flowers in a vase sat on the corner of the desk. Pens were arranged by color in a holder probably made by some child as a project. The woman pointed to a chair at a table stacked with books and newspapers.

"We need to talk." She sat in her chair across from him and leaned forward. "When I started to ask around for information on your grandmother, I was stonewalled. No one would talk to me. Worse than that, several people told me it was a dead issue and not to speak of it. Matt, what happened? What do you know?"

Matt didn't allow himself to react as he opened his notebook. "Here's what I know. My grandfather died in September 1947 and was buried somewhere around here. I'm going to check the church records to see if there's a family plot."

"I checked with Marian at the Historical Society. They've made a list of all the graves in every cemetery or family plot in the county. There is no record of Samuel Orin Sullivan or Katherine Sullivan." Selma rubbed her hands down her skirt, smoothing the worn material in a frustrated gesture.

Her response mirrored his feelings. At every turn, he discovered dead ends. He went on, reading from his notes.

"I'm not surprised. It seems that in the fall of 1947 after my grandfather passed, the entire Sullivan family disappeared from Millerton. Two of my uncles reappeared near Columbus, Ohio. My cousins, who were very little help, were born in Columbus. Emma and her husband, Thomas, moved away from Millerton in 1947 for his job, according to my cousin Anne, Thomas's daughter by his first wife. Emma and Thomas had three children after they married.

That made six in all. Anne was the only one who showed any interest in the family history, but she didn't have any information about Emma's life. They were told her parents died, and no one questioned it. She did remember going to a funeral as a small child. She thinks it was probably my grandfather's. She was very vague about it and remembered they stood in the sun for what seemed to be a long time, then left. She never saw who it was."

He flipped to another page of his notes. "Martha and David Kincaid lived in Bowersville, West Virginia, where Uncle David worked as a foreman at the foundry there. Later, Uncle Thomas found David a job as a manager for a building supply company, and they moved to Columbus. That's all she knew. Thomas and Emma didn't talk much about their life before Columbus."

Selma nodded. "That takes care of two sisters. How many siblings were there?"

"There were five total: Martha the eldest, Emma next, then Lucas, Henry, and Joseph—my father." Matt ticked them off on his fingers. "I don't know when Lucas and Dad came to Columbus. My guess is it was around '48 or '49. I read letters written between Katherine and Samuel at Uncle Lucas's house. The Bible I found on my father's desk made me wonder about my roots. I tried to ask my uncle, Henry Sullivan, but he won't talk about it, either." Matt bit his lip, wishing he hadn't added that information.

She looked up and grinned at him. "Any relation to the candidate for President?" she joked.

"What a question." Matt's laugh sounded high and false in his ears. In a small town like this, word would spread fast. "We need to find where they buried Sam and what happened in 1947 to split up the family."

Selma tapped the top of the pen against her lower lip, drawing Matt's attention to its fullness. His throat went dry until she spoke. "I suggest we start with the church." She stood, reached for her purse, and dropped a pad and pen inside.

Matt followed Selma out of the library after informing the woman seated at the desk that she was leaving. The woman gave Matt a long stare that left his hair on end. He forced himself to smile at her and reached for the back of Selma's elbow to escort her out the door.

"The Methodist Church has been here since the town's inception. It's straight across the square from here." She pointed to a spot where he could see the steeple peeking above the large, old oak trees.

Matt walked beside her and nodded at people who appeared out of nowhere to stand along the sidewalk. They gave the two long looks as they passed. Some called a greeting to Selma, and she replied in kind but didn't stop to chat or introduce him.

Children and mothers sat on the benches, a gazebo big enough to hold a good-sized band, and a few trees for shade graced the town square. They passed the city hall with the police station at one end and the library at the other.

Opposite the square, a long building housed a few small shops. Barker's Market and the attached parking lot took up a portion of the block to the south of the square. Across the main road into town, a couple of large, two-story houses anchored that block. The church rested on a side street that ran at an angle out from the corner of the square.

At the corner, they crossed toward the wrought iron fence surrounding the old cemetery. Selma explained, "Only people are buried here with a family plot. The newcomers or young folks are buried on a hill just outside town."

She led the way around the church to a door on the side and pushed the doorbell. A muffled ding-dong answered, followed by heavy footsteps a moment later. The footsteps came to a stop on the other side of the curved, wood plank door. A small door at eye level swung open, and part of a lined face with bushy eyebrows over blue, watery eyes peeked through the metal grate over the opening.

"Pastor, may we come in? We have some questions about the cemetery that I'm sure only you can answer," Selma shouted.

The eye first looked at her, then at Matt. The little door shut, and the large door squeaked open. A voice told them, "Come in, children."

A portly older man who smelled of cigar smoke and body odor stepped aside to allow them to pass down a narrow hallway. "Go on in and make yourself comfortable." He turned into a side door, and Matt heard muffled voices in conversation.

Selma whispered as they walked, "That was Pastor Bob. Pastor Mike's a lot older and probably lived here during that time."

The heavy steps returned down the hall, and Pastor Bob met the two in the middle of the sitting area. A threadbare couch covered with worn quilts lined one wall. Two wing-backed chairs faced each other with a rag-tied throw rug in the middle.

Pastor Bob waved his hand at the couch. "Sit, please. Sit. My bunions are killing me." He collapsed into the chair with indents that came from the familiar body. "You know who I am. Please, who are you?" The man wheezed the words, and Matt wasn't sure he would live through the end of the conversation.

"I'm Selma Greeley, the librarian here in town. This is Matt Sullivan."

The pastor's head swung so fast to look at Matt; the younger man thought it might turn around his clerical collar. "I know you, my dear." His bushy eyebrows furrow closer to make one large unibrow. "Sullivan, you say?"

"Yes sir," Matt answered.

"I think there was a family of Sullivan's here at one time, but they moved." He turned to stare at the wall, away from Selma and Matt.

"We're trying to find out where they buried Samuel Sullivan. There are no records from the church listing his burial place, but I was wondering if you might know if he was buried in an unmarked grave here in the cemetery."

"He wasn't buried here." His voice was firm.

"Then do you know where he's buried?" Matt leaned forward, his voice hopeful. "I want to find my family, and I've traced my roots to Millerton. I know he died September 1947."

"Have you been to the farm?" Pastor Bob asked, his tone far too mild to be genuine.

"No. Where is it?" the two asked simultaneously, then grinned at each other.

"It's about two miles south of town. The road makes a sharp right. There's an overgrown fence, and I don't know that you can even go up the driveway. I don't think the mailbox is even there. Look for that curve. Tall trees line the drive if I remember." His brows furrowed for a moment, then relaxed.

"Pastor Bob, do you know anything about what happened back then? Why would my family have just upped and left?"

Pastor Bob waved his hand in the air as if clearing smoke away from his face. "I'd just moved here. I don't know anything about your family. I do know there's a Sullivan homestead as I met your grandmother there once. I suspect your grandfather might be there."

"What did you talk to my grandmother about?" Matt queried.

"It was so long ago, and I don't remember." His answer was too quick for honesty. Matt pursed his lips and frowned.

"Can you ask Pastor Mike? He was here then." Selma gave him a sweet smile.

"I can ask. Why don't you two come with me? He gets a little lonely with just me for company." The older man shuffled down the hall and guided them through a doorway.

CHAPTER 12
MILLERTON, WV
August 2000

SELMA AND MATT FOLLOWED PASTOR BOB INTO the room, and Matt was glad he wore a light shirt. The room was hot, even for a summer day.

Bob pulled a wooden chair close to the quilt-padded rocking chair. "Mike, these young people want to know what happened to the Sullivan family. Do you remember why they left town after their father died, and do you know where he's buried?"

The old pastor was a diminished version of the large picture on the wall with his name under it. This version had shrunk to a misshapen caricature of what he'd been. When he spoke, his voice was raspy and weary. "Sullivan. Sullivan. I know that name."

Bob turned to Matt. "What was your grandfather's name?"

"Samuel Sullivan. He died in 1947."

"I know when he died." Pastor Mike snapped the words, the weariness vanishing.

"Where was he buried?" Matt prompted gently.

"I wasn't there. The boys and Ben dug the grave. They brought Sam from the hospital to the mortuary, and he was buried immediately at the farm. No one but the family, Ben, and Cassie were at the funeral. I got a report from the mortician."

"Who were Ben and Cassie?"

"The Lundgrens. Uppity neighbors. They lived down the road to the next driveway. They moved here from up north somewhere. Never did fit in, but Katherine liked them, and they protected her."

"Protected her from what?" Matt frowned, his stomach sinking.

A coughing spell prevented him from talking. He pulled a plastic mask attached to an air tank over his nose and took long pulls of air.

Pastor Bob stood and ushered them to the door. "I think he needs to rest. When he talks too much, he starts coughing, and it takes its toll. Mike has lung cancer," the man explained in a hushed tone.

Selma stopped at the door, so he couldn't shut it. "Pastor Bob, we need to know more about what happened that summer and fall. When did you move here?"

"I came that fall for a few weeks. Then I was asked to return a few months later after the New Year."

"Please ask Pastor Mike if he remembers anything thing that can help us find what happened to Katherine Sullivan," Matt pleaded.

The older man nodded and began to push the door closed, giving them no choice but to leave.

On the sidewalk, Matt looked at his watch. "It's only two o'clock. Do you have to get back, or can you show me where the homestead is?" His voice held hope and added a smile, hoping the combination would convince her.

Selma gave a little chuckle. "Sure, I can go."

They drove out of town; Selma gave Matt directions. When they neared the two-mile marker, Matt watched for the curve in the road and the fence.

"It's just up here." Selma gestured to the yellow caution: curve sign. "Stop over here." Matt followed her lead and pulled into a small turn-off just after the sign before turning off the car.

With the thick foliage choking the bend of the road, Matt couldn't see either fence or driveway, and he scowled. "Are you sure this is it?"

"I should've remembered this was the Sullivan homestead. I came here as a child and played by the creek and sat on the back porch, wondering why anyone would leave that beautiful place. It didn't dawn on me it was the same place until he described it."

"You lived here as a child?"

"Just visited." Selma opened the door and climbed out.

Matt followed but didn't see much of a fence. It took him a minute, but closer inspection revealed a few posts poking above the flowering weeds. Between the two of them, they pushed shrubs and weeds aside to make a path. Matt followed close behind Selma as they made their way up what once was a dirt driveway.

After passing the last overgrown tree along the drive, Matt saw the two-story house. The windows were broken or missing, and the front porch roof barely hung onto the house. The supports lay like a drunken man's legs. His heart tore at the neglected shell of what once was a family's home, his family's home.

"Let's try the back door." Matt took Selma's hand and smiled as she didn't resist. The contact was a welcome warmth to replace the sadness he'd just experienced.

They pushed and stomped a path in through the vegetation to the back of the house. The rear porch appeared in much better condition than the one in front. An old wringer washer and a refrigerator with its round generator on top sat to one side of the back door. Both were completely rusted.

Matt helped Selma climb to the porch deck before he turned and looked across the field. Over waist-high weeds and wild grass, or wheat of some sort, he saw the barn. Most of the shingles were gone, and bare wooden slats baked in the heat like dried, sagging bones. Large doors hung open on their hinges as if waiting for the next gust of wind to release them to their final resting place. Matt shook his head as he turned to face the house with its secrets.

The damp smell of old smoke lingered as they stepped cautiously into the house. The large kitchen was intact, save for one scorched wall. Selma followed Matt's footsteps past the staircase to the living room where the fire had claimed most of the outside wall, leaving the fireplace in one piece. He looked up to see the space above him open where the fire had burned through the floor, leaving a large hole. Shreds of curtains falling from the rod fluttered just over the lip of the hole, giving the impression of reaching fingers.

A couch and two chairs, burned beyond any salvation, lay collapsed on the floor, their upholstery moth-eaten and thick with decades of dust. From Matt's vantage point, it looked as if the fire had started near the living room's fireplace and spread outward from there.

"Why would someone start a fire outside the fireplace?" He spoke aloud without thinking. His lips tugged downward in a deep frown.

"Maybe a log rolled out and caught a rug on fire." Selma stood beside him and pointed to the dark spot at the edge of the hearth. "It looks like the fire spread this way and then caught the curtains. Maybe they couldn't put it out." Matt made his way across the flooring, testing each step before putting his weight down, and stood on the floor joists. It looked as if the whole wall went up in flames before the fire moved to the front of the house, catching more rugs and then the sofa and chairs. This was a big fire. It moved fast.

"I never went in the house when I was little. Just sat on the back porch and used the wooden swing." Selma gingerly stepped into the room, but Matt grabbed her arm and pulled her back, holding her shoulders, so she stood with her back to his chest.

"I don't think the floor is secure." Matt pointed to the broken floor trusses near the fireplace. "Stay behind me; we'll stay on this side of the house. It doesn't look as damaged." He moved her behind him but held her hand at his waist. The pair then walked down the hall, testing the floor as they went.

Matt backed to the safer part of the floor and looked into the dining room on the other side of the stairs. Shards of broken dishes littered the floor around the room. Something about them caught his attention, and Matt picked up a shard to examine the pattern. He frowned.

"What is it? Did you find something?" Selma stepped around him and held onto the only chair left at the table.

"When I was at my uncle's house, I found plates, cups, and a bowl or two in this pattern. I thought it was odd that he would have chipped plates and glasses in his hutch." He held up the ceramic shard with the flower pattern on it. "This is the pattern on the pieces in the hutch at my Uncle Lucas's house."

"He must have come back," said Selma.

Matt shook his head. "Lucas said he rescued what he could and hid it.

Later, he brought them with him to his new house."

"That's so sad." Selma walked around to the hutch and pulled the drawers open. They were empty.

"Selma, look around. If your house burned, wouldn't you at least take what you could to start anew? If you couldn't rebuild, you'd take all the things that hadn't been too damaged, clean them up, and use them. Then why was everything left? This table, for example, is fine except for the weather and time. The chairs look as if they were vandalized, not burned. What's left of the curtains is still hanging, and the rugs are still on the floors. It's as if they ran out of the house, took what they could carry, and never came back." Matt paused, the frown still on his face as he stared around himself at the ruins of the house. "I don't think they left voluntarily. Do you think maybe Katherine died? Left them? All this creates more questions." He shook his head and rubbed his neck, frustrated.

Selma nodded. "At least the questions can be more specific now. We need to find out where they went and why."

Matt moved to the stairs, surveying them. The stair horse was intact, and some of the risers were in place. He pulled on the banister and found it solid.

"You're not going up there," said Selma. It was more of an order than a question. When he looked over at her, she was scowling at him, concern drawing her brows together.

"I have to see what was left." He stepped on each step carefully, letting his weight adjust. At the top, he stepped onto the floor and bounced a little. It seemed to hold, but he moved with caution nonetheless. The fire had ruined whatever room had been on his left, leaving portions of the burned floor joists exposed.

In the first intact room, a couple of mattresses lay on the floor with no bedding atop them. Wallpaper printed with soldiers still clung to the old plaster despite being faded and stained with smoke and water from a leak in the ceiling. A lone chair leaned against the corner, and an old-school desk lay on its side nearby. Printed on the wall were the names LUCAS, HENRY, and JOSEPH. Mattresses lay on the floor. One long dresser sat along the remaining wall, and Matt moved to see anything that remained inside. The floor cracked under his weight, and he retreated, his heart leaping into his throat.

"Matt! Are you okay? Get back here!" Selma's voice echoed to him up the stairs, demanding and fearful. He grimaced, though it became a smile half a second later. It was a long time since someone cared about his welfare. A glance in the last room revealed pink walls and one mattress on a broken bed frame, minus the bedding. Nothing was in the closets.

When he returned to the main floor beside Selma, he heard her sigh. "I'm safe," Matt reassured her, smiling toward the woman.

"What'd you find?"

"More of the same. There were mattresses but no bedding and no clothes."

They moved beyond the dining room and passed a bathroom whose door was broken and hanging. At the end of the hallway, Matt and Selma discovered a final bedroom.

Here they found a double bed, a swollen chest of drawers, and a vanity with the mirror broken and lying at an angle against the wall. Again, there were no clothes in the closet. Maybe they had been stolen by squatters?

"This must have been Sam and Katherine's room." Matt's voice was almost a whisper, and beside him, Selma nodded.

Uneasiness overcame him, and Matt turned away from the room with the sudden urge to escape the closed confines. "I'm going to check out the barn." Matt strode out of the house and jumped off the porch, Selma following close behind. He turned to lift her down with his hands at her waist. She didn't resist, and Matt took that as another positive. "Wait here for me."

"No way. I want to see what's there, too." She hiked up her skirt and followed in his steps through the grass.

Animals, probably deer, had made a trail around the barn and into the backfield. The two followed it, veering off to walk through the hanging doors. The sun shone through the missing roof, revealing the empty interior. Wild Grass and weeds grew in the stalls, a few flowers blooming in shafts of afternoon light.

They moved through the main aisle toward the back and a door Matt assumed led to a tack room. Instead of harnesses or equipment to tend the animals, they found a metal bedstead with no mattress. Hooks on the wall held nothing but a hammer, a rusted saw, and some grooming brushes that lay scattered on the table attached to the wall.

"Nothing useful here." Matt turned to leave, but Selma grabbed at his shirt and pointed to the wall.

"Look." Notches gouged at intervals into a door frame. Next to the notches, names and dates were carved or burned into the wood: Lucas- 1934, Henry-1937, and Joseph-1940. Above them, a ways were more notches with the same names and different dates until 1948, where they stopped.

"So they left in 1948. I wonder where they would have buried my grandfather." Matt murmured as he looked around the barn. There was an empty, wild sort of beauty in this place. The two walked through the tall grass along a path from the corner of the barn toward some trees. It looked to Matt as a good place for a grave.

After a fruitless search of the small grove, the pair turned back to the barn to investigate the other side of the field.

As they rounded the house, a gunshot rang out. The bullet hit a tree only a few feet away from Matt. Without thinking, he grabbed Selma's arm and dragged her to the ground with him. "Don't move." When he sought her face with his eyes, her gaze was wide and frightened.

They lay on the ground, Matt covering Selma and hoping no other shots. Their breaths were fast and loud in the silence.

"You're too heavy," she gasped and tried to squirm out from under him, but Matt pinned her in place with his larger body. He wanted to keep her there. She felt good.

"Okay. Stay low and crawl on your elbows to your right to the corner of the house. I think whoever it is, is behind us." Matt lifted his head a little, looking in the direction the shooter might be.

"Right." Selma's voice was breathless as she answered, and Matt saw her throat convulse as she swallowed. The woman slowly pulled herself toward the house using the weeds and tall grass as cover, followed by the man.

Once they reached cover, Matt rose, but Selma grabbed his shirt and hissed, "Get down!"

"I just want to see if anything is moving toward us."

Another shot tore apart the corner of the house just above Matt's head. With a startled yelp, he dropped back onto his belly and slunk further behind the wall.

"Who would want me dead?" Matt's voice was shaking as adrenaline pounded through his veins.

"Maybe it's me?" Selma's voice choked like she was holding back tears. Her face was pale as she crouched behind the meager safety offered by the crumbling wall.

"Not likely." He didn't want to tell her about Tim, but the thought ran through his mind like a freight train. Would his Uncle Henry go so far as to kill him to keep him from finding out about his grandmother? They lay there in silence for about an hour before Selma started to get up.

"Stay down," Matt ordered, reaching for her to try and forestall her movement.

"No." She slowly stood up, and when nothing happened, the woman moved away from the house and looked around. Matt climbed to his feet beside her, but there was no gunfire.

"Stay low to the ground and move to the car." Matt didn't want to take any chances with their lives to explore the property further. Taking her hand, he stooped over as far as he could and followed their previous track back to the road.

Everything around them was quiet except for the sounds of birds calling back and forth to one another through the trees. The two ran to the car and sagged into their seats, doors locked. Despite the adrenaline from the shooting, neither wanted to linger. Matt made a quick U-turn, and the dust blew behind them.

On their way back to town, Matt ground his teeth. "I'm going straight to the police." White-knuckled fingers wrapped around the steering wheel as he focused his attention on the road.

"I'm going with you," Selma's response booked no argument. She directed Matt to the opposite end of the library and city hall parking lot, where he followed her into the door with a plaque marked "Police Station."

Inside, they walked the hallway painted Ming green, an institution color popular too many years ago to count. Selma turned into a doorway and knocked on the jamb. "Lavon?"

Matt stood in the doorway, feeling uncomfortable. The situation stirred memories of Tim's death to the forefront and the long hours he'd spent being questioned by the officers on the case.

The large man behind the desk looked up and saw Selma. His face lit like a Christmas tree. "Selma, darlin'!" He started to come around the desk, but she backed up to stand in front of Matt.

She introduced the two men. "Lavon, this is Matthew Sullivan. Matt, this is Sheriff Lavon Shelton."

Lavon stepped closer to Selma, maneuvering her to the side as if to get closer to Matt. The man's move wasn't lost on Matt, he responded to the outstretched hand and the powerful grip in the most polite manner he could provide under the circumstances. He gave the customary squeeze, but Lavon did not let go and dedicated himself to crushing Matt's fingers. Matt refused to engage him and winced.

Selma, watching the interchange, stepped up and hit Lavon's arm. "Knock it off, Lavon. There's no need for a pissing match."

Lavon gave a practiced look of sorrow and backed up a step. "Now, Selma, what can I do for you?" He winked.

"We were up at the old Sullivan homestead, and someone took a shot at us.

"A couple, to be sure," Matt added.

"Someone shot at you? Did you see who it was?" He moved quickly for a man of his size and girth as he returned to his desk. Lavon was close to Matt's age, maybe a little younger, but his sedentary job showed the beginning of a thick middle. Matt saw the counter behind the Sheriff's desk held an old coffee maker a box of donuts.

"Yes, someone shot at us, and no, I don't know who did it. The first bullet hit the tree on the other side of the driveway and then the side of the house right above our heads." Selma's voice wavered a little.

Matt liked how she portrayed them as both being in danger, not just because he had probably been the target.

Lavon eyed him. "You think someone deliberately tried to hit you?"

"It sure looked that way. We weren't doing anything wrong. I don't know if anyone owns the land because it certainly isn't being taken care of."

"Do you want to file a complaint? I mean, it isn't hunting season, but you know them, hill boys. They don't need a season to hunt." He gave Selma a long look.

"That's true, but this time they got a little too close, and there wasn't anything about us that screamed wild animal," Selma retorted. She'd moved to stand across the desk from Lavon.

Lavon pulled some papers from a file and pushed them toward Matt. Selma grabbed them out of his fingers, walked to another desk, and sat down. She filled out the papers and spoke only when she wanted to define something. Matt stood beside her and watched her fill in the blank spaces with the details of the attempted shooting.

Lavon got up and sat on the corner of his desk, watching the two with an eagle eye. "How long are you staying in town?" he asked Matt.

"I'm not sure yet. It depends on what I find and if people are willing to talk." Matt didn't look up from Selma as he answered.

"What do you want to know?" Lavon persisted, trying to draw Matt from Selma's side. Matt caught onto the ploy but remained where he was, leaning over Selma. He wouldn't have moved to spite the sheriff.

"I'm looking for information about my grandmother."

"What's her name?"

"Katherine Sullivan."

"Hmm. I don't know anyone living around here by that name. You've been to the old Sullivan farm, but they left long before I was born. Don't know what happened to them."

"Neither do I, but something happened here to make them leave."

Selma finished writing and held the pen for Matt to sign on the line at the bottom. "Matt's staying at the inn. If you find who was shooting at us, you can call Matt or me."

"What are you going to do?" Lavon let the paper slide from his hand into the full basket marked IN on the corner of his antique wooden desk.

"I'm not sure; we haven't discussed it. Lavon, I hope to hear you find the culprit and give them a good shaking. They could've killed us." Selma turned to the door.

"I will." Lavon followed them and held the door open as they walked toward the door.

Matt walked with his hand at Selma's waist, his fingers lightly touching her side. She didn't seem to mind, and he held the door for her as she got into the car.

CHAPTER 13

MILLERTON, WV

July 1947

KATHERINE PACKED SEVERAL BOXES WITH eggs and cheese along with the pies and cakes she had made. She slid the last cake into place just in time as Cassie pulled into the driveway and honked the horn.

"Joseph, Henry! I'm leaving town; stay close to the house," Katherine called.

She started to pick up the box, but Lucas forestalled her, putting his hand on top.

"I'll carry them out for you," he said.

When she lowered her hands, the young man lifted the cargo with ease.

Lucas walked in front of her, meeting Cassie at the rear of the utility sedan, holding the trunk open. She smiled at Lucas, but he didn't return the greeting. Cassie looked at Katherine with a concerned and confused expression. Katherine just gave a quick shake of her head.

Lucas shut the trunk and turned to his mother, walking with her to the passenger door. "Ma, don't talk to anyone there but the Barkers."

"Lucas, what is wrong with you? I have to be friendly, or else I won't make any sales."

The boy ran his fingers through his hair, leaving it sticking out at odd angles from his head before grabbing the door handle. "Ma, the men in town—" He paused and clenched his teeth but didn't look at her.

"I know what they are." Katherine smoothed her son's hair down and noted it was time to give him a haircut. "They're just lazy louts. I don't pay them no mind."

"Ma, you don't know 'em. I've heard 'em talkin'. Stay close to Miz Cassie. Do you have your knives with you? I don't know what they have planned, be careful." He was worried, and it gave Katherine a sense of love she hadn't felt since Sam left two weeks ago.

"I do and thank you for thinking of me. I'll be careful." When he gave her a look, she went on, "Honest, Lucas. Thank you for letting me know what to expect." She patted him on his shoulder as he opened the door for her.

After she settled in the front seat, Lucas leaned down to look into the car, "Miz Cassie, you be careful and stay close to Ma." He didn't wait for her answer but shut the door and strode toward the back of the house.

"What was that all about?" Cassie asked as she shifted the car into gear and headed down the driveway.

"Lucas heard the men of our fair town have something planned for me. He didn't know what or wasn't going to tell me, but it wasn't good." Katherine frowned. "I don't like it. If Lucas knows something, that means he's been sneaking into town without me knowing. He must've taken the horse."

"You can't fault him. He's young in years, but he acts older than some of the adult men in town. I wish he wouldn't have stopped going to school."

"Cassie, I've been meaning to talk to you about that. I'm thinking of pulling all the boys out of school. Henry came home and said the children were teasing him and Joseph. No fights yet, but if you'd be willing to tutor the boys, and that includes Lucas, I can pay you in bread, eggs, and cheese."

Cassie didn't respond right away. "Let me think about it. I loved teaching, but when Ben wanted to get away from city life and live off the land, I had to put that dream aside." She looked upwards for a moment, grinned, and gave Katherine a full smile. "I thought about it; I'll do it. Have Lucas bring the boys over in the morning."

"Thanks, Cassie." She reached over and squeezed her friend's arm. The two were quiet the rest of the way into town, though the silence was companionable. They pulled into the drive beside Barker's store, and Cassie killed the engine.

The two women picked up the boxes from the back of the car and started climbing the steps. Men lounged on the porch and made rude noises as the women made their way up the steps.

Ollie, one of the louts on the porch, moved over to the door and opened it for them in a show of mock gallantry. Cassie stepped through with a polite little smile, and Katherine followed, but Ollie's arm dropped across the doorway.

"Hey, darlin', mind if'n I stop by your place tonight? I'll come around late so's the boys are asleep." An ugly leer twisted his already ugly features.

Katherine didn't look at him but ducked under his arm. Ollie worked alongside her husband for many years, and he'd known his place when Sam had been there. She wasn't sure exactly when that had changed, but at some point since Sam's departure for his new job, Ollie decided she was going to be his woman. Ollie's hand moved faster than she expected and gripped her buttock, pinching hard. Katherine scowled, trying to escape his reach.

She moved inside as Cassie came to her rescue, taking the box from her. Katherine whirled to face the large man through the screen with her hands on her hips. "Ollie, you step one foot on my property without your wife at your side, and you'll find yourself full of buckshot." She made the threat loud enough so the other good-for-nothing bums on the porch could hear every word.

Katherine turned and followed Cassie to the counter, behind which Robert Barker carefully transferred the cakes into the cooler next to the pies. Cassie grinned, but Katherine couldn't manage a smile after the attack by Ollie. "Miz Sullivan, I'll be happy to take your baked goods for sale. What were you thinking on a price?" asked Robert.

"Fifty cents each." She spoke with conviction, hoping there would be no argument.

"I was thinking of selling them for that amount. Let's say twenty-five cents."

"Forty-five." She countered.

"Thirty." Robert leaned on the counter, watching her expression. "Forty-three."

Robert raised his eyebrows. "Thirty-eight."

"Mister Barker, this is my last offer. If you don't want it, I'll take the cakes and pies home. Forty."

Robert grinned. "I like you, Miz Sullivan. Forty, it is." He held out his hand. Katherine shook it and gave a slight smile.

"Can you bring me some more on Friday?" he asked. "I have most of my shoppers buying through the weekend. It would be a good time to sell the ladies their dessert for Sunday dinner. What the hubby doesn't know won't hurt him."

Katherine picked up a few staples for the cakes she would make for the weekend before waving farewell to Mr. Barker.

At the post office, she pushed open the door with its tinkling bell and dropped her weekly letter for Sam in the mailbox.

"Miz Brewster, do you have any mail for me?" Katherine spoke through the metal bars that separated the lobby from the sorting room.

From around the corner, Mrs. Brewster stuck her head out. "No, Miz Sullivan, I do not. How's your husband doing?"

"Oh, just fine. He's staying with Martha and David in Browerville, and he likes his job. I know he misses us, and I sure miss him."

"That's nice." She turned to Katherine and looked through the bars to see if anyone else was in the room. Behind her, a whistle from a teapot blew. Mrs. Brewster jumped, then held her hand over her ample breast. "That gave me quite a scare! I'd better get it." She turned and hurried around the corner of the wall of tiny square slots that represented the town's population.

Katherine left the post office and met Cassie near Barker's for the trip home. They didn't talk much during the drive; Katherine had too much on her mind.

After Cassie dropped her off, Katherine walked up the long driveway to her house. She didn't feel like walking through the hot kitchen, taking a detour into the field. She followed the path into the woods.

The shade of the trees was refreshing after the hot sun beat down on her head, and she could hear the forest animals moving away from her as she made her way deeper into the forest. She stopped and drew in a deep breath of air and hesitated.

Smoke. It smelled like fire. Fear ripped through her body; any fire could destroy all their homes and gardens. She followed the scent through the woods that opened into a nearby clearing. Trees had fallen and formed a border. In the center of the square, a burned patch of grass and timber caught her attention. She moved closer, staring at the burn pattern. The fire had started in the center, and wood was added to make the fire bigger. Someone dragged logs away from the main blaze to make spokes of fire burning toward the edge of the clearing. Who would do this? Playing with fire wasn't funny. The slightest spark could ignite the entire forest and then jump to either her farm or Ben and Cassie's.

A quick exploration of the burned areas found them cool to the touch. At least it was safe for now, anyway. Katherine looked around the area for clues about the person who'd been there. She found footprints larger than hers, and whoever it was must not have been too heavy.

Relieved the fire was in no danger of reigniting: Katherine retraced her steps toward home. As she came around the barn, she found Henry and Joseph in a tangle.

Separating the two, she shook them both by their collars. "What is going on here?"

"He called me a bad name."

"I did not!" Joseph yelled.

"Listen, both of you! Since one spoke it and the other knew what it was, you both get your mouths washed with soap." Katherine started walking toward the house with the boys hollering for leniency. She let her grip relax, and they took advantage of it, running a few feet from her.

"Ma, we're sorry. We don't need no soapin'."

"Then I suggest you get your chores done so you'll be ready to eat when I ring for dinner." They took off running toward the barn.

Katherine spotted Lucas standing at the edge of the woods and watching what happened. She looked his way, smiled, and gave him a shrug. He shook his head as he watched her walk to the house, then made his way to the barn after the boys.

After dinner, she told the boys her plan for their schooling and that Cassie had agreed. Henry and Joseph looked at each other, not sure if they should be happy or sad. The idea of going to Cassie's house was a treat, but doing any schoolwork took the joy out of the visit. After a short discussion, they agreed to it, picked up their plates, and headed for the sink.

When they were out of the room, Lucas looked at his mother. "I take it I'm expected to take the boys to Miz Cassie's?"

Katherine stared at her oldest son with his light brown hair, brushing his shoulders. She suspected that the girls were attracted to his looks and blue eyes but put off by his aloof attitude.

"Yes, Lucas, I want you to go, too, and not just to sit and watch them study. Cassie is going to tutor you so that you can graduate. I don't want ignorant children. You will get your diploma."

She waited for an argument, but he just grinned at her. "Okay, Ma."

Katherine sighed. That was one hurdle cleared. "Lucas, be careful in the woods. I found a large burned area. Someone could've started a forest fire there. Keep an eye out for anyone suspicious. It wasn't too far from the house, and that scares me."

Lucas stood and stretched. He was serious. "I'll keep a lookout for anyone.

I'm going to the barn to get some sleep."

Katherine stood and dumped the last of the dregs of her cup into the sink. She pulled the pot from the stove and emptied the day-old coffee into the sink. There were times like today when she forgot Sam wasn't here to drink the other half a pot during the day.

"You have a bed upstairs," she said to her son. "Why are you sleeping in the barn?"

He shrugged and sauntered to the door. "It's quieter. Night, Ma."

"Good night, Son."

Katherine rinsed the pot and turned it upside down on the counter. She took one last look at the room to ensure everything was in its proper place before she turned the knob that cut the light.

In the bedroom she and Sam had shared, she sat on the bed and stared out the window. A half-moon shone to give the woods and pasture outside a bluish tinge.

A figure loomed in front of the window, blocking the view. Katherine threw her body to the far side of the bed. On her knees, she slid the shotgun from its place beside the bed. She slid her hand under pillows and pulled her knives from their hiding place.

A knife blade slit the screen of the half-open window, and a large hand pushed it up all the way.

Katherine waited in the darkness as a leg moved over the sill into the room, followed by a body. A man stood inside, looking around to adjust his eyes. She recognized him. It was Ollie. Large, bulky, Ollie.

"Ollie, you have thirty seconds to get your body back out that window before I blow you full of buckshot."

He stopped and tried to follow her voice in the darkness. "Baby, come on out."

"Ollie, get out right now. I don't want you here." She raised her voice and spoke firmly over the thud of her heart.

Ollie moved to the bed, following her voice. He leaned a knee on the mattress and tested the springs.

"You don't have a squeaker here. We'll do just fine." He started to crawl over across the quilt toward Katherine, but she backed away and stood up.

"I warned you, Ollie. Get out!" She pumped the lever, and Ollie froze.

"I'm not leaving until I have you. The guys have talked about you, and none have the balls to come here. I know you want me. I saw the way you tried to keep from watching me."

"Ollie, you're an idiot. I don't look at you because I don't like you."

"Don't say that!" He roared and lunged over the bed toward her.

Katherine hit him along his head with the barrel of the shotgun, then backed away. He fell off the side of the mattress, and she pulled the knife from its sheath.

"One more move and this knife will find your balls. Then you'll handin' them over to Clemmie in a bag."

Ollie tried to stand up, but Katherine slammed the shotgun barrel into the side of his head a second time. He collapsed to his knees and moaned, his hands holding his head.

"You hit me!" As soon as he had gathered himself, Ollie lunged across the bed for her again. This time she pulled the knife and slammed it up to his throat as he grabbed her arms.

He grunted, and his fetid breath made her gag. "You think you can do it? Go ahead," he taunted, but she could feel him shaking.

Katherine ground her teeth and shoved him with all her might. He stumbled backward, and she slid the knife across his throat. It cut his skin, and he let go of her, his hands going to his neck.

Katherine pointed the barrel back at him from across the room. "I mean it. Get out of my house and never come back!"

"I'm going to have you." His voice wasn't as confident as it had been the first time, and she could see the whites of his eyes in the dim moonlight.

"Ollie, give it up! You aren't going to have me. Leave before I have to shoot you. You'll have to go to the hospital. You know Clemmie will be mad at you, and all your friends will be laughing."

Ollie stopped. He stood at the end of the bed and looked at the shadowy frame holding a gun. "I just wanted your lovin'. I loved you since we were youngins, and you never paid me any mind." He pleaded his case. "I got Clemmie pregnant, and her Pa comes after me with a gun." The man moved away from Katherine, and she lowered the gun a fraction.

By this time, Ollie was pacing like an animal, more focused on his story than on her. "Katie-girl, I saw you today, and I knew Sam was gone. I just couldn't get you outta my mind. I'm sorry. I'm sorry Clemmie and the girls hate you. You're so pretty, and they're jus' jealous. I know it doesn't help none that we men just go on and on about you and wished our wives could cook like you, and bake like you, and make love like you."

"How do you know how Sam and I make love?" Katherine burst into his monologue.

"One of the boys was in the woods and came across you and Sam making love. He tol' us you was hollerin', and Sam was hollering—"

"Enough Ollie. That was a lie. Sam and I have never made love here in the woods. That was all made up for your benefit. So that's why the women won't speak to me. I should just shoot you now and put you out of your misery, but that's too good for you."

She took two steps and pointed her knife at him, but he backed up with his hands raised in a warding gesture. "That little slice across your neck is just a warning to you and your misfit brothers in crime. Don't mess with me and no more talkin' 'bout me and comparing me to your wives. You tell them lazy good-for-nuthin' porch mannequins they better not be doin' it, either. In fact, ya'll better buy some flowers from Daisy and take them home to yore misses and apologize. I better have a good response from yore wives, or ah'll tell 'em myself."

She didn't worry about proper talk. Ollie wouldn't have understood it anyway.

Ollie backed up to the window. "Now, Katie-girl."

"Stop calling me Katie-girl. I'm Katherine to you! I don't live in the hills anymore; I live like proper people, and so do you. Clemmie's dad got you that job, and you better start actin' like a proper man and not like someone who just walked down from the hills. Now git." She motioned toward the window with the gun. Ollie scrambled through it, landing with a grunt and groan of pain. She watched as he lumbered around the house out of sight.

Katherine lay on the bed. The confrontation ended, and tears fell from the corners of her eyes. All this time, she just wanted to be accepted by the women of Millerton, but she was doomed before she had a chance. Had Sam known about all this and never told her? He wouldn't want her feelings hurt. He must have heard the comments made by the men. Most of them had worked with him at the plant.

All she worked for, schooling and trying to talk proper, telling Cassie to correct her if she lapsed back into slang, made no difference. They all hated her. She knew they were snobby, and Cassie said not to mind them. To realize they despised her because of something she had no control over cut her to the quick.

No matter what Katherine, she knew it would never be enough. What did all that matter? Sam was gone, and she had no idea when she would see him. Unless he could make good money, and she could sell her baked goods, chances were that they wouldn't be able to join Sam for years. Katherine buried her head in the pillow and cried heartrending sobs.

CHAPTER 14
MILLERTON, WV
July 1947

A WEEK LATER, CASSIE DROVE LUCAS AND THE boy's home from their lessons. They tumbled out of the car in a flash and headed to the fields. Cassie shook her head, laughing at their antics as she joined Katherine on the porch, shelling beans.

"Those boys are as smart as a whip, especially Lucas. That boy would go far if he put his mind to it. He could be a teacher; he's good at helping Henry figure things out. What surprises me is the knowledge he has of farming. I ordered some books from the library for him. I don't know all that much, but I know there are magazines and books on agriculture techniques that he might be able to use." She collapsed in the Adirondack chair Sam had made.

"So you think he might be smart enough to go to agricultural school? Is there a school for that?" Katherine stopped snapping beans and leaned on the large metal bowl. The thought of one of her boys attending school beyond what the law required had her heart almost bursting with pride.

"Sure there is. They study animals, feed, plants, what manure makes better compost, and how to switch up the plants, so all the same nutrients aren't taken out of the ground. Its real science, Katherine, and I think Lucas would be a whiz at it. I know he wants to learn more, but I think he's afraid of something. I'm not sure what."

"Lucas? Afraid? He isn't afraid of anything I know."

"I'm not talking about things like reactions to a snake or bear. I'm talking about how he thinks. He might be afraid to leave you and go off to school. He's lived here all his life, and moving to a campus away from home is a pretty big step for a country boy. It's one thing to have people know you here in a small community. He'd be like a fish out of water on campus.

"I think Ben and I could help out there. We could take him to see some of the schools around here and introduce him to several professors. I'll have Ben talk to some of them when he goes in for his meeting." Cassie stretched and yawned.

"You want some iced tea?" Katherine started to get up, but Cassie waved her off.

"Thanks, but you're bowl deep in beans. I know where the tea is. I'll fill your glass and mine. I'm sure you have some pie or cake or something I can piece out for us to enjoy." A far from innocent grin covered Cassie's face, making her look more mischievous than helpful.

Katherine laughed. "Yes, I saw a recipe for a Dolly Madison cake in one of those magazines you brought over. I made it this morning."

Cassie was on her feet as fast as one could move out of a slanted back chair. "Where is it? I saw that coconut-covered cake picture. I want a taste!" She didn't wait for an answer, but the slam of the screen door behind her was the only response.

Cassie was the only friend Katherine had. She thought about what she knew of her friend and Ben. They had moved here from Philadelphia, and she'd helped Katherine with her speech and how to act and walk. The two women had laughed until their sides ached as Katherine practiced walking with a book on her head and drank tea with her pinky finger extended at the proper angle. Katherine smiled at the memory and snapped more beans into the bowl.

Cassie had told Katherine, she and Ben's families were from the upper crust of Virginia, but they left it behind to live in the country. Katherine watched Ben climb the hill twice a month to learn things from the hill folk, and he, in turn, taught them something about a world outside their own. He taught them by example, not by dragging books they couldn't read like the government social workers who demanded they send their kids to school. She and Sam had many a laugh over his interactions with her relatives.

Cassie returned with cake and tea. Katherine put down the handful of beans and her memories.

Once they settled into their seats, she told Cassie about Ollie's attack.

Cassie bolted upright. "Why didn't you say something before? We have to go into town and tell Sheriff Shelton. Ollie must be punished for this."

"I can't." Katherine stared at her slice of cake. "Ollie's Ollie; not too smart, but he acted on something I guess he heard from other men. He left crying and begging me not to tell Clemmie. I handled it my way, and I'll see the reaction when I go into town. My guess is Ollie won't open his mouth, and I won't be getting any more sass from him." Katherine took a bite of the moist layer cake, closed her eyes, and hummed. "This is good."

"I won't tell you what I think of that ideas, but it's your decision." Her fork hovered above the cake, and she cut into it with reverence. "Are you kidding me? It's delicious! This cake would take the blue ribbon at any contest." Cassie scooted to the edge of the chair with wide eyes. "Let's do it. Let's make some of your pies and this cake, and submit it to be judged in the fair."

"How can I do that? Are you going to take me to the fair?"

"Of course! I would love to see those women in town when you walk into Barker's with the blue ribbon. I could just see Miz Shelton, Miz Beacon, and her little busybodies when you sport that ribbon for them. I don't think any of them have ever even sent something to the county fair."

"Speaking of the fair ladies of Millerton, I found out why they're so again' us." Katherine's hands returned to breaking the beans.

"Against us," Cassie corrected.

"Why they are so against us. Ollie spilled it all that night. Seems like-"

"It seems like."

"Okay. It seems like. I can't tell the story if you keep buttin' in!" Katherine protested, pointing a bean at Cassie with every word.

"Butting in. I'll be quiet now." Cassie took a big bite of cake and chewed slowly, a smile on her face. She waved her fork for Katherine to continue as she worked on the mouthful she'd taken.

"I was saying. Ollie told me the women in town don't like me because all the men do. Like the stupid men they are, they haven't been exactly quiet about it to their wives." Katherine hunched her shoulders as if expecting a lash to come across her back. When she didn't hear anything from Cassie, she looked up. Cassie was concentrating on licking the last of the frosting from her plate. Katherine burst out laughing.

"What?" Cassie eyed her over the rim of the plate. "It's too good to leave any evidence." She set the plate on the porch next to the glass of tea. "Katherine, I knew that."

"You did? You knew and never said anything? How could you not tell me?"

"How do you feel now? Does it answer all your questions and make you feel warm and fuzzy inside?" Cassie countered.

"No, but—"

"No buts. I didn't say anything because Sam asked me not to for just that reason."

"Sam knew about this? Well, that shouldn't surprise me, come to think about it. He did work in the plant with them." Katherine felt disappointment like a knife in her chest.

"Yes, he had to put up with a lot of harassment from the guys about you. At first, he wanted to fight them all, but what would that accomplish? He dug in his heels and worked harder. That's why he got promotions over the others.

"He worked hard and kept his mouth shut to you, too. He didn't want to see you hurt. It was bad enough you talked about how you felt when the woman snubbed you. But you still wish their approval for some reason.

"You worked on your speech, how you dressed and acted more refined. It just rubbed the women the wrong way all over. Now that I think about it, you were right not to tell the sheriff. It would just make things even worse."

Katherine let her hands drop into the bowl of beans. "I can't win, can I?"

"What do you want to win?"

"I left the hills to be a different person. To be treated like a real person should be treated. I get here, and it isn't any different. They still think I'm a Hillbilly, and because I have something they feel they don't have, I'm the bad person. How do I get past that?" Katherine pleaded.

"You don't, and it doesn't matter. Think of it this way: you're better than they are, and they know it. They feel inferior to you, and because of that, they want to drag you down to believe you're something beneath them. Don't do it. You're a great mother, seamstress, and baker. You don't have to apologize for that to anyone, especially them. Stand tall, remember the book on your head, and let them try to be your friend. Not the other way around." Cassie pounded the arm of her chair like a preacher.

Katherine smiled, straightening her back. "Let's take the cake to the fair."

Cassie waved her hands in the air and moved her feet like she was riding an air bike, then hollered like she was one of those holy rollers from the other side of town. Katherine put the bowl of beans on the porch and laughed so hard she had to wipe the tears with her apron.

CHAPTER 15

MILLERTON, WV

August 2000

SELMA SUGGESTED WHERE TO GO NEXT. "LET'S go visit Emily Smith. She owns the bakery shop and has lived here all her life. She'll remember what happened. We've had a friendly relationship over the years." She opened the door of the car before Matt could do it for her. He shut, rounded the car, and climbed into the driver's seat.

Selma gave him directions to drive the corner. They circled the square, and Matt parked in front of a shop with various baked goods in the window. The pair left the car, and he took a moment to enjoy the view of the tempting-looking array of treats.

The bell jingled as they opened the door, and the smell of cookies, cakes, and bread mixed in an aroma that triggered Matt's memory. He remembered the smell when he came home from school to loaves of bread and a pie on the shelf. He grinned, and his eyes went straight to the case shelves. They were overflowing with all the goodies he could imagine and a few he hadn't. Matt made straight for the curved glass and leaned against it, his hands spread across it as if hugging it.

Selma laughed as she tugged at his arm. "Come on. She'll have to sanitize the glass now."

Mrs. Emily Smith came around the corner and saw Selma first, then Matt. She watched him for a few seconds with amusement dancing in her eyes and then smiled at Selma. "There's a boy in every man when it comes to baked goodies. What can I get you, sir?" She stopped across the counter in front of Matt.

"I'd like—"

"Mrs. Emily, we need some information." Selma moved to Matt and tugged on his arm again to draw his attention back to the reason they were there in the first place.

"Oh, I'm sorry. I'm Matt Sullivan, Ma'am. My grandparents and family lived here in Millerton back in the forties. There's something about them leaving here that I'm trying to find out. Would you know anything about them?" Matt leaned on the glass, not wanting to leave the trays of warm treats.

The bakery's owner stepped back a couple of steps and looked from Selma to Matt. The smile she wore turned to a frown. "Why do you want to drag that mess up to people? It was bad enough it happened. We all want that forgotten."

"What happened?" Selma and Matt spoke at the same time.

"What's your family told you?" She narrowed her eyes at Matt.

"Nothing, and that's the problem. My father died, and my uncle won't tell me. I know my uncles don't know where their mother is or what happened to her. They have some sort of issue with this town. I want to give them some peace before he dies, that his mother didn't abandon him and his brothers."

"Are you sure she didn't?" Mrs. Emily shot back.

Matt and Selma looked at each other, then back at Emily. "What?" Matt asked.

"Are you sure she didn't abandon them? Times were hard back then. Food was scarce, and there wasn't much money to buy groceries, let alone pay the bills. Having three hungry young boys took a toll."

"Are you saying my grandmother voluntarily left her three boys? Abandoned them? I can't believe that." Matt stepped away from the glass counter; the baked goods no longer appealed to him.

His mind whirled. He hadn't considered that scenario. Would his grandmother walk off and leave her boys in a town that was as poor as she was? It was inconceivable.

"Where did the boys live if she just left them here?" he questioned.

Mrs. Smith eyed him. "One lived with the Mellon family, and one went the Garland's who arranged for him to live with the McClure's up in Jersey. The one with the Mellon family ran away."

"What about the third boy?" Selma spoke up.

Mrs. Smith frowned for a moment. "I don't rightly know now. He was older, and I think he ran away too. I heard he got in with some gypsies."

"How did you know he went with gypsies?" Matt asked.

Mrs. Smith drew her shoulders up in a defensive gesture, and her frown deepened. "I just heard it, that's all."

"Do you know what happened to Katherine Sullivan?" Matt pressed.

The woman moved some things around behind the counter without looking up. "That's all I'll tell you. It would be best if you just took what I said and left."

Matt felt the anger rise inside. He pulled a pad from his pocket and jotted the names she told him for later, but he didn't give up that easily.

"I'm sorry you think I would take your word for it and leave. How do I know what you're saying is the whole truth?"

The netted head of the bakery owner snapped up. "Are you accusin' me of lyin', boy?" she shot back at him.

Matt cocked his head to one side. "I didn't say that. I said that I'm not sure you're telling me the whole truth."

"No matter how you word it, you think I'm lyin'. I think you better leave and don't come back. I don't need your business."

"Now, Mrs. Emily, don't do that." Selma pleaded with her, but the older woman spun on her heel and disappeared into the back of the bakery, leaving Matt and Selma alone in the store.

In the car, Matt gripped the steering wheel, his knuckles white. "I don't believe my grandmother would've abandoned her children, but I don't know her. I don't know what she was facing. I do know this happened after my grandfather died because Lucas said his father was dead and buried." He leaned his forehead against his clenched hands.

Selma reached out and grasped his arm with her delicate fingers. "We'll find the truth. Others know what happened. We have to find someone who will talk. Let me take you to dinner. It isn't much, but the food is as good as home-cooked. You can get a turkey dinner with all the trimmings almost every day of the year." She patted his hand. "Come on. Food is what you need."

Matt complied and followed her directions to the diner near Main Street, which divided Millerton. He parked alongside the old cafe and looked at Selma for confirmation.

She gave it in the form of a nod. "You can't beat the food; that's why the lot's full."

After disembarking the car, Matt followed her into the noisy diner to an empty booth.

Several rows of red plastic-covered booth seats lined the room. Matt ran his palm over the duct tape covering the rips. The tables sported aluminum trim with speckled tops in red, grey, and a single green one next to them circa 1950.

As soon as the customers at the front saw them and fell silent, the rest followed. Selma frowned at the now quiet townspeople and raised her hands, palm up.

"What's up with you people? It isn't like you haven't seen a stranger. I'll bet every one of you knows who he is and why he's here. Now we want a good, hot dinner. So go back to your talking." No one spoke. "I mean now," Selma barked, putting her hands on her hips and giving them each an almost threatening look.

The conversation returned at a low buzz with many a furtive look cast in their direction. Matt raised his eyebrows at the familiarity and command Selma had over the patrons. "What was that all about?"

Selma shrugged. "They're just nosey."

"Did you have to yell at them like that?" he whispered across the table. "Maybe we should go somewhere else."

"Are you going to let them win and make you leave so they can go on talking about you?" she challenged. "They'll babble about you whether you're here or not. We need information, and this is where we throw out the challenge." Selma then called to someone behind May. "Coffee, please. Two, Izzy." She didn't ask if he wanted coffee, and it didn't bother him to have her order for him.

Matt reached for the menu, but Selma jerked it from his hand. "Are you allergic to turkey?" she demanded, not smiling at him anymore.

"No..." He raised an eyebrow.

"You're going to try the turkey dinner. Once you eat it, if you want to try something next time, you can." Selma nodded to someone just out of his peripheral vision, then smiled at him. "I didn't mean to come off as bossy; it's just the best thing here. I hope I didn't offend you."

"I'll let you know if I'm offended. You intrigue me."

"That's a different approach. I haven't heard that line before." Selma smiled, and her eyes twinkled.

Matt swallowed, forcing himself to look away from Selma's teasing glance, and stared around the room. He noticed that most of the patrons had ordered the turkey dinner and were in varying stages of demolition. He loved turkey; if it was as good as it looked, and Selma insisted it was, it wouldn't be hard to eat it the whole thing. There were many plates with meatloaf and fried chicken, basic comfort foods in a diner that the citizens seemed to frequent. It would have been pleasantly familiar if he didn't feel like the center of attention.

"So you think some of these people might know what we're looking for?" Matt leaned close and spoke in a low voice as he reached for the sugar shaker. He already poured cream from a cow-shaped pitcher into his cup. The mixture turned a promising color.

"I think we're going to find out what you're looking for, Matt." Selma's voice wasn't loud but remained conversational. "I'm sure there's someone here who knows why the Sullivan family left town. When they know we'll pay for that information; we won't have to wait long for someone to come forward."

Matt's eyes widened. They hadn't talked about paying for information. What was she thinking? What kind of money were they talking about? Before he could ask her about it, a plate slid across the table in front of him. The words stuck in his throat.

A mound of mashed potatoes, turkey, and dressing smothered with gravy filled the large plate, accompanied by a generous spoonful of corn and a scoop of cranberry sauce in a paper cup on the side.

Matt picked up the fork and dug into the dressing. It was the hardest to make with any skill. The right combination of sage with a complement of celery and, upon chewing, the taste of chestnuts assaulted his tongue. He closed his eyes for a moment in bliss. The gravy filled the cracks as he raked in a forkful of potatoes. Matt didn't bother trying to talk; he just enjoyed the turkey dinner without conversation.

"I knew you'd love it." Selma's voice was distinctly satisfied as she spoke around a mouthful of tender turkey. Matt couldn't disagree with her.

When the plates were clean and his hunger satiated, he smiled at Selma. "It was good, but I want to talk about this reward you're offering. We didn't talk about that."

"We'll discuss the money when someone comes forward with something to offer." She didn't seem to be worried about the amount or whether or not he would pay.

"Selma, I don't have money for a big reward. If you're talking about a hundred dollars for good information, I'll go along with it, but I'm not handing out money for every tidbit of information someone tells us. It has to be something we don't already know and something that directly leads to me finding what happened to Katherine."

"I agree. We just passed the information of the reward out there. Now we see what falls out." She tilted her cup to empty it.

The waitress hurried by with the pot of coffee and refilled their cups. "Did you mean what you said that you would pay for information?" She whispered.

Matt looked up to see a woman in her late twenties. How would she know anything about a family who left here more years than she had been alive?

"What've you got, Izzy?" Selma asked.

"I heard a story, but it was a long time ago. I have to ask around and see what I can find out. But you'll pay? How much?" she whispered.

Selma shrugged. "That depends on how reliable the information is. You know my number, and you know Matt here is staying at the Inn. You call one of us when you have something." Selma took another swig of coffee. Izzy moved away with her pot.

Matt watched the young woman move among the tables, pouring coffee until she reached a table with an older couple. She spoke to them, and the woman shook her head. Izzy was persistent, but the woman shook her head again and stood to her feet before making her way to the door. The man stood and fumbled for his wallet without looking at the waitress, leaving Izzy at the table as he made his way to the front counter. He put the bill and some money next to the register. Matt saw Izzy blink back tears as she walked out of his sight toward the front of the diner.

"That's interesting," Selma muttered, her voice thoughtful as her eyes stared after Izzy.

Matt turned to look at Selma. "What's interesting?"

"The couple Izzy talked to was Ron and Cecelia Delany. Her mother is Rose Mellon. Didn't Emily say that one of the Sullivan boys lived with the Mellon family? Izzy is Cecelia's niece. She must've heard some of the stories and wanted Cece to talk to us. My guess, knowing Izzy, is she needs the extra money. That good-for-nothing man she married is gone again, and it's not easy to raise their daughter. Let's wait a few days and then call on Cecelia and Miss Rose."

The bell over the entrance rang. Selma's eyes narrowed as she looked over Matt's shoulder. "The Sheriff's here."

Sheriff Lavon Shelton stood in the doorway for a moment and frowned at the patronage in the diner. Over the past half an hour, people came in, filling all the seating in the diner, leaving nowhere for him to park himself. Lavon's gaze wandered over toward Izzy. "There a town meetin' here I didn't know about or wasn't invited to?"

Izzy didn't look at him. "There isn't any room, Sheriff unless you want to boot some of these people out the door." She waited for his answer. Lavon looked around the room, his frown deepening as he hooked his thumbs into his belt. Matt noticed some of the good citizens of Millerton fidgeted and wouldn't look at Lavon. The conversation became a murmur, and the sheriff made his way to their table.

Selma looked up when he stopped next to her. "Hello, Sheriff."

"Looks like all the tables are filled, don't mind if I sit here and share, do you?" He didn't wait for an answer but dropped his butt onto the vinyl next to Selma.

She gave him a grimace, which he ignored, and retreated to the wall of the booth. Selma tried to put her purse between them, but Lavon grabbed it in his fist and dropped it at her feet.

"Just set it on the floor, honey. It's clean. I know Dempsey mops the whole place each night. Feels the cushions for loose change, too." Lavon moved closer to Selma, crowding her with his bulk. Matt felt a little uncomfortable but couldn't say anything.

"How's the research coming along? Saw you went to the bakery but didn't buy anything. Didn't see anything you wanted?" There was a slight sneer in Lavon's voice that Matt ignored.

"Now you're following us?" said Selma. "Come on, Lavon, this is just a research project. What interest would a sheriff have? Unless you have some information at your office that you aren't sharing." This time, she looked up at Lavon.

"If I did, why would I give it to you?"

"Why wouldn't you? Is it something worth hiding? Wasn't your uncle the sheriff or chief of police back then? Did he keep records?" She leaned toward the sheriff. Lavon looked down at Selma as if she were an amusing toy, a smug expression coloring his features.

"My uncle, Beau Shelton, was the sheriff back then. He kept real good records about everything. I think he secretly wanted to be a writer. If you want to come over, I can dig them out, and we can go through them."

Matt's hackles rose at the overly friendly invitation, but he checked himself. Why would he care if Selma was interested in Lavon Shelton? Selma was fun to talk to and sexy. The thought gave Matt pause. Was he attracted to her? Yes, and he thought she might feel the same way about him, but he wasn't sure. It was too soon to tell.

"I know Matt, and I would love to look at the records your uncle kept. What time would you like us to come over?" Selma replied, a far too sweet smile on her face.

"Honey, I didn't invite him." He looked across the table at Matt and grinned. "You do understand the invitation was for the lady alone?" Matt refused to take the bait. Instead, he locked his eyes on the other man until the man in uniform looked away.

Selma pushed the empty plate across the table as Lavon waved Izzy away for the third time.

"How about now that you've finished eating? It's still early, and we can take as long as you need to get it done." The innuendo grated on Matt, and he clenched his teeth.

"Sorry, I have another engagement. I have to decline."

Matt pushed the arrogant sheriff. "I would love to read through your uncle's diaries or journals. Could I stop by and pick up a few to read tonight?" He smiled, and his voice rose just a little while asking the question. It didn't matter because everyone had focused on the conversation. Lavon looked at his watch. "Sorry. I'll have to cancel that offer, too. I have to go to a meeting. See ya later." After a pause, he added, "Selma."

The sheriff slid out of the booth and left the diner, his expression thunderous. When the door slammed shut on the man's heels, a pregnant pause filled the room before any conversation started again.

Selma spoke, though her head remained bowed. "Matt, I have to go to the library and check on the closing. Some paperwork needs doing. I'll do it tonight in case there is a new lead after our dinner announcement."

He could see her eyes moving to watch the crowd, not moving to leave. "This is ridiculous," she muttered.

Matt pushed his plate away, and Izzy appeared to collect it. "Dessert?" she asked. Matt shook his head, and so did Selma.

Selma retrieved her purse and slid across the seat to stand beside the table. She turned to the other diners. "Y'all better tip Izzy real good tonight. No dimes and quarters. She busted her butt pourin' ya'll's coffee so that you could sit and listen. She needs the extra dough, so don't skimp." She stared at them until some heads nodded.

Matt followed her to the counter and paid for the dinner, but Selma slipped Izzy a bill rolled up so no one could see what it was, not even him. He then guided Selma to the car and drove her to the library.

"That was a good dinner, but I can't say much for the entertainment," Matt offered as he pulled into the library parking lot.

"I'm sorry for that. I guess there isn't enough excitement around here, so the residents take it when it comes." Selma turned to face him across the car seat. "I'm not sure what happened to cause this sort of response. We have someone shooting at us on one side, and on the other, a town with a lockjaw. Are you sure you want to keep on this quest?"

"Yes," Matt answered without a pause. "But I think you need to keep your distance from me. I don't want you involved or hurt. Besides, the sheriff seems to think the same way, but for other reasons."

The woman didn't answer but opened the door, waving Matt to stay seated. The light illuminated the two.

"When you finish, do you want me to come back and take you home?" he asked.

Selma laughed and gave his cheek a quick pat, but before he could react, she slid out of the car. "I've been in and out of this place for as long I can remember. No, I'll see you tomorrow."

Matt watched her walk into the building, then drive away. At the inn, he turned the key in the door lock and flipped on the light. The bed wasn't as pristine as the first time. Taking a more thorough look around the room, he settled into the chair to remove his shoes. His suitcase wasn't entirely in the closet where he'd left it earlier. One of the drawers hadn't been closed all the way. Whoever searched his room tried to be unobtrusive, it didn't work. After freeing his feet from his shoes, Matt took a few steps to the dresser and pulled the drawer open to see his clothes had been moved but not missing.

He turned around to his briefcase. While it leaned against the desk, it faced the opposite direction. As a lefty, Matt made sure the lock stayed on the left side. Pulling the briefcase out, he rested it on the desk and opened it, examining his folders to ensure the contents were present. One thing was missing: the paper with the information and the newspaper clippings he saved from his uncle's with names of the town's families underlined and crossed through.

Matt walked downstairs to the common area, where he knocked at the door that led to the owner's suite and waited.

The older woman opened the door after a few moments. "Mr. Sullivan. Is there something wrong?"

"Mrs. Millard, were there any visitors here today? other than people who were registered?"

"Why, yes. The sheriff and his deputy were here. He said the deputy needed to do a safety inspection for my insurance card. We had some tea and sandwiches." Mrs. Millard's smile was sweet.

"Did they stay long?"

"I had time to tell Sheriff Lavon about my husband's dream of owning a hotel."

Matt heard from Selma about the story, and he should be cautious about being invited to listen to it. The story could be about an hour long. "Thank you, Mrs. Millard. By the way, how long have you lived in Millerton?"

"We moved here in 1950. My husband found this home—"

"Thank you." Matt turned away and retraced his steps to his room. Grabbing his jacket and keys, he headed down the back stairs.

A thought stopped him in his tracks. Who was he going to tell? The sheriff had to be in on the search; going to him would be redundant. If he told Selma, it would put her in the same position. Matt returned to his room with a deep sigh of frustration and lay in the rumpled bed wide awake.

CHAPTER 16
MILLERTON, WV
August 2000

MATT ATE A QUICK BREAKFAST AT THE DINER the following day without speaking to anyone but the waitress. His wanderings took him out to the Sullivan farm. Matt parked across the road from the entrance. Taking the chance to go onto the property by himself was a profoundly bad idea, and he knew it. It wouldn't be difficult for someone to ditch his car or his body out in these woods.

A memory struck him: the couple who lived down the road from Katherine. The Lundgrens, friends to his grandparents. Matt put the car in gear and moved slowly along the road to the next driveway.

Someone mowed the lawn recently and kept up the house better than his grandparents' home. He turned into the driveway and pulled into the parking area near the front porch.

The door opened, and a man dressed in faded overalls, a plaid shirt, boots, and a floppy brimmed straw hat emerged. He stood at the edge of the steps and stared at his visitor. A rifle lay across his arm.

Matt took a deep breath. Was this the person who took a shot at Selma and himself? He had to take a chance and get out of the car. With no small amount of concern, he pushed open the car door and climbed out, lifting his hands in a placating gesture.

"Hello. I'm Matt Sullivan. Can I talk to you?"

At the man's nod, Matt moved to stop near the bottom of the steps.

"You related to the Sullivan's in the farm over yonder?" Matt could see tufts of grey and brown hair sticking out over the man's ears under his hat. The wrinkles on his face set his age to be between sixty and seventy.

"Yes, they were my grandparents."

"Heard you were asking a lot of questions."

"Yes, I am. I want to know what happened to my grandmother." The man motioned for Matt to join him on the porch. "Have a seat."

"Are you related to the couple who lived here and were friends with my grandparents?" Matt sat in one of the four oversized rocking chairs on the porch.

"Nope. I moved in here fifteen years ago. The house was empty, and I needed a place to live." He filled his corn-cob pipe with what might've been tobacco and lit it. Matt bit back a grin. The older man looked just like Jed Clampett on Beverly Hillbillies' TV show. "I moved in and kept the place clean and up kept. Sheriff lets me stay as long as I pay something toward the utilities."

Matt wondered if the bank owned the house.

"Do you have a name?" Matt asked.

"Doesn't everyone?" The man gave a dry laugh and continued, "Clare. Clare Williams."

"Clare, was there anything left here in the house that might give me a clue where the couple moved to?"

The older man puffed on the pipe, smoke rose to the brim of his hat, then drifted away and disappeared off the porch. "There was a letter settin' on the kitchen counter addressed to a Lucas Sullivan."

Matt took a breath, so he didn't jump on the slow recollection. "What happened to the letter?"

"I saved it in case the man came for it."

"Could I see it? Lucas is my uncle." Matt leaned forward in the chair.

Clare studied the younger man for a moment, frowning until finally, he nodded. "Shore." The older man pulled his body to stand and went inside. There was some noise before the screen door opened, and Clare handed Matt an envelope. It was old but clean as if no one handled it much.

"Would you be opposed to me opening it?"

Clare stared down at Matt, his brown eyes boring into the younger man's as if searching for some hidden secret. He nodded and resumed his seat.

Matt carefully slit the flap with his pocket knife. The glue was old and gave away easily. He pulled out the single sheet. The date at the top was July 1948.

"Lucas,

Ben and I have waited for you to come back and get us. I know you ran away, but we thought you would come here where we could help you.

We talked to the sheriff to find out where he sent Joseph and Henry. He told us he was in charge until the judge arrived.

We never saw the judge or heard of a hearing. The boys disappeared just like your mother. No one will talk to us. I'm sure you found the same thing. The only thing I heard was someone saw your mother being put into the sheriff's car late one night, and he drove her out of town. We can't find where he took her.

Lucas, we stayed here as long as we could. Ben has been offered a job in California. I am leaving our post office box number there for you to contact us. I hope to hear from you or one of the boys.

All our love,

Ben and Cassie Lundgren

"Thanks for letting me read this. Would you mind if I took it to my Uncle Lucas? For some reason, he won't talk about what happened on that day." Matt paused as he thought over the years. He never heard his father or uncle talk about their parents, and he didn't remember ever asking his father or mother about his parents. A frown creased the edges of his mouth as he wondered why. "I'm hoping to find someone here who will tell me what happened on that day."

"People 'round here are buttoned up tighter than a preacher's collar." Clare chuckled at his joke, and Matt smiled. "I'd say you don't have much chance of finding that out unless there's someone around that was there as a kid, and their parents have passed. It could be you need to go up the mountain. They might know sumpin' up there."

"How do I get up there? Is there a road I should take or someone I should see?" The path he'd seen behind the Inn popped into his memory.

"I wouldn't try it on your own. I'll see if there's summin' goin' up that can take a message."

"I'd appreciate that. I'm staying at—"

"I know where you're stayin', and I know yer a burr in the sheriff's saddle. He wants you out of town bad. Seems you caught the fancy of our little Selma. Now she's a right good girl, that one. If she likes you, I'd be careful you hurt her none. Just a kindly warnin'."

"I don't plan on hurting her. I like Selma, and she's been a lot of help to me."

"You run along back to town. I'll see what I can find out for ya."

"I thank you, Clare, for the comfortable chair and the company."

"I'll sell you a chair if you want. I get a good deal of money for 'em. Sell quite a few to Barker's Market to sell to tourists. Not that many come through Millerton. I have better luck in Connersville. They're on the highway."

Matt grinned as he walked to the steps. "Now that's good business sense." The trip back to Millerton was quick, and Matt parked next to the Inn.

Instead of heading inside, he took a walk toward the town square. The school playground was filled with kids in the late afternoon sun while their mothers sat in the shade, conversing. They glanced his way, and then their heads moved close as if sharing a secret.

Matt bypassed the bakery and had no reason to enter the hardware store. After crossing the street to Barker's Market, he smiled when he saw the rocking chairs on the porch with sale tags hanging from them. He climbed the steps.

Inside the store, it didn't look like time had passed. Maybe the nostalgia of the past era brought more money into the store. Matt noted many of the items were current logos and new products. Toward the back, he found an old pop machine with a glass door that contained glass soda bottles. Matt stood, looking at the metal caps of the bottles pointing his way.

"It works, but the bottles are seventy-five cents now. Not ten like in the old days," a voice broke the silence. Matt turned to see a man close to his age come from behind the counter. "You're Sullivan, aren't you?"

"Matt." He held his hand out.

"Don. Don Barker. My grandfather ran this store back in the day." "How long have you been here?"

"I was born here. My parents met at school and married."

"I guess you don't know anything that happened back then."

Don perched his hip on the counter. "When I heard you were looking for information on the Sullivan's, I dug into Grandpa's ledgers and found a few things. Your grandmother supplied eggs, cheese, and baked goods to the store. Grandpa bought cakes, pies, rolls, and such from her. Most of what she sold went on account of her grocery order. I got the feeling Grandpa had a soft spot for her; he paid more for her items than he did any others." He gave a little chuckle. "She must've been some cook. Everything she brought in sold that day or the next for a tidy profit." Don laid an arm across his thigh. "I found no more sales or purchases after March 1948. The account still had a balance, but a month later, Grandpa wrote CLOSED, and that was it."

"March 1948. That gives me something new. I should see what the newspapers at the library have." Matt spoke more to himself than Don.

"I called my aunts. They married and moved away. One told me she remembered being on the porch with her mother when the trucks came. A little while later, there was some commotion in the square. She saw the Sullivan boys carried away and said she'd never forgotten the screaming. She couldn't see their mother. My grandmother pushed my aunt back into the store and sent her to the back room." He shrugged. "I don't know if that's any help."

"What trucks?"

The man frowned. "I have no idea. I'll ask her and see what she says."

"Every little bit is a piece to this puzzle. I appreciate the information." Matt smiled and shook his hand.

Don looked him over a moment, then looked toward the door. "Now, there isn't a lot of excitement around here. I'd say half the town is too young to remember, and the other half might have been around back then. I'll give you a little warning: It's apparent you're ruffling some feathers around here. Whatever happened affected quite a few people. Not to mention, you're cutting the sheriff away from his girl."

Matt gave him a weak smile. "What can I say? She finds me fascinating, or at least what I'm doing has her captivated."

Don gave him a little boxer's punch in the arm. "I can't say I'm sorry to see it. I—"

The bell over the front door jingled, and a police officer stepped in. Don turned on his heel and returned behind the counter. "What can I do for you, Deputy?"

"Nuthin'. I just wondered if this man was botherin' you any?" The officer stood with his feet slightly spread and one hand resting on his gun belt.

Matt cocked his head. Was this a joke? The officer didn't smile. Matt walked to the cooler, pulled out a couple of bottles of soda, and paid for them all under the watchful eye of the deputy. Matt gave Don a nod and walked past the silent centurion out into the summer heat.

"It's like the TV show, In the Heat of the Night," Matt muttered to himself as he headed back to the Inn.

When Matt met with Selma that night, he told her what Don had revealed but left out the deputy's visit.

They sat comfortably on the Inn's porch. Mrs. Millard had been out twice already with iced tea and pie, but didn't return when she hadn't been invited to join them.

During a lull in the conversation, Matt looked over at Selma. "You intrigue me." He rocked back on the chair and laced his fingers behind his head.

"I do? Why?" Selma wore a pink-and-blue geometric patterned sundress that stretched over her breasts and covered her knees.

Matt kept his eyes where it was safe: looking out at the stars. "You have a great rapport with the townspeople. You teach at the high school. But you have ability far above what you use here. Why stay?"

Selma didn't answer right away, then turned to him. "I love this town. I've lived near here most of my life, and after I got my teaching degree, the school superintendent wrote to me and asked if I would teach here. As did all the graduating classes, I got a letter stating we would get a stipend if we took jobs in rural areas. Some fringe benefits came with the two-year commitment. I went online and, out of curiosity, looked up this area. They were looking for a teacher, so I signed up and just stayed." She shrugged.

Matt nodded. "Admirable." After another pause, he asked, "Would you ever be willing to leave?" He almost held his breath, but he needed air while she thought.

"If the right incentive came along."

Matt let out the breath he held. That was at least promising.

When Matt drove Selma home, it was well after ten. The time had escaped them both during the long evening, but from what Matt could tell, she hadn't minded. He sure hadn't. Spending a lazy summer evening in such pleasant company was a rare treat for him.

Matt parked the car, headed to the back of the Inn, and went to the door leading to the back stairs. At the door, he realized the light that usually flooded the lot earlier was now dark. The light bulb must have burned out. He'd mention it to Mrs. Millard in the morning.

Before he reached the stairs, dark forms appeared beside him. One grabbed his right arm and another, his left. They dragged him off the porch to the back of the house, where anyone driving into the parking lot wouldn't see them. Matt protested as best he could, but fear choked him. Were these men the ones who had shot at him and Selma?

While Matt hung helplessly between the two, a third form appeared from nowhere and drove a fist into his side and kidney. Before he could catch his breath, another blow struck his jaw with shattering force. The pain kept him from making a sound. His vision blurred.

"I tried to be polite before, but I guess you need more encouragement." Even in darkness, Matt recognized the voice and the hulking, overweight form of Sheriff Lavon. Matt felt the man's fist plow into his middle. The man stepped back and delivered another blow. Another man took his place, and the blows continued.

When Matt awoke, he felt soft bedding. Pain stabbed his body. He tried to turn his head, but the throbbing increased, and he stopped the movement. It was dark, or maybe he couldn't open his eyes.

"So you're awake." Lavon's voice cut through the pain. Matt tried to open his eyes but gave up.

"You're gonna stop seeing Selma. She's mine, and I plan on having her all to myself. She's going to accept my proposal and marry me. Now she's focused on this foolishness, and that's just confused her. I can't have that happening. I want you to leave. I want you checked out tomorrow morning. You tell her that you have all you need, and you're going back where you came from, ya hear?"

Matt licked his lips and tasted blood. Every breath was an effort.

He whispered, "What? Did you agree with me? I thought you did."

Matt heard heavy steps of boots as they thudded to the door, followed by the creak of hinges closing. He struggled to raise his head to make sure he was alone. He lay back on the pillow, closed his eyes, and gave into the pain in his head.

Was this what happened to Tim? Had Lavon somehow been mixed up with whoever tried to stop him from finding his grandmother?

Someone pounded at the door. The sound came from far away, and he tried to call out. The doorknob rattled, and he heard Mrs. Millard's voice. "Mr. Sullivan, open this door. Are you all right? I heard something going on back here."

Matt groaned an incomprehensible noise.

"I'm coming in, Mr. Sullivan." He heard the rattle of a key in the lock, followed by a gasp and quick footsteps to his side. "Mr. Sullivan, are you alive?"

He wasn't sure if she could understand him, but Matt tried to reply. It came out as a garbled collection of sounds.

"I'm calling Selma." Mrs. Millard ignored the injured man's attempts at a protest and used his room phone to call Selma. After a brief conversation, the older woman patted Matt's hand in a motherly fashion. "Selma's on her way."

Unable to argue, Matt tried to nod but allowed himself to sink into the darkness.

CHAPTER 17

MILLERTON, WV

August 2000

SELMA CHARGED UP THE BACK STAIRS OF THE DEW Drop Inn and toward the landing, where a very distraught Mrs. Millard waited for her.

"He's bad, Miss Selma. Someone beat him up bad." The old innkeeper pointed to the open door.

Selma ran to the room and stopped a few steps inside, stunned by what she saw before her. As soon as her mind began working again, her quick footsteps brought her to the bed. Matt's face was puffy, bruised, and bloody. One arm lay cradled against his chest.

"Matt," she whispered.

Matt stirred, but only one eye opened enough for him to see who was there. "Shelma. Sorry."

"You're sorry? Who did this to you? Tell me right now!"

"He couldn't see them. It was too dark." Lavon spoke from behind her. In her concern and surprise for the state of her friend, Selma realized she must have missed the sound of his heavy footsteps on the stairs.

Selma whirled and faced him. "What are you doing here?" She stood stiff, her eyes boring into his.

"I saw your car fly past me way over the speed limit. I thought I better come and see what had you in an all-fired hurry." Lavon's large hand wiped at his brow, his gut bouncing a little as he gasped for breath after hauling himself up the stairs in a hurry.

"Don't go there, Lavon. I know who did this. I just wanted to know if he knew and could talk about it. You better get yourself gone. I won't put up with this."

Selma turned back to Matt and spoke loudly, her voice calmer and gentler. "I'm going to get you up and to the hospital."

"He'll be just fine. You can leave him in my care," Lavon ordered, his eyes met hers dark with defiant anger. He spread his legs and folded his thick arms over his protruding belly. Despite being physically fit, Lavon's weakness for the peach cobbler at Randy's Diner showed around his belt line.

"Like I would do that after what you did?" Selma spat the words at him like bullets out of a machine gun.

"I didn't do anything," he protested and gave his head a little toss, allowing his mullet-styled hair to move against his thick neck. He then held out his hands, knuckle side up for her inspection.

"You may not have dirtied your hands, but I know Bo, Cletus, and Clint did it for you." She leaned over Matt. "Put your arms around me, and let me lift you."

"Ribs." Matt gasped as he tried to lift his one arm. "Ribs, arm, broke." He motioned to the one lying on his chest.

Selma frowned. "Call Izzy," she ordered Mrs. Millard, who picked up the phone.

Lavon moved to stop the call.

"Don't even think about it." She threatened.

"Leave him alone. I'll have the boys take care of him."

Selma snorted, then glared at the sheriff. "Lavon, you may think you can order me around, but that day is over."

Tears gathered in her eyes as she focused again on Matt, and she blinked to keep them back. Behind her, she heard Levon stomp out of the room, grumbling under his breath.

While Mrs. Millard called Izzy, Selma slipped into the bathroom and pressed a speed dial number on her phone.

A few minutes later, Izzy ran up the stairs, followed by a still-sulking Sheriff Lavon. She carried a small bag and gasped when she saw Matt. "Who—?"

"Never mind," said Lavon. "Get him wrapped up as best you can. We have to get him into my car and to the hospital."

Matt shook his head, trying to protest.

"We don't have a hospital here in Millerton, but there's one in Connersville. Lavon can drive ahead of me with his lights flashing so we can get there faster." Selma reassured Matt.

"You think I'm going to do that for you? You're out of your beautiful, sweet head, darlin'. Now let me help you get him up."

He started forward, but Selma patted her jacket, stopping him cold. Her eyes were hot and mad as she stared him down. "Don't you lay a finger on him. Mrs. Millard, bring me some aspirin and water, please."

When the woman was out of the room, Selma turned to Lavon. "You're going to do as I ask and stay out of the way, and if I were you, I'd watch my back and tell all three of your little posse to watch theirs."

"You threatening me, girl?" Lavon took a step closer, straightening himself to his full height and puffing up his shoulders in an attempt to remind her just how small she was to his size.

"I never threaten, Sheriff. You'd best remember that." Her calm voice and cool gaze didn't waver. Lavon turned on his heel and stomped out of the room and down the steps.

Selma and Izzy got Matt up on his feet and out to the stairs.

"This isn't going to be easy, Miz Selma. He's hurt bad," Izzy said, a worried frown coloring her young face. Selma knew she'd been watching the whole exchange with the sheriff, but the girl had the good sense to keep her mouth shut. For now, at least.

"I know, Izzy, but it's the best we can do in the circumstance."

The process of walking him down the steps left Selma in sympathetic tears. Matt gasped as he clung to the railing with white-knuckled fingers. Izzy had wrapped his other arm over his chest. After what felt like an hour of pained groans and many pauses for breath, they reached the outside door.

They loaded Matt into her car, which she'd parked sideways to the door. Selma lowered the front seat to recline. Matt relaxed, his breathing becoming more manageable. Lavon stalked over to stand at the back door, and his three deputies ranged around the trunk.

"Lavon, you might want to step aside," Selma ordered as he stepped in front of her. She slid around him as she moved around to the driver's door.

"You aren't going anywhere with this man. I'll have one of the deputies drive him to the hospital." Lavon started to wave his hand to one of the three deputies but stopped mid-gesture.

From between the other parked cars, men holding rifles stepped into the beams of Lavon's cruiser's headlights. The sheriff's eyes widened as several heavily-armed men strong-armed his deputies and confiscated their weapons with little effort.

"You boys are barkin' up the wrong tree here. Y'all don't want to mess with the law," Lavon warned in a loud voice. "This ain't your business."

"Lavon, you messed in my business. These are my kin," Selma informed the sheriff. "My boys here don't rightly care for your law around here. It seems like you bend it to suit you. This time, you bent it too far for my conscience. I'm taking this into your backyard, and we'll play by your rules." Selma spoke to one of the men closest to her. "Just make sure they aren't dead or found too soon. You saw what they did to my friend." She got into the car, carefully shifted it into gear, and pulled out of the Inn's parking lot.

Despite her bold words, Matt noticed her fingers shaking. Had she really just done that?

Matt's tired voice cut the silence. "You're related to people in the hills?"

"Yes. Does that bother you?" She never took her eyes from the road.

"Why should it? My family comes from this town, too. You're one tough woman." He tried to laugh, but the low chuckle turned into a pained wheeze.

Selma felt a stab in her chest. "Is that good or bad?"

"If it didn't hurt so much, I'd be grinning from ear to ear." Matt gasped as the car leaned into a curve.

"Relax the best you can. I'll handle the talking unless you want to sleep."

"No. Talk."

She took a few minutes to gather together the words she wanted to use, then began to talk. "My family knows your family up on the hill. I'm not saying they would want to come down and visit you, but I sent word to see if any of them knew what happened to your grandmother."

The road to Connersville curved like a writhing snake, and no matter how gently she drove, she could hear Matt gasp with each turn. The rattling, wheezing quality of his breath was concerning. Broken ribs were dangerous, and if one of his lungs collapsed out here on the road, Selma didn't know if she could do much to help him.

"I'm sorry about what happened. Lavon assumed way more than he should. I've never let him think that we were any more than friends, and I use that term loosely."

When Matt didn't answer, she looked over to see his eyes closed. He was unconscious or asleep. Selma grit her teeth, pressing her foot on the gas and pushing the car as fast as she dared.

Relief flooded Selma when she pulled up to the doors of St. Vincent Medical Center's emergency room. After a couple of honks, the EMTs ran out to see what was needed. After a brief conversation, they helped Matt onto a gurney and wheeled him through the doors. Selma parked the car, and after some interference with the admitting nurse, she found him in a curtained room.

"How is he, Doc?" she asked. The doctor shook his head. "Not good. I think he has a concussion and some broken ribs. He's pretty beaten up."

A uniformed officer walked past the curtain, nodding in polite greeting to the doctor and Selma. "I saw this man brought in and wondered what happened?" He stood, expecting an answer.

"I think it's pretty obvious what happened," Selma returned dryly.

"Do you want to file a report?" he asked.

"We already did. It happened in Millerton." Her response was short and curt.

The officer nodded and made some notes on a pad of paper before leaving.

The doctor shut the record file with a snap. "I can give him pain meds, but he will need to rest for a couple of weeks. I'm ordering x-rays and an MRI."

"Weeks?" Matt protested in a weak voice.

"You're awake. You aren't going to feel like moving much for a while, Mr. Sullivan. I want to keep you here for a day or so, at least to monitor your concussion. Millerton is too far from a hospital to bring you back here in a hurry if something isn't right."

Matt grunted a sour expression on his face as he slumped back into the pillows with his eyes closed. A nurse and orderly slid through the curtain and wheeled the gurney out of the enclosure. Selma tried to follow, but the nurse stopped her at the door.

"Unless you're married, I suggest you let us get him ready for bed. Then you can come in until he goes to sleep."

Selma nodded and retreated, wandering out to the hall where she discovered a small sitting area not far from Matt's room. There were two vending machines, one for soda and snacks, a couch, and chairs. A television hung on the wall playing some late-night infomercial.

Selma settled into a chair and called Mrs. Millard to let her know they wouldn't be back that night, also that Matt had a concussion along with broken ribs and more bruises than she wanted to count.

Mrs. Millard expressed her sympathies and then paused for a moment, hesitating to ask the next question. "Do you know where the sheriff is? There's been a problem, and everyone's been looking for him. He was here when you left, but no one has seen him since. Cletus and Bo are missing too." The older woman's voice petered out, inviting a response.

"I'm sure that they'll show up sometime. They may have had a call out to the hills." Selma kept her voice even and calm. "Phone service can be spotty up there."

"All right. I'll hold Matt's room for him. I can't understand who would do such a thing to him and right here in Millerton. That just isn't like folks here."

After a few more minutes of Mrs. Millard sputtering about the beating,

Selma escaped the conversation. Once she hung up with the innkeeper, she traced her fingers across Matt's phone. She knew he had a brother and a sister, but not their names. Making a decision, Selma flipped open the phone. She brought up the contacts and found them listed under the abbreviation ICE.

"So thorough. In Case of Emergency." Selma found herself smiling despite the circumstances, and she selected the first contact. ICE#1 listed 'Sam Sullivan' and his number. She pressed the green button and waited.

It rang a few times with no answer, and she had just lowered the phone to disconnect when she heard a groggy voice speak into the receiver. "Hello, Bro. Do you know what time it is?"

"Are you Matt's brother?" she asked. Then she heard a pause and a rustle. In the background, a muffled female voice asked, "Who is it?" and the male replied, "I don't know," followed by indistinct conversation.

"Can you talk? The battery's low on his phone, and I don't have a charger handy." Selma walked to the window, hoping for better reception.

The male voice returned. "I'm here. Who are you?"

"My name is Selma Greeley. I'm helping your brother with his research. Is this Sam? Can I call you that?"

"Yes." Sam's voice no longer sounded groggy.

"Matt's in the hospital in Connersville, Kentucky. Some thugs mugged him. He's in the hospital and recovering."

"Tell me where he is. I'm going to drive down right now." There was activity beyond the phone.

"Are you sure you want to do that? It's late. He's sleeping and can't talk to you right now anyway. You'd be better off waiting until morning. He's at Saint Vincent Medical Center, Connersville, Kentucky." Selma gave the address from the card the admissions nurse had given her. "They moved him from ER to a room. He's got more tests scheduled for tomorrow morning, but he's stable for now."

There was more background conversation before Sam's voice returned clearly into the receiver. "I'll come down tomorrow, then. You're right about it being a long drive."

"I don't want to stop you, but do you think Matt will want you to do this? I can keep you informed, or you can call the hospital tomorrow and check on him."

A long silence stretched over the line; so long, Selma glanced at the screen to make sure they hadn't lost the connection. Finally, Sam's voice came over the line again. "What happened?"

"It's a long story. Let's just say some jerks took it on themselves to try and stop Matt from getting the information he's looking for."

Sam swore. "I told him this was a foolish idea. We don't need to find a grandmother who abandoned her family." The harsh tone startled Selma, and she frowned in response.

"I don't believe your grandmother abandoned her family. I'd explain, but the battery's about to die. I'll write your number down and call you the moment I know anything."

After another long silence and a big sigh, Sam declared, "You best call me in the morning, or I'm calling the hospital."

"I will."

"What did you say your name was?"

"Selma Greeley. I'm the librarian in Millerton."

"Okay. I remember Matt telling me he was going to meet someone in that town."

After saying goodnight, Selma pressed the red disconnect button, then shut the phone down to preserve what battery life was left.

A nurse walked into the waiting area and approached Selma, sitting down on the couch next to her. "He's resting now." The woman looked to be close to her mother's age. Short, light brown hair drawn away from her face in a loose tail, and the brown eyes crinkled at the corners when she smiled.

"I'll stay here for the night. If he can leave, I'll drive him back to Millerton tomorrow." Selma stifled a yawn.

The nurse nodded then asked, "What happened to him?"

Selma looked at her and raised her eyebrows at the seemingly ridiculous question.

The nurse nodded with an amused chuckle. "Okay, he was beaten up.

That's obvious, but is he going to be safe going back there?"

"Yes."

"His chart says he's from Columbus. What's he doing in Millerton that would get someone mad enough to do this to him?"

"Do you know people in Millerton?" Selma's brows lifted. The town was small, and she expected she'd know anyone the nurse did.

The woman sat back. "At one time. I was a nurse at an asylum in Weston, Kentucky, and took care of a woman who used to live there. It was a sad situation. I heard the town had her committed on trumped-up charges. Her family never came to see her, either. They didn't visit or have any contact with her, at least when I took care of her. She talked a lot about her life there and her husband. She never said a bad thing about the people or her family. I wondered why she'd been committed."

"That's so sad. Who was the woman?"

"Her name was Kathy."

Selma sat up and reached out for the nurse's arm. "Kathy? Matt's looking for his grandmother whose name was Katherine. I wonder if she's the same person. What happened to her? When did she die? Where is she buried?"

"Hold on there, girl." The nurse laughed and held up her hands in surrender. "As far as I know, she's still alive. They closed the asylum and moved most of the patients into other places."

Selma pulled a notebook from her tote and began writing. "What was the name of the home she moved to?"

"I don't know, but I'll find out for you. If Kathy's related to your friend, and she's still alive, it would be a wonder. I want to be there to see it. Kathy was such a sweet woman; she deserves to have some happiness. By the way, I'm Rita."

"I'm Selma. Thanks so much for talking to me, Rita. I'm sure Matt will appreciate the lead, even if it doesn't turn out to be his grandmother." A yawn split Selma's lips, and she covered it with a hand.

"Why don't you get some sleep in Matt's room? It'll be quieter in there." Rita smiled at her, patting Selma's knee before getting up and bustling off toward the nurse's station.

Selma slipped into Matt's room and curled in the chair. A moment later, Rita appeared with a blanket and pillow for her.

Selma woke a few hours later when the nurse came in to check on Matt. She watched as the nurse asked him questions to evaluate his mental state after the concussion. When he answered them to her satisfaction, the nurse handed him a little cup of pills and some water. Matt swallowed them down and immediately fell back asleep. Selma sighed. All seemed well, and she relaxed in her chair.

Selma woke when another nurse entered the room to perform the same battery of questions. She checked her watch after seeing the sun backlit the shade. When she stood to stretch, a package fell on the floor. Inside were a toothbrush, paste, comb, and a small bar of soap.

After eating breakfast in the cafeteria and feeling refreshed, she headed back to Matt's room. He remained sleeping.

Nurse Rita appeared in the doorway and handed her a folder of papers. "Here's what I found when I called my friend at the nursing home. She told me after making me promise you wouldn't tell anyone where you got the information. Katherine Sullivan is ninety-six years old. She lists no immediate family, but her file mentions a husband, Samuel Sullivan, deceased. No family was ever visited or contacted the asylum about her. When anyone asks her about her family or life, she says, 'They're all gone.'"

Rita turned the page over, a sad look on her warm features. "She's not insane. There was never a good reason for her to be there. I don't know what she was like before she came to the asylum, but from the day I met her—and was in her seventies by then—she helped with patients. She knew more about them than the staff did. Staff came and went, and Kathy would butt heads with new staff who tried to put her in a box and label her insane. She put them in their place, and everybody else backed her up. Does this sound like the woman you're looking for?"

Selma read the notes, looked up at the older woman, and smiled. "I don't know anything about her, but you've made this girl ecstatic. When Matt wakes up, he'll want to jump out of that bed and be on his way. Where exactly is she?"

The woman's happy expression faded. "I'm sorry. I haven't been able to find where they sent her. The information is all confidential. I got this from an old file that my friend found." She patted Selma's hand. "Don't worry, honey, I'm on this. We'll find her. Now go back to sleep. He's doing fine."

Selma relayed the good news to Matt the following morning while he ate breakfast. He was still in pain, but finding information about his grandmother blunted some of its sharpness.

After Matt finished eating, Nurse Rita stepped into the room and shut the door behind her. "I have some bad news." The two occupants watched her and expected to hear Matt's grandmother was deceased, but all she said was, "You're Henry Sullivan's nephew, aren't you?"

Matt's eyebrows furrowed. "Yes, but what does that have to do with anything?"

"I'm not supposed to be here, but I heard in passing that someone called the media and told them that a Sullivan boy was here in pretty bad shape. I don't know how they knew who you were, but you can expect the media circus to arrive within the hour."

"I need to get out of here." Matt swung his legs out of bed, but when he tried to sit straight, he sagged back against the elevated headrest with a pained sound.

"Lie down and let me think." The uniformed woman paced across the room a few times while Matt tried to raise himself without help, but he gave up after several unsuccessful attempts.

"My aunt lives ten minutes from here. Let me call her and see if you two can stay with her. She's a retired nurse, and she'll protect you like a mother hen." Rita punched the numbers into the cellular phone she took from her pocket.

Within a couple of minutes, she had arranged everything. "Now, how are we going to get you out of here?" Rita cracked the door open and looked up and down the hallway. She tapped her finger on her chin for a few moments, considering the options. "No use waiting around, I guess. Let's get you on your feet." She wheeled a chair next to the bed.

Rita and Selma stood Matt upright as gently as they could. By the time they'd finished, his face was white around his mouth, where he strained against the pain.

"I don't think this is going to work." Selma stood next to Matt, supporting him as he leaned against her.

"I'm going to take Selma to the desk after we get you dressed." Rita and Selma assisted Matt to sit in the chair. Sitting proved too much, and he gagged, forcing them to return him to bed. Rita disappeared through the doorway and returned with an armload of clothing Selma didn't recognize.

Rita's mouth tightened at the corners. "Not doing so good?" Selma shook her head.

"Okay, Plan B. I don't know how to tell you this, but he just died." Selma raised her eyebrows in surprise.

Rita left the room again and returned shortly, followed by a strapping young man. Tucked under her arm was Matt's chart. "Lie still, buddy. You're going for a ride. This young man is going to help us get you on the gurney." Rita instructed.

With the help of Rita's friend, they transferred Matt onto the gurney and strapped him down to prevent him from jostling too much, then draped the whole thing with a sheet, including his face.

"Can you breathe okay?" Selma whispered where his ear should be.

"Yes. Barely. I'm fine."

"Lay still; we're on the move," Rita ordered.

Selma opened the door, and she composed her face in an expression of restrained grief as she walked down the hall after the gurney. They bypassed the nurse's station without incident and made their way to the elevator. Once the doors slid shut, they let out a collective sigh of relief.

"The only way to get you out of here without being caught is through the morgue," Rita explained as she pressed one of the floor buttons.

"The morgue?" Both Matt and Selma responded together in dismay. Matt wiggled on the gurney, trying to throw off the sheet in distress.

CHAPTER 18
CONNERSVILLE, WV
August 2000

"HEY, NONE OF THAT." RITA REARRANGED the offending material over Matt's face. "The driver is a friend. I told him a little story about how this guy is waiting for you to come out so he can finish the job. Greg was more than happy to secret you out the morgue door and take you to Aunt Mabel's house." She winked at Selma, who wasn't sure if the wink was for the trick or if the guy was a very good friend of Rita's.

It wasn't long until Matt was in the ambulance, and the nurse had Selma's keys. Rita would leave as soon as she made sure Plan B became Plan A. Just as Rita had said, they reached their destination in ten minutes.

Mabel, a tall, thin but strong woman, had Matt situated in bed and ensured he slept comfortably. She made tea for her and Selma. "Now, young lady, I want the whole story. Don't spare the details."

Selma gave her a short version of what happened, leaving out that the identity of the perpetrator.

After hearing the story of why Matt was in the hospital, Mabel's brows furrowed. "Why would anyone want to beat some guy up because he was looking for his grandmother?"

"That's something the authorities are looking into." Selma made a point to sidestep the details of that quagmire.

"He's safe here. I don't know how anyone found him, but we'll make sure he stays safe."

Matt woke from strange dreams he couldn't quite recall to dull pain. It had to be the drugs. He tried to piece everything together. The memory of the trip from the hospital and Selma at his side came in bits and pieces. He turned his head to see if she was in the room.

One eye was still swollen shut, but the other opened to see a small room in country plaid and quilts. Matt lay in a double bed covered with a handmade Amish quilt. The pillows felt soft, and the fresh smell of the outdoors in the room filled. Blinds covered the window but allowed some of the sun to peek around the edges.

The door creaked as someone turned the glass knob and pushed it open. It was a woman, older than the nurse he had at the hospital, but there was a family resemblance. She wore a hot pink sweater over a white blouse and grey slacks.

"Are you awake?" She spoke in a low voice.

"Yes."

"How are you? Are you comfortable, or do you need something for pain? My name is Mabel." She came to him, and he felt her cold hand on his forehead. He almost smiled; it reminded him of his mother when he was young.

"So far, so good, but wow, the dreams are crazy."

"Sorry, there isn't much I can do about that." Mabel smiled, handed him some pills, and eased him up to drink water from a straw.

"You're a nurse," he stated.

"Retired. The training comes in handy. I teach basic first aid to new moms and children at the elementary school."

"I appreciate your kindness. I don't want you to get into any trouble."

"Don't worry about that. This is the most exciting thing that's happened in years. It's good to get my blood pumping fast once in a while."

Mabel smiled as she tucked his blanket under the mattress and fluffed his pillow. He fell asleep before she finished and headed out the door.

When Matt woke a few hours later, he felt a little better. His phone lay charging on the nightstand. He called the hospital in Columbus to see how Lucas was doing.

"Boy, I've been trying to get a hold of you. Where are you?" Lucas asked, but before Matt could answer, another voice came over the line.

"Matthew, where are you?"

"Who is this?" Matt was pretty sure but asked anyway.

"Your Uncle Henry."

"Aren't you supposed to be out campaigning?" Matt barely held the sarcasm in check.

"I am. That's why I'm here. I stopped in to visit my brother. I've heard some interesting information about you. Where are you?"

"That isn't open for discussion right now," Matt answered.

"I heard you were in a hospital. What happened?" There was a concern in his uncle's voice.

Matt ignored the question. "Someone called the media from the hospital I was in, and now I'm in hiding. Why don't you tell me the truth? Where is Grandma Sullivan?" His voice rose in frustration, but a cough caught him, and the pain from the action kept him from continuing. He handed the phone to Selma, who entered the room when she heard his voice.

"This is Selma Greeley. Matt's in too much pain right now. He can't talk." She used her librarian voice: curt with no emotion.

"What happened to him?" Henry demanded his voice a roar over the phone.

"He was mugged." Her tone was short, and her words clipped.

Henry stopped yelling, and Matt couldn't quite make out what he said next, though he heard the voice on the phone.

"Four men jumped him and beat him up," Selma added only a little to the previous information.

More noise from Henry.

"This was a beating. I'm sure there was no conversation. Let me say that, despite your reticence, we are getting closer to finding your mother. If you have any information that would speed this up, it would be much appreciated."

"I have nothing to tell you. I told Matthew I knew nothing. He doesn't believe me."

"You came to Millerton, and no one would talk to you about your mother? Why? What happened that was so awful that no one wants to talk about it?" Selma asked.

"I don't know. I don't remember anything, and Lucas won't talk about it." There was some background conversation, and then Selma heard a door close, and it was quiet.

Henry's voice returned. "I stepped away. Lucas was becoming agitated at our conversation. He doesn't want Matt finding anything."

"Why doesn't Lucas want his mother found? What could have happened so awful she can't be forgiven?" Selma moved out of the room when she saw Matt's eyes closing. He'd swallowed a pill not long before the call.

"Are you Matt's girlfriend or something? I shouldn't be talking to you."

"It's not your concern about our relationship. Matt hired me to help him locate his grandmother. We will find the truth; someone always talks," Selma promised.

"They haven't for all these years. I doubt they'll start now." The wry tone sounded through the phone.

Selma pressed, "Why didn't you get together with your family after you left them?"

"Are you some a reporter?" Henry demanded.

"No. I said I'm helping Matt find the truth."

"Do you know what happened to the last person that helped Matthew look for the truth?" Henry's sharp voice asked. Selma heard a cautioning voice in the background. "Hush, I'm not saying anything." He spoke away from the phone. "Miss, he was found in a river tied to a cinder block," Henry spoke into the phone again.

Selma quietly disconnected the call, pressed the vibrate button, and put the phone in her pocket. Her heart pounded in her chest. She'd just been speaking to the man who might be the next President of the United States. He'd just threatened her, hadn't he? Who had ended up in the river tied to a cinder block?

CHAPTER 19

MILLERTON, WV

AUGUST 1947

WHEN CASSIE AND KATHERINE ENTERED the town of Millerton, small groups of people gathered in the square. Another crowd stood in front of City Hall.

Cassie parked in the lot beside Barker's Market. The two women walked to a group of women talking.

"What's going on?" Cassie asked Winnie Mellon.

"Oh, my! It's terrible. Ollie and Clemmie's house caught fire. It was destroyed," Winnie wailed, wringing her gloved hands.

"Winnie, don't exaggerate," Sarah interjected. "It wasn't destroyed. The back wall of the kitchen caught fire. Most of the kitchen is ruined, but Ollie and Clemmie got the kids out. The neighbors helped put the fire out before the fire department got there."

"How awful. Is there anything we can do for the family?" Katherine added, but the women ignored her comment.

"We're going to cook some meals for them until they can get a new kitchen. I hope they had insurance," another added.

The women moved off, leaving Katherine and Cassie standing alone on the sidewalk. Cassie frowned at the women walking away, then turned to Katherine. "I guess we better get our shopping done. They don't need our help. Too bad. You could've whipped up quite a feast for Ollie and Clemmie." She slipped her arm through Katherine's, "Please forgive me if I'm not too sad about the situation." The two walked up the steps to the store.

Inside, the store was abuzz about the fire. There wasn't any new information, but the consensus those rehashing the story said a match caught the trash in a can, on fire. The flames had engulfed the back wall by the time the neighbors saw it and woke the family.

"I'll bet Ollie was smokin' on the back porch and tossed his match in the trash can," someone guessed.

"Ollie doesn't smoke, but he could have had someone visitin'," another offered.

"Ollie says he and Clemmie didn't go to the back porch last night. They were at the church for the prayer meetin', came home, put the kids to bed, then went themselves. They were sleepin' when the neighbors started poundin' on the door," the voice of authority said.

Cassie and Katherine grinned at each other and went separate ways to shop.

Mrs. Barrett peered through the bars in the post office as she slid the expected letter to Katherine. "How's the mister?"

"Just fine. We're hoping he'll come home for Christmas." She nodded at the woman and tucked the envelope in her pocket as she left.

Katherine walked across the crowded square to the hardware store. Sheriff Beau Shelton stood in the middle of the aisle, talking to the owner. Katherine slipped down the first aisle and made her way to the shelf with the items she needed. She gathered them in the basket when she felt someone behind her. Katherine stiffened and turned to see the sheriff.

"Hello, Katherine. How are you today?" His voice was low and smooth as honey, and it grated on her nerves. Turning to face him, she put the basket between them, holding onto it with clenched hands.

"Here, let me carry that for you." He reached for the handle, but she backed out of his reach.

"I can handle it, Sheriff. Thank you." She didn't use his first name.

"Oh, I'm sure you can handle anything." His voice went even lower, so only the two heard the words.

"Sheriff, I need to pay for these items and get back to Cassie. She's going to be wondering what's keeping me." She backed up to go around the shelves to the other side.

Sheriff Shelton took hold of the handles of the basket and tugged, not letting her escape easily. "I said I'd carry this to the counter for you. Now don't make my momma a liar when she taught me to be a gentleman." He didn't let go, and Katherine had no choice but to release her hold on the basket or have a tug-o-war right there in the aisle.

He stepped aside for her to pass by him and followed her to the counter. Katherine could feel the sheriff's eyes following her movements, and a hard, cold knot of anxiety twisted itself in her guts.

Joe, one of the local kids, rang up her purchases. Before she could take out her money, Beau spoke up. "Put it on my tab, Joe."

"Yes, sir."

"No, thank you. I won't be beholden to anyone." Katherine pushed several crumpled bills across the counter. "Joe, you'll take this money." Her voice had the authority of a mother.

Joe looked from one to the other, his gaze lingering on Katherine. He finally took the bills and handed her the change. Beau grabbed the basket as soon as she let go of it. To her dismay, he followed her out of the store.

On the sidewalk, she turned and held out her hand for the basket. "I'll take that now."

"I don't think so. I'll carry it to the car." He held out his arm for her to take and walk beside him.

Katherine rebuffed the offer and seethed as she walked stiffly beside him. At the crosswalk, she felt his hand touch her back to guide her across the street. At the curb, she side-stepped out of his reach.

The population of Millerton took notice of the two as they crossed the square. Whispers followed them, and Katherine ground her teeth in frustration. She made the walk with long, purposeful strides, trying to keep a proper distance between herself and the sheriff despite his advances.

Cassie waited at the car, her arms crossed. Her eyes narrowed as she watched the two then opened the trunk as they approached. She gave Katherine a look, silently asking if she was all right.

"Hello, Mrs. Lundgren. It's good to see you in town today." Sheriff Shelton smiled in a fashion he figured disarming.

"Thank you, Mr. Shelton. I heard there was quite a ruckus last night with the fire at Ollie and Clementine's house." Cassie slammed the trunk closed after Katherine placed her purchases inside.

"It was unfortunate. It seems to have started with a match in a trash can. A gas can be found on the porch, which no one could account for seems to be the source. The whole back wall of the kitchen went up. Ollie said he never put a gas can on the porch. I wonder how it got there." Beau looked at the two women.

"Sounds like you have your job cut out for you, Sheriff." Cassie motioned for Katherine to get into the car. "I hope you catch whoever did it."

"What was that all about?" Cassie asked, glancing in her rear-view mirror.

"I don't know. The Sheriff was at the hardware store when I got there and grabbed the basket from me. Then he wanted to pay for my order."

"Did you let him?"

"No! If Joe hadn't taken my money, I would've left and come back later."

Katherine still felt anger at being handled by the sheriff in such a manner. "He carried my basket, had his hand on my back, and walked next to me across the square. It'll be all over town." She groaned, draping an arm over her eyes. "I don't know what his game is, but I don't want any part of it." It sounded like a wail.

"Katherine, don't take all this personally. You're better than all these people. You know what you want and are willing to make sure you and your children get it. They only see the hierarchy here. When Sam sends for you, you can be anything you want to be."

Katherine nodded and felt her pocket for the latest letters that Martha and Sam sent. A comfort to her as if he were right there beside her the whole way home.

After dinner, and with the dishes washed and put on the shelf, Katherine sat on her bed and opened the letter from Martha first. She saved Sam's letter to read later. The dim overhead light illuminated the paper. It was dated three days ago.

Dear Mother,

This is a hard letter to write. I know you will be getting one from Dad, but I don't know which one will reach you first.

We've lived with Dad's coughing for a while. It's been worse lately, and the company doctor made him go and get it checked.

Mother, Dad has TB. They sent him to a hospital yesterday. I wanted to call you, but I didn't want to leave a message with anyone or send a telegraph.

Katherine set the letter on her lap. A cold chill spread through her body, and her heart stopped. She couldn't think. Sam has TB. The disease is often called consumption because, by the time the person died, there was nothing left. She lifted the letter in trembling hands.

We cannot speak to him or see him. We were told to get tested by the doctor to see if we were carrying any of the diseases. The doctor said we are fine but should be tested every year for a while to make sure.

I will let you know more when I find out.

Love,
Martha

In a rush to read the letter from Sam, Katherine picked up the second envelope and slid her finger under the flap. It came up easily.

Dear Katie-girl,

I wish I could tell you good news that I found us a place, and I was making enough for you all to come to Browersville. That ain't gonna happen. I won't be comin' home without a miracle, and we know how often that's happened for us.

I've had that annoying cough for a few years now, and we figured it was the sawdust. It wasn't. It was TB. You and the boys are going to need to be tested.

I'm so sorry I bought all this for you. You won't be able to speak or see me anymore except through a window. I think I would rather you remember me as I was when

I left and not what I'll become. The doc says I won't be handsome anymore.

Tell Lucas he needs to step up and become the man of the house now. He'll have to take the duty of running the farm. Ben'll help. Tell Henry and Joseph I love 'em and to be good to you and become men that would make me proud. I'm goin' to write each of 'em a letter of their own.

I love you, Katie-girl, an' I won't stop. I know you, and you'll mourn me when I'm gone. I don't want you to stay alone. I want you to go out and find another man that is worthy of you. No one from Millerton, though. Get Cassie to take you to Charleston and get a job there, where you can find a man that'll love you as much as I do.

I'll write again.

Love always,
Sam

Katherine lay on the bed and gave into fear and despair. Her heavy sobs woke the boys, and they stood outside the door. Lucas sent them away and came into the bedroom his parents had shared.

Lucas sat on the bed and touched her shoulder with nervous fingers. When she didn't respond, he began to rub her back. Katherine turned and cried even harder, wrapping her arms around him.

"What happened? Is Pa dead?" He feared the worst.

"Not yet."

Lucas's body went completely still. He finally pushed his mother away so he could see her face. "Not yet?" he prompted.

"Your father has TB. Lucas, they have him in a hospital, and we can't see or speak to him. The only way we can talk to him is with letters."

"Letters." Lucas's voice sounded odd. He let Katherine lie back down on the bed. "Ma, I'll be back."

Katherine didn't see him leave as she buried her face into Sam's pillow and cried until she fell asleep.

Katherine moped around the farm for days when she was able to get out of bed. Finally, Cassie drove up the dirt drive in a cloud of dust. She jumped from the car, waved for the two younger boys to stay in the car, and bounded the two steps to the porch.

"Katherine! Where are you?" Cassie swung the screen door open so hard it banged against the wall.

"What! What happened?" Katherine wiped her hands on the dishtowel as she rushed out of the kitchen. "Are the boys okay? Is it Ben?" Her heart pounded with worry for her boys. Since learning about Sam's sickness, she'd begun to expect terrible things would happen to her sons.

"Nothing's bad. Just grab your purse and come on. We are going into town for ice cream!"

"I have things to do." Katherine frowned, resisting Cassie's fingers as she tried to drag her friend out of the house.

"Nope. You've moped around here long enough, and you're scaring the boys into thinking they've lost their mother as well as their father. We're going to show them that you're alive and well. Let's go. It's only for an hour or so, and then you can come back."

Katherine looked around the kitchen for an excuse. There was nothing that wouldn't keep until she got home. "Okay, fine." She grabbed her purse and followed Cassie.

When she got to the car, she saw two heads bouncing behind the front seat. "Where's Lucas?"

"I don't know. He brought the boys over for school but didn't come in. The boys didn't know where he went." She shifted and sped down the track to the paved road. Cassie didn't seem worried, though, and her bright smile, combined with the exciting giggling in the back seat, forced Katherine to relax.

They pulled in and parked behind the ice cream parlor. Inside, a buzz of conversation halted the minute Cassie, Katherine, and the boys entered. All eyes followed them around the small shop. Cassie remained defiantly cheerful and ignored the town hens as they ordered their cones and went outside to sit on the benches in the park.

Katherine went still as the sheriff sauntered toward them and stopped in front of the women.

"Nice to see you, ladies." He touched the brim of his hat in a polite gesture. "Have you heard the latest?" He put a boot on the bench seat next to Katherine and leaned his arm on his knee, looking at the two women.

"No," Cassie answered. Katherine concentrated on her ice cream, refusing to look at Beau.

"We've had a rash of fires lately. I don't know how so many people can be so careless all of a sudden. The post office caught fire last night."

Both Katherine and Cassie turned to look at the building attached to Barker's Market. They shared a common wall but separate doors.

"The outside wall of the post office caught fire and burned last night. It started at the door. Someone poured everywhere to make sure it caught. Good thing I was doing my routine checks and saw the flames shooting up over the roof. The fire department showed up, but it was too late. It didn't get to Barker's because a cinder block wall dividing the two spaces. You know anyone that might want the post office burned down?" The sheriff looked at the two with a quizzical eye.

Despite his mild tone, Katherine heard a faint undercurrent of accusation in his voice. Scowled into her Rocky Road. "No, sir, I don't. I have no reason to want that. It's the only connection I have to my husband, and that connection is important. Will it be open someplace else during the rebuilding?"

"I don't know. I think the Post Office will have to send a mail truck over from Connersville. I called the Postmaster General to inform him what happened. They're sending a team out to investigate." He straightened a little and looked at Cassie, who eyed him with disdain. "Katie-girl…"

"Don't you dare call me that." Katherine's head jerked up, and she glared at Sheriff Shelton. "Never call me that."

He dropped his foot to the ground but didn't move away. "All right, if that's what you want. I want you to know that you can call me anytime you need anything."

"I don't have a phone, and I can take care of myself. By the way, how's Cynthia? Is she moving around in her wheelchair yet?" she retorted.

The man's expression soured. "She's still not able to move much, but other than that, she's fine. Afternoon, ladies." He touched his hat brim as he moved back a few steps and headed away.

Once he was gone, Cassie shook her head. "I can't believe the post office burned. First Ollie's, then this. Do we have an arsonist or what?"

"An arse-what?" Katherine grinned as a picture came to her mind.

"Ar-son-ist. It's a person who sets fires. It could be to gain insurance or a reward. There's usually some reason they feel justified in getting even. Arsonists are different from a pyromaniac. They're a person who lights fires just to watch them burn."

"There's a name for people who play with fire?" Katherine took another bite of her ice cream.

"Yes. Pyromaniacs have a sickness. They like to control things usually because their world is out of control somewhere. Arsonists want to punish someone." Cassie finished the last of her ice cream. "Tell the boys we're going to try on hats." She stood and waited for her friend to join her.

Katherine called to the boys and told them where they were going and to stay in the square. A group of men stood talking in the middle of the sidewalk not far from the post office remains. The women heard the conversation long before they reached the group.

"I'm tellin' ya. There's something bad goin' on. I saw fire burns on the grass beside the school and in the woods. It's gotten outta hand." One man spoke to the others.

"I saw some burn marks down by my field," another man added.

"One of my fences was burned. At first, I thought it was lightnin', but now I'm thinkin' it might'a been on purpose," a plaid shirt-clad farmer mentioned while the others nodded.

"First Ollie an' now the post office burnin'. I'm thinkin' the sheriff outta know about these other burns and start lookin' for someone who likes to play with fire."

The picture of the burns she'd found in the woods came to Katherine's mind, and she wondered if she should mention that to the sheriff, too. The two women split and walked on each side of the group without acknowledging the men. One of the men turned to Katherine with a concerned frown. "Miz Sullivan. Sorry about Sam. I hope he'll be all right."

Katherine stopped, turned, and stared at him. "What about Sam?"

The man looked surprised. "Um… Ah-'bout him being sick an' all. Sorry." He turned back to the group, who looked away as though guilty of something. Katherine thanked him for his concern, but her mind raced with questions.

How did they know about Sam? She hadn't talked to anyone but Cassie and Ben about what had happened. She knew Cassie wouldn't tell anybody. Struck by the need-to-know, she turned back and planted herself in front of the man who addressed her.

"What did you hear about Sam?" she demanded.

"Nothin'. It was a mistake."

"I don't think so. You were pretty sure there was something wrong with Sam. How did you know?" She turned her eyes to the rest of the men and pinned them with her gaze.

They fidgeted and then broke under her long, cold stare. Finally, one man cleared his throat. "Our wives told us Sam had TB." The others nodded.

"I see. Well, you're right; he does. He's in treatment, and we're praying for the best. I suggest you put in a prayer for him yourselves. After all, most of you worked with him, and he was contagious." Katherine turned her back on them and stalked off, her head high in defiance.

"How did they know?" she asked no one in particular.

Cassie, who had stopped to watch the confrontation, shrugged with a frown on her face. "Who had access to that information?"

"No one but me read that letter." Katherine stopped and remembered how easily the flap on the envelope opened. "When I lifted the flap, it came open easy as if the glue wasn't holding it. What if Missus Barrett was reading the mail before she put it in the slot?" She thought for a minute. "How long does it take to get mail from Millerton?"

Cassie stopped in the middle of the sidewalk at the question. "A couple of days. Sometimes the next day if they have a good run."

"It takes three to four days for Martha and Sam's letters to be in the slot. I bet she's been reading all my mail, that snake! What if mine isn't the only mail she's been reading?"

"Are you sure? That's against the law." Cassie took Katherine's arm and pulled her back down the street toward the square where Sheriff Beau stood talking to a man on the corner.

"I wish I could whistle loud," Cassie muttered as she pulled her friend along the sidewalk.

A loud whistle pierced the air, and everyone stopped and turned to see who had made the sound, including Beau Shelton.

Cassie stopped and stared at her friend, grinning. "Thanks. You're going to have to teach me to do that."

Katherine didn't smile back; she focused on speaking to the sheriff.

When Beau noticed the two women headed his way with a purpose, he broke off the conversation and met them halfway with a questioning frown.

"Sheriff, we've discovered something disturbing. It seems there are some in this town with information that could only be known if someone had opened a letter and read it inside the post office." Cassie crossed her arms, and Katherine copied her.

"What are you talking about?" Beau frowned.

"Don't act stupid. It seems the whole town knows Sam is sick, and the only way they would've known that is if the postmistress opened the letter, read it, then shared the news. Now that's illegal, and I think that the present postmistress should be removed from that position and prosecuted."

Cassie wasn't exactly quiet in her accusations, and people nearby had already turned to look. Katherine could almost see their ears twitching, looking for the next bit of juicy news.

"I think we need to discuss this privately." The sheriff motioned for them to follow as he tried to guide them somewhere with fewer people. They didn't move, and he had to come back to them. "Come on, ladies, do we need to talk about this now?"

"Yes. These people need to know the postmistress has been reading their mail and sharing the contents with their neighbors." Cassie raised her voice so the people standing close could hear every word. There was an inhale of breath, and whispering began.

Beau pushed his hat further upon his forehead and scratched his head, an annoyed expression on his face. His eyes moved toward the crowd gathering.

"You need to question her, then call the judge and have her indicted. That's only right. It's no different than someone going into the bank and robbing it. We trust the bank to protect our money just as we trust the postmistress to protect our mail. Don't you agree?" Cassie looked around to see others who heard and nodded.

Their expressions of concern and anger had the sheriff rubbing his neck in agitation. Sheriff Beau Shelton was sweating, and Katherine was sure it wasn't the warm sun. "I guess if you put it that way, I'll have to bring Shirley in for questioning."

He turned away, muttering as he strode down the sidewalk. The rest of the onlookers stood talking while others followed the sheriff. Katherine and Cassie retreated across the park, calling the boys.

Katherine rubbed an oiled rag scented with lemon across the wood in the living room when she saw the sheriff's car come up the drive. Pausing her chores, she stepped out on the porch and waited for Beau to come to the porch.

He arrived at the bottom of the steps, looking up at her. Her stance warned him not to come any closer.

He cleared his throat. "Can we sit and talk?"

Without comment, she moved to the chairs and sat in her favorite. Beau climbed the steps and sat across from her on the rail.

"Tea?" It was an automatic offer, and she bit her tongue, hoping he refused.

He shook his head. "I met with Shirley. She's sorry. I reprimanded her and had a meeting with her friends, and admonished them about being gossiping harpies. I told them there could be some jail time for all the ladies as an accessory to the crime. They all broke down and cried. They said they had no idea it was wrong."

"That's a lie. Reading someone's mail and then passing it to others? Not wrong? Those women aren't that stupid." Katherine waved her hand in dismissal of his comment.

"Cassie came in this morning and filed a report on what happened and demanded that Shirley be prosecuted. If this is what you want, you'll have to come in and file one, too. I think she's been punished enough. Her husband died in the war, and she's trying to raise her children. She needs that job."

Katherine's face flushed, and her fingers curled into fists before she forced herself to flatten them against her legs. "I should feel sorry for her? Me? I have a husband who's dying, I have three boys to raise, and I have no job." She stood and walked to the railing and leaned on it, staring down the dirt road to the highway. "Who knows how long she's been reading my letters, let alone other people's letters?"

"She said this was the first time." Beau's voice was placating, and he lifted his hands in a defensive gesture.

A rude noise left her throat. "This isn't the first time. If you believe that, I know a piece of swampland I could sell you. I'll bet she's been reading everyone's mail and sharing it with her friends. It's a fact she got caught spreading something around that was none of her business. It was my business."

Katherine stood and wrapped her arms around her body. Tears rose, and emotion choked her. "I haven't even come to grips with it. I have to find a way to feed my family and live. If Sam doesn't—" Her voice broke, and she wiped her face with the edge of her apron to try and hide the tears. "If he doesn't come home, we won't have a home or a place to live, and I will not go back up the mountain." Her words became hard with determination as she spoke the last words.

Beau eased off the rail and stood by her, laying a hand on her shoulder. She didn't move away. "I'll do all I can to help. I know Barker will buy any baked goods you make for him. He already buys eggs and butter. I'll talk to the others. It might be that Mabel at the hotel would buy some of your baked goods instead of having them shipped in from Clarksburg. As far as Shirley's concerned, do you want to go on prosecuting her?" He squeezed her shoulder again. "I'm here, Katherine. If you need a shoulder to cry on or just to talk, I'm here."

Katherine heard the words, but she knew there was an underlying motive to his offer. Nothing came without a price to Sheriff Beau Shelton.

She wiped her face and stepped away. His hand dropped to his side. "Thank you, but I'll make it. Somehow, I'll find a way to survive. I'll think about Mrs. Barrett. If you can think of something that serves the purpose for both of us, I'll consider it. You still have to deal with the town and how they feel about her nosiness."

"I will. Will you be at the church social on Sunday?"

"Yes."

"You gonna give me some idea 'bout what you're packin' your lunch in?" He leaned a little closer to her, his breath stirring the top of her hair.

Katherine stepped aside and passed him. "That wouldn't be fair. No, I'm not bringing a lunch this time. Sam isn't here, and I don't want to eat lunch with someone else's husband."

"Now, Katherine, that isn't fair. The menfolk are lookin' forward to bidding for your lunch and eating with you. We've lost to Sam a few times now, but this time, one of us will get that chance to eat one of your fine dinners. I suggest you change your mind and come prepared."

Katherine frowned at the almost threatening tone of his voice. "What if I don't come at all?"

"If you want me to turn in Shirley, I'm sure you'll be there and bring a lunch box." He took two steps to her and wrapped his big hand around her arm. "I'm going to win that lunch with you. I'll do whatever it takes to make sure that happens."

Katherine jerked her arm away and rubbed it. "Is this how you treat women? I can see why your wife isn't getting any better." She opened the screen and let it slam behind her as she stomped into the house.

Lucas stood in the middle of the hall as she entered. He didn't speak but watched out the front door as the sheriff went to his car. The tires spit gravel as the sheriff disappeared, leaving a cloud of dust behind him.

"He isn't going to give up until he has you," Lucas spat.

"Don't talk like that. It isn't going to happen. I would never allow it. I love your father, and I'd never do something like that to him." She walked past her son into the kitchen.

Lucas stood there for a long time, then hollered down the hallway, "I'm going out to the field."

Katherine watched him go into the barn with a sigh before she returned to her baking.

CHAPTER 20
MILLERTON, WV
September 1947

KATHERINE TOOK THE ENVELOPE FROM CASSIE, who picked up her mail in Connersville. She sat beside her friend as she suspected the worst. The letter wasn't from Sam; it was from the sanatorium in Clarksburg where he was staying. She didn't talk to her friend as she read the typed words.

When she finished, Katherine silently handed the paper to Cassie, then laid her head against the back of the chair. Cassie looked at her friend and reached out her hand, and squeezed it. The tears ran down both their cheeks.

It was an impersonal letter from the sanatorium doctor explaining Sam's death. It detailed his care, the date and time he'd been pronounced dead, followed by options for his burial or transportation and a phone number to call for instructions.

Katherine took the pony cart to the church parsonage and knocked on the door with a heavy heart. She had wanted Cassie to go with her, but her friend had other plans and hadn't been able to get away from them.

The door opened, and a short, stocky man in a priest's collar answered.

"Hello, Katherine, I've been expecting you since I heard about Sam. I'm sorry for your loss." Pastor Mike stepped aside and motioned for her to enter. Katherine hesitated. She didn't trust the pastor. He'd come out to the homestead a few times to "visit," but he touched her too much and in a way that felt too familiar. After a moment, she set foot inside, knowing she had no choice if Sam was to receive a proper burial.

"Please, come in. Sit down." He touched her back and walked close to her as she walked down the short hall to the living room.

Katherine escaped to a chair rather than the couch he intended for her to sit on. "Pastor Mike, I'd like to make this short. I want to know the cost of the funeral and a plot for Sam." It all came out in one breath.

Pastor Mike Blake smiled as he came around to pat her shoulder, his fingers sliding across her neck. "We don't need to rush this. I have a pot of boiling water for tea, or I can make coffee if you want."

Mike was shorter than Katherine's tall frame but had a barrel chest and thick arms under his black shirt. She had heard he was a fighter, maybe a boxer or a wrestler in his younger days.

"No, thank you. I need to know the cost. I don't have a lot of money, but I know I can sell some things to make up the difference."

"It's nothing for you to worry about. It can all be taken care of." Father Mike walked into the kitchen, and she could hear him putting things on a plate.

Katherine was afraid. She had overheard a couple of other women in Barker's telling how Pastor Mike hugged and touched them when they came for counseling. It seemed he made sure he sat next to them and kept his arm around them during the meeting.

One woman had spoken of a time when her husband was in the hospital. Pastor Blake had driven her there, and then on the way back, he stopped and said he needed to relieve himself, but he wasn't doing that outside her door. She had turned her head away, and when he got in the car, she clung to the door until they got to her house.

Katherine didn't know how these pastors got to stay or if no one complained. She certainly wasn't going to let him get away with touching her. Her fingers felt for the familiar knife in her boot and at her waist. There was a third at her wrist, hidden by her sleeve. Carrying weapons came as natural to her as breathing and was one of the few habits she had kept after leaving the hills.

Pastor Mike returned. "Here we are, just a few cookies and some tea." He set the tray on the coffee table in front of the couch. "Come and sit here by me. It would be easier to reach, don't you think?"

"I'm fine right here." Katherine sat stiffly on the chair. "What's the cost of a funeral?"

The pastor leaned toward her a little; his eyes were cold. "I'm going to have to insist you come and sit on the couch. I can't be yelling across the room all the time." The expression relaxed into the genial guise he wore. He picked up the teapot and poured two cups. "Sugar? No? Milk or lemon?"

She shook her head again.

He held out the cup for her, but Katherine didn't move to take it. "Come now; I don't bite, at least not hard enough to hurt." He chuckled as though he'd made a joke.

Katherine still didn't move.

His eyes became hard again, his mouth stern as his lips pressed together. "Mrs. Sullivan, if you want to do business with me, you need to be amicable."

Katherine considered her position and stood, reaching out to take the cup from him.

The minute she had the cup and saucer in her hand, Pastor Mike clamped his hand around her wrist. The cup tipped, spilling hot tea onto the floor. He ignored it, continuing to tug her forward toward the couch. Though she tried to resist, she couldn't break his hold. "I said sit," he ordered.

Steely fingers guided her to the couch, and Katherine sat rather than fall. The moment she was beside him, the pressure on her wrist released. "That's much better." He sat close but didn't touch her. He replaced her cup and poured tea into it, handing it to her. He poured tea into a cup for himself, adding some milk and one cube of sugar.

"Katherine, I'm sure Sam was a good man. However, life goes on, and we must find a new path. Let's first close out the old life. We can have a nice service, and I know Monty has a reasonable price on a coffin."

He named a price, and Katherine held her breath. It was more than she could afford, not even in a year of Sam's pay, and now that was gone. What was she going to do? The cost for Sam to be brought home, the coffin, and then the funeral. Where would she get that kind of money? If she didn't, her Sam would be buried in an unmarked grave in some potter's field.

Katherine turned her face away and stared at the wall of bookshelves. She didn't see the books. "I can't afford that." She touched her lips to keep them from trembling.

"Now, Katherine, you're worrying too much. I'm sure Monty will be accommodating if I tell him to be, and I can work out something on the funeral price. Now drink your tea." He reached to squeeze her knee.

She sipped the tea. It didn't taste like tea; there was some strange, medicinal flavor to it Katherine couldn't place. She put the cup to her lips and pretended to swallow while spitting the tea back into the cup.

"What, exactly, do you have in mind for working out a price? I can supply you and Monty with eggs and cheese. Would a year be sufficient? I could do some mending, and I could make you a couple of shirts. Would that be enough?" She set the cup and saucer on the coffee table and sat back against the arm of the couch as far away from Pastor Mike as she could. Her mouth felt strange.

Pastor Mike leaned forward to pour more tea into his cup and shifted closer to Katherine, his knee touching hers. "That would be a start. I was thinking more of personal service. Some hands-on, if you get my meaning."

"I'm not sure I do. Would you like some house cleaning? I thought the janitor service for the church did your cleaning, too." She hoped she had put off what would be an indecent offer. She wanted to gag, jump up, run and scream out the door, but she had to finish what she'd started. Some part of her had to know just how far Pastor Mike Blake was willing to take this. Her insides began to shake.

Mike put his cup and saucer on the table and laid his hand on her knee. "Katherine. I'm thinking more of a personal service about twice a month for a year to start. We can negotiate after that. I want to seal this bargain today." He began sliding his hand up her thigh, taking the material of her skirt along with it.

"If you don't remove that hand. you're going to have it sliced off." Katherine tried to stand, her voice coming out higher than she would have liked.

His hand didn't move, and his fingers tightened. Then before she blinked, he pushed her down into the cushions despite her warning. He started to move his other hand toward her breast, but she slid the knife from her waist into her fingers and held it to his throat.

"Don't move that hand another inch," she ordered through clenched teeth.

He looked her in the eye, and in a flash, he grabbed her wrist and pushed her back into the corner. Rather than being afraid, like most men would have been, Pastor Mike scoffed at her. "Don't play me a fool, woman. I grew up on the streets, and I know how to fight dirty." He flung his leg over her lap and held her there as he pried the knife from her stiff fingers, almost breaking them in the process. "Give it up, Katherine. You're not going to win."

His arm came up under her chin, pushing down hard enough to cut off her air. Katherine stopped fighting, forcing herself to wait until he relaxed his hold. This wasn't the first time she'd had to discourage an unwanted attacker.

"Now that's a good girl." He smiled and leaned close to her neck, his mouth pressing against her skin in greed.

She lowered her hand, feigning submission, and let the knife in her sleeve drop. The moment he lifted his arm from her neck, she caught the blade in her palm and plunged it into his side. Pastor Mike gasped, and she felt the edge of the knife strike bone, maybe a rib. Without hesitation, Katherine yanked it free and drove it again higher and harder. Then, with all her might, she pushed at him, but he didn't move.

Pastor Mike's eyes grew glassy with anger and pain, and he roared and swung his fist and hit her across the face. Katherine's head rolled to the side as pain exploded across her cheek, but she kept her focus. The man reached for the knife he'd dropped. As he rose, using her for leverage, Katherine raised her knee and drove it into his groin as hard as she could.

He fell back against the settee arm, ripping her bodice where he gripped it in his fist. She used her free hand in an uppercut. He lost his balance and landed on the floor. While he lay there stunned, she used the toe of her boot to kick him between the legs a second time, and he doubled over on his side, crying out as blood stained his shirt.

Through the haze of pain and fear, Katherine heard someone pounding on the back door. She pulled the edges of her dress together and picked up her knives, wiping the blood on his shirt. She turned toward the front door, opened it, and peeked out. No one was there.

She crossed the porch with a great sigh of relief and ran halfway to her buggy when Beau Shelton came around the corner.

"Katherine! Stop!" He pounded after her and caught her around the little arbor that covered the gate leading to the parsonage. When the sheriff gripped her wrist and tugged her toward him, he saw the red mark on her cheek and then the way she held the front of her dress.

"Where is he? "His voice sounded hard and angry in her ear.

Beau wrapped his arms around her shaking body, and Katherine let him. She held the tears back as long as she could, but there was only so much she could do to stem the tide. "He's inside. You better call the doc. I stabbed him."

"What did he do?" Beau's arms still held her in comfort. Unable to keep a strong front any longer, she began to sob, leaning into the sheriff's chest.

"H-he attacked me. He said—he would work out Sam's funeral costs if I s— serviced him twice a month for a year. I would never do that to Sam's memory, no matter what the cost was." She pulled away, suddenly feeling the need to run and never look back. "You'll just have to arrest me." Katherine ran for the buggy and swung into the seat; her eyes blurred with tears. She didn't even notice her hand and arm covered in blood until it slipped on the reins.

Beau grabbed the leather lead. "I'll be out to get your side of the story after the ambulance gets here. You go home now."

He let go of the reins, and Katherine turned the horse with a click of her tongue. She and the horse cut across the back streets to reach the shortcut towards home.

Once she arrived at the homestead she and Sam had built together, she slid from the saddle and threw the reins around the back porch rail before heading for the outhouse. Inside, she emptied her stomach. The foul taste wasn't only from the bile but from whatever Pastor Mike had put in the tea.

The following day, Cassie brought her the news Pastor Mike had taken a sabbatical for a few months.

The interim pastor, a man by the name of Pastor Bob, took over the funeral arrangements in place of Pastor Mike and sat in Katherine's

living room. He was a small man, younger, and quiet. The pastor occupied a seat across from Katherine and showed no interest in being closer than that. It was an arrangement that Katherine found both refreshing and comforting.

"Pastor Mike has told me that you wished for a public funeral and burial in the church cemetery." He cleared his throat and looked at Katherine, Lucas, Ben, and Cassie before continuing. "It is our decision, now that Pastor Mike is leaving us for a time, that you shall have a quiet funeral and burial.

"The body will be transferred to Millerton. Monty will bring it out in the hearse and not charge you anything. I'm sure none of us want the taint of TB to spread.

"The doctor says you're all cleared of the disease, but no one in town wants the possibility of coming in contact with it. I have spoken to the sheriff, and he has allowed a waiver for you to bury your husband on your own property. I hope this will meet your needs as it's the only choice you have unless you want to bury him in the Clarksburg potter's field." He didn't offer any other option to his order.

Katherine sat stiffly on the wingback brocade chair, her hands clasped tightly in her lap, as she stared straight ahead and not at the man dressed in black with his little white collar that he tugged at every few words.

"Mrs. Sullivan did you under—"

"That can be arranged. I'll have Lucas pick up the waiver from the sheriff. We'll dig the grave ourselves. Ben will instruct Monty when to bring the coffin." Her voice interrupted him, calm and monotone.

"Thank you for understanding. Pastor Mike is indisposed at the moment and in need of bed rest for another week. If you want him to officiate, I'm not sure he can make it." The short young man moved from side to side. Sweat rolled in streams down his ruddy cheeks and into his collar.

"That won't be necessary. We'll handle the words ourselves," Ben answered for Katherine as he moved to her left between her chair and the reverend. Lucas stood beside her on the right, his hand on her shoulder.

The balding man stood, nodded, and excused himself as he replaced his hat. No one spoke when he let himself out the front door.

Once he was gone, Ben squeezed Katherine's shoulder in a gentle show of support. "Lucas, I think we need to get the boys and dig us a grave. Where do you think you'd want it?"

Katherine couldn't answer, but Lucas spoke his voice low. "At the edge of the garden is that stand of trees. They grew in a kinda circle, leavin' an opening. I think Pa would like it there, and he could rest under the trees. I'll make a bench, so we have somewhere to sit and talk."

At those words, Katherine choked on the emotion that welled inside, and she reached out to Lucas, tears streaming down her face. "You're your Pa's firstborn son. He was so proud of you. I know that whatever you make will be your best, and we'll be proud to sit there." She tried to hold back the sobs but couldn't, and she buried her face in the embroidered handkerchief.

Lucas bolted for the door, barely getting it open before the tears he struggled to hold back flowed down his face.

Cassie sat between the two younger boys, who cried also. Their tears flowed, and their noses ran unheeded as they buried their heads in her lap. Outside, it began to rain. It seemed to Katherine that the whole world mourned the passing of Samuel Orin Sullivan.

CHAPTER 21

CONNERSVILLE, WV

August 2000

MATT PRESSED THE SPEED DIAL FOR HIS SISTER Kathy's phone. After she answered, he called Sam for a three-way call.

"I'm fine and will be heading back to Millerton as soon as the doctor gives me the go-ahead." Matt forced his voice to be lighthearted. He'd been a week at Mabel's house and felt far better than he had when he arrived.

"You come right home." Kathy's voice sounded stern.

Matt sighed. He loved his sister, but she would not appreciate the reality. "I'm fine. I'm close to finding Grandma Katherine. I have a few leads to put together. I'll tell you everything as soon as I have the whole story." He squeezed Selma's fingers where they laced through his own. She squeezed back, smiling at him in a way that made his heart skip a beat.

Kathy's voice drew him back to the real world. "Who was the woman who called Sam? She said she was working with you." Kathy's voice came through the phone a bit more demanding than curious.

"You'll be meeting her. She's been beside me the whole time."

"Is there something I should know?"

"As soon as I have confirmation, you'll know." He looked at Selma, glad she couldn't hear the conversation.

Sam broke into the conversation then. "Take care, brother. Be safe."

"Thanks, Sam. I will. I'll call you both when I have more information. Bye." Matt disconnected before Kathy could ask him more questions.

After discussing it with Selma, they agreed it was time to get back to work. They didn't want to impose on Mabel longer than they had, and both had the itch to follow up on the lead Rita had given them.

"They love you very much." Selma leaned over and kissed his uninjured cheek.

After breakfast, the pair made their excuses, and Mabel wrapped him up in a chest bandage and gave him a pain killer for the trip back to Millerton. She packed a lunch that would last for dinner and waved as they left.

Matt slept the entire trip. Selma, thankful the rain poured on the windshield and made the drive slower than usual. When she saw the front of the Dew Drop Inn, she relaxed her grip on the steering wheel as she pulled into the parking lot.

Selma called Mrs. Millard when she had cell service. The Inn owner waited on the porch when Selma turned into the parking lot.

"I moved Mr. Sullivan's things to the bedroom downstairs. You can walk up the ramp and into his room from the porch." She rushed to Selma's side, holding a large umbrella over the three of them as Matt slowly stood.

"Thank you, Mrs. Millard. That's very kind of you. I don't think I could've made it up those stairs."

"The room down here is much larger, and he'll feel more comfortable." She tripped along behind them, holding the umbrella just barely over their heads.

When they entered the room, Selma sat him on the bed, pulled Matt's shoes off, and tucked him under the covers while the older woman looked on, clicking her tongue.

"I don't understand what happened. For days, the sheriff was absent, and now he has some bruises on his face. He hasn't been out much. He's in his office, so I've heard."

At the door, Matt saw Selma look back at him. She was probably tired of him. "Go home and take a nap yourself. You can come back later. I'll keep an ear out if he calls for help. I've had plenty of experience with sick men." Mrs. Millard winked at Selma and followed the young woman to the porch. "I'll have some dinner ready for you when you come back."

"You don't have to do that. You only provide breakfast and a snack," Selma responded as she stepped off the porch to her car.

"Never mind 'bout that. Just go home and get some shut-eye."

Selma smiled as the little woman shook her apron, went inside.

The porch wrapped around the Inn, and Matt could walk from his room and relax in a chair facing the street or the yard as it dipped into a small valley before the foothills took over. He avoided the back of the Inn.

He had no visits from the Sheriff or his deputies, although Matt saw the Sheriff's car drive past the Inn a few times during the week—especially when Selma's car was present.

Matt's bruises turned a yellowish tinge a few days later, and some of the scabs were gone, leaving a red reminder. He still favored his ribs, but he could move and breathe easier.

"Let's go back to the diner and see if anyone's feeling sorry enough to give us some information," Selma offered as she sat next to him on the porch.

Matt looked over at her. She pulled her hair off her neck in some twist with chopsticks stuck in it to hold it up. He had no idea how it stayed up with those sticks in it but chalked it up to feminine magic. She wore a sundress with straps that widened at the top like a bit of a sleeve. Historically, he was sure it was a dress from the 1950s or 1960s. Either decade, she sure was cute in it.

Selma sat with her feet tucked under her, and her sandals lay on the porch. She was comfortable, and he felt comfortable with her. He could talk to her with ease. They had many things in common.

When he had a relapse, she sat next to his bed, ran back and forth to get him food and drink, or helped him to the bathroom. She stood outside the door, but it was the only time he felt uncomfortable with her. She'd never said a thing about it and helped him back to bed.

Matt answered her question. "If you think it's a good idea, let's do it."

She gave him a big smile in response, and his heartbeat a little faster.

When they arrived at the diner, the occupants ignored them as they sat in a booth near the front. The only waitress in the room continued to speak to a couple who finally got up and left. The woman turned to glare at Matt and Selma, then pointedly turned her back on them.

"What's up with her?" Matt asked after the recalcitrant waitress took their order. Despite how much he'd enjoyed the turkey, he decided to try the meatloaf this time around.

"She's a 'friend' of the sheriff's." Selma wiggled her fingers in air quotes as she said the word.

"We know where his interest is." Matt's tone was dry and humorless. "I guess I passed the test, and now I'm accepted." He gave his head a slight nod to the diners, who showed little to no interest in the couple.

"I wouldn't go as far to say you're accepted, but you're one to be avoided. The people in this town won't talk. It's driving me nuts wondering what they're hiding." Selma stopped talking when the woman dropped their plates on the table.

Matt looked down at his dinner. The meatloaf looked black. There was nothing worth eating on the plate. The few green beans were visible in the gravy. The runny potatoes spread across the plate. He looked at Selma, who looked at his plate then yelled, "Dana!"

No one came out from the kitchen. The other diners stopped talking, waiting to see what would happen. Most of the men craned their necks to see what was on Matt's plate.

Selma picked up his plate. "Gary. Get out here," She shouted as she strode to the counter and pushed between two regulars. They got up and took their plates to a nearby table rather than be in her way.

An older man came out of the kitchen, wiping his hands on a towel. He frowned at Selma and pushed his stained, white paper cap to the back of his head as he stopped at the counter.

Before Gary could ask her what the problem was, Selma tipped the plate on its side and let the contents slide onto the counter. Potatoes and gravy ran to the edge nearest Gary and then over the side. Gary jumped back, swearing.

"This is what Dana served to a guest in our town. Is this the kind of food you serve? Is this how you want someone treated in our town? We don't have enough tourism as it is, and this is how we treat people?"

Gary's face turned red. "Dana, get your ass out here!"

Dana stepped out and came within a couple of feet of Gary. She crossed her arms and stared Gary down. She smirked at her boss.

Gary looked at her, and with his beefy arm, made a quick sweep that sent the mess across the counter at Dana. It splattered her from head to toe. Potatoes and gravy, beans, and meatloaf pieces slid down her face and apron. Dana yelped and began swearing as she surveyed the mess. Her face grew red, and her eyes narrowed first at Gary and then at Selma, who had trouble keeping a smile from her lips. Finally, Selma choked and lifted the back of her hand to her mouth to hold back the laughter.

Dana glowered around at the rest of the occupants of the diner. Some laughed out loud at her. She stamped her foot and swore again. "You'll be sorry for this!"

"Dana!" a voice bellowed from behind Matt, who turned to see a tall man in overalls with long, white hair and a red handkerchief tied around his forehead, Willy Nelson style. "You go home and clean up. I'll see you there." His demeanor brooked no argument.

Matt looked back at Dana, who pressed her lips tightly, whirled, and stomped out the door. The rest of the customers went back to their dinner and talked in quiet tones.

"Go sit down, Selma. I'll bring you a new dinner." Gary sighed and turned back to the kitchen.

"Sorry for the trouble, Gary," Selma offered. He waved his hand in the air and disappeared.

Matt turned back to the booth he vacated. The tall man who ordered Dana to leave stood in his way.

"You have her look," he said to Matt in a soft voice.

"What?" Matt looked up with curiosity.

"You have your grandmother's looks—her eyebrows, eyes, and narrow face."

"You knew my grandmother?" Matt took a step toward him, his interest piqued.

"Yes. Katherine was my cousin. She left the hills and made a better life for herself and her family. I went to visit her as a young boy. She told me to leave the hills and go to school and look higher than just eking out a living making moonshine." He leaned a little on the back of the booth.

"Do you want to sit down, sir?" Matt hooked a chair with his foot and pulled it close to their booth, ignoring the action-induced pain.

The man sat heavily in the chair and looked at Matt. "You're hurting, boy. I heard all about it."

Matt ignored the comment, "You knew my grandmother and my father. Do you know why they all left Millerton in 1948?"

The older man shook his head. "I was still up in the hills when I heard the family was gone. I went to their house but found it burned. While I was checking the house, Lucas found me and yelled at me to get away. I tried to talk to him, but he waved a gun at me and ordered me off the property. I went into the woods and hid. He unlocked the door and began to carry out some boxes. I stepped out and called him again, calling him Cousin Lucas and asking if I could help. He looked at me for a long time, then told me to grab the end of the box.

"We carried boxes into the woods to a shed he'd built into the side of the mountain. It was pretty good for a townie. I brought him food and spent some time with him. He never said what happened, only that the sheriff took his mother and brothers away."

The man leaned his elbows on the table. "He told me to take care of his things and not let anyone steal them. He'd be back to get them; then he was gone. I kept watch over the hut, but I checked on the place a few years later, and it was empty. There were a few books Lucas had left for me and a thank-you note. He taught me to read and write, and that was a priceless gift to me."

Matt watched the man as he told his story. His hair and clothes were clean and pressed. He spoke clearly without dropping the 'g' at the end of words, and somewhere along the line, he had left his life in the hills.

"What do you do for a living?" Matt knew the older man had nothing that would help his search, but maybe there was a way he could get his Uncle Lucas and this man together.

He smiled. "I was drafted at the end of the Vietnam War. I could shoot and knew more about surviving in the wild than most other boys, so I quickly moved up the ranks. When I got out, I took the few men left of my platoon that was good at surviving. We started our own business. We hire out as guides, taking men and women on treks into the mountains for hunting and fishing. We also take those who want to learn survival up to the mountains." He grinned. "You'd be surprised how many people wanted to learn to survive, especially before Y2K."

Matt nodded. He'd had some interest in the subject himself at one time. "Is it a profitable business?"

"We do well and have some former servicemen who joined our company and do the same thing in their areas of expertise. I get to do what I love: I hunt, fish, teach others, and make money at it."

Matt held out his hand, and the other man took it with care. "I know my uncle will be proud when he hears what you've done. What's your name?"

"Finn. Finnbar O'Malley." He stood. "You take care, now." He nodded at Selma as she returned and left.

"Is that Dana's dad?" Matt wondered aloud.

"He's her uncle. Finn lives here in town part of the time when he's not out on one of his treks. Dana stays in an apartment over his garage." Selma tipped the glass to drink the last of her sweet tea.

As they left the diner and headed to Matt's car, the two heard a noise—a whispered voice.

"Miss Selma. Psssst!" It was Izzy. She hunched down next to their car.

Selma turned as Matt continued around the car and climbed into the passenger side. Izzy followed them and squatted beside Selma's open door.

"I tried to get Cecelia to talk to you. Miss Rose, Cece's mother, has been here for years. She has cancer and is in hospice care. I work as a caregiver on the weekends, and Miss Rose said she wanted to talk to you." She indicated Matt.

"Me? Did she know my grandmother?" Matt leaned over as much as his body would allow seeing Izzy in the darkness.

"She told me she has important news for you, but Cece won't let you come to visit. She says it's too hard on her mother's health." She looked up at Selma.

"See what you can do. We'd need to talk with Rose." Selma patted Izzy's shoulder. "We promise not to upset her."

"I will. I can't make any promises. I wanted you to know what she said." She stood disappeared into the darkness.

"That was promising. We'll need to talk to Cece and get her to let us speak with Rose," Selma said, glancing over at Matt as she slid into the car.

Matt nodded in response and leaned back in his seat with a sigh, trying to dismiss the aching in his ribs.

"I'm beginning to wonder if this is all just a wild goose chase. Maybe it would be best for everyone if I left town for good." He stared at the buildings along the route back to the Inn.

"So you think you wasted your time here?"

Matt heard more into the question than what it sounded. He looked at Selma. "No. I don't feel I wasted any time I have spent with you and getting to know you. If I learn nothing about my family, meeting you was worth the beating."

Selma pulled to a stop beside the Inn. "So, I'm still worth a beating?" She raised her eyebrows at him.

Matt frowned and wondered if he'd worded that wrong. "Ah, um, meeting you was the best part of my coming here." He hoped that made whatever he said before better.

"Me, too. I'm disappointed that we didn't find out what happened to your grandmother. I'm happy I met you."

The next day, Selma finished up a few chores she'd let slide when she heard a knock on her door. Turning off the vacuum cleaner, she walked to the door and opened it to find Cece standing on the step outside.

"Can I help you?" Selma asked.

Cece, older than Selma, returned to Millerton after her husband retired. She cared for her mother and was close to her grandbabies.

"I think it's more about me helping you. My mother demands I bring you and your friend to the house today. I've resisted, thinking the strain would be too much for her, but she's insisting. Whatever it is, she's made herself sick over it. Can you both please come?" The woman fidgeted as she spoke and looked up and down the street.

"Would you please come in?" Selma stepped back to give her room to pass.

"My car's in your driveway. Everyone will know I'm here. Just tell me yes or no." Her words were a matter of fact but a little ill-tempered.

Selma swallowed her annoyance glanced at her watch. "I'll call Matt, and we can be there in about an hour or so?"

Cece nodded and left. Selma punched Matt's cell number.

CHAPTER 22

MILLERTON, WV

August 2000

MATT MADE HIS WAY UP THE STEPS TO MISS Rose's house, Selma at his side. His heart pounded with nervous excitement. Selma stood beside him, her presence a comfort. It felt right, them together, her arm through his as if they were a couple.

Cece, wearing black slacks and a print shirt covered with the front of her cardigan, clutched in her fist as she let them in. "She's been agitated all morning waiting for you to get here. I hope this wasn't a mistake." Cece pressed her lips together in distrust. Her eyes narrowed, but she stepped aside for them.

Matt and Selma followed the woman into what once served as the dining room, now converted to a bedroom. Izzy stood by the bed of the frail woman. Her eyes showed concern and hope.

The woman in the bed lay with her eyes closed and took breaths from an oxygen mask. Her thin wisps of hair were almost invisible against the stark white of the pillowcase beneath her head.

"Should we come back later?" Selma whispered.

The woman's eyes opened at the sound of voices, and her gaze took in the two standing at the foot of her bed.

She pulled the mask away from her face as she spoke. "Come." She motioned for them to come closer. "Sit." She indicated the chairs by her bed. "You, too, Cece, this is for you too."

Cece perched on a chair beside Selma, who sat next to Matt and waited. Rose indicated for Izzy to raise the head of the bed a little. "This is a long story. I need to tell it while I still have time." Rose took a breath from the mask before continuing. "I don't want this hanging over my head for eternity. You're looking for your grandmother, Katherine. I don't know where she is, but I do know a little about what happened." She swallowed and took a pull of air from the line in her nose.

"I was fifteen. There was a big meeting in town. Something about food boxes to be handed out that day from the government: everyone who received a letter was there to get a box. We kids were sent to the school playground and were not paying attention to what the parents were doing. "All of the sudden, there was a ruckus when the trucks came to town.

We ran to see what was going on. The Sullivan boys were inside the cab, and they were black from soot. They got out of the vehicle and ran to their mother. The next thing I knew, Joseph Sullivan was brought kicking and screaming to my father, who threw him in the bed of the truck. Father said if he moved out of it, he'd be hogtied for the rest of his life. Joseph stayed there, crying, with my brothers holding his arms so he couldn't run away. I waited, too, trying to calm him, telling him it would be all right. I saw Henry crying, and he also was put into the car with the McClures. A couple of the men grabbed Lucas, but he fought and ran across the square. I saw him come back around the corner of Barker's Market and watch what went on.

"Joseph came to our house. My parents told him his mother wouldn't be coming for him. He'd be given room and board in exchange for working on our farm." Rose paused, and Izzy gave her an ice chip to suck on as she gathered herself and took deep breaths of oxygen.

Cece stood up. "Mother, this is too much. I think they should leave so you can rest." She spoke as if the matter was closed, and her expression echoed the sentiment.

Rose waved her away. "Sit down, Cece." The woman's face showed firm resolve, and her eyes glimmered with determination.

"Young man, your father was a good boy. He missed his mother, and no one would tell him where she was. My parents told him his mother abandoned him and didn't want anything to do with him. Joseph cried every night and didn't want to eat. He didn't want to work. My father took a strap to him until he got up and ate his food and went to do chores in the barn."

The memory sent tears that leaked from the corners of Rose's eyes. Her voice choked a little. "I tried to comfort him, but he just cried all the harder and louder until my dad ordered me to leave him alone.

"A few weeks later, Lucas came to our farm while I played. He stood at the edge of the field and called me over to him. He warned me not to tell my parents he'd come and wanted to know how Joseph managed. I told him not so good; he missed his family. Lucas asked if I could find a way to bring Joseph to see him. I agreed.

I knew Lucas from school. The girls secretly admired him, but he was aloof and paid them no attention. Here was this handsome, older man, and he was talking to me, asking me, not my brothers, to help him." There was a secret smile on her face.

Matt glanced at Cece to see her frown.

Rose continued, her voice gaining strength. "My older brothers built a fort in the woods when they were young. When they got older, they abandoned it. I took Lucas there to hide and wait for Joseph."

Matt was surprised his uncle never mentioned Rose McClure. He did remember their last name underlined with a black pen in some of the newspapers.

"I made sure Lucas had blankets and would bring food to him. We sat and talked. He never treated me like a kid. When Joseph slipped out at night to meet Lucas, I followed him. I told myself it was to make sure he got there and back safe, but I wanted to make sure that Lucas didn't leave." She began coughing, and Izzy patted her back, giving her more ice chips. Cece again tried to stop her mother, but Rose waved her back and continued.

"I spent a lot of time at the fort with Lucas. My mother and father were busy on the farm, and as long as I got my chores done, I was free to roam.

"In late summer, about four weeks after he came to the farm, Lucas was gone. When Joseph didn't go to the fort, and I discovered Lucas wasn't there, I confronted Joseph. He shrugged and told me Lucas had some business to do and would be back.

Joseph was better after that. He didn't cry or fight when he had to do chores. I kept watch at the fort, and weeks later, Lucas returned. I was so glad to see him. He treated me as an equal, not just some dumb girl of fifteen. I fancied myself in love with him." She looked at Cece, who stared at her hands as if all this were a waste of time.

"Four days later, on a Sunday, Joseph was sick and couldn't go to church. He was in the outhouse and refused to come out, so Dad let him stay home. I was worried about him the entire time we were at church and the potluck afterward. I tried to get Dad to take me back to the farm to check on him, but he wouldn't. As soon as we were back at the house, I checked on him, but he wasn't in his bed. His blanket and pillow were gone, and so were his clothes.

I ran through the woods and down to the fort, but it was empty, and there was no evidence anyone had ever been there. It was as it was when I first showed it to Lucas. He'd turned the table over, broke the leg he fixed, and threw a fine layer of dry dirt over everything.

"My father and brothers followed me looking for Joseph, too. They asked why I would even think to look for Joseph at the fort, and I told them I'd shown it to him and thought maybe he'd run away here.

"When everyone else left, I looked around for any sign Lucas might have left me a clue where he went. I was sure Lucas wouldn't just disappear without a word of some sort. I found a matchbox on the ledge. I opened it up and pulled out a piece of paper.

"It said one thing: 'Thank you for all you did. I wish you all the best. L' I was mad and hurt. I went back to my room, threw myself on the bed, and cried. My mother came up and wanted to know what was wrong with me. I lied and told her I loved having a younger brother, and if Joseph didn't come back, I would miss him."

Rose stopped talking. The silence went on for a minute or two. Izzy checked her, then nodded to Cece she was okay.

Cece ran her fingers through her short, gray hair with a frustrated, concerned expression on her face. She stood and leaned over her mother, laying her hand on the thin, brown-spotted arm. When Cece started to speak, Rose opened her eyes and continued in a rush, as if she needed to finish the story in a hurry. Her fingers gripped Cece's hand.

"A couple of weeks later, I was sick." Cece didn't move away from the bed. "I would wake up in the morning and throw up. At first, I thought it was the flu. I would sneak crackers or bread to settle my stomach.

One day, Mom sat me down. She noticed that I was growing out of my clothes. I couldn't get my skirts buttoned, and I began wearing my jackets all day long. I cried. I didn't know what was wrong with me. She asked me some questions, then took me to the doctor who confirmed it: I was pregnant.

My parents were mad. No amount of screaming or threatening would get me to tell who'd done it, either. They had had no idea Lucas had been around. My lips were sealed and have been until now." Cece tried to pull her hand away, but Rose gripped it in both of hers, keeping Cece by her side.

"My parents sent me to my Aunt's house in Clarksburg. When I managed to escape her eagle eye, I ran to the drugstore for soda. I met a man there named Daniel. We walked to the park. He talked to me and told me that he would marry me and give me home if I kept my baby instead of giving it up. He was nice to me, and like Lucas, he treated me with respect. I agreed.

He called Dad and Mom and told them he wanted to marry me before the baby was born so it would know its father right away.

My parents were angry and refused. I cried and begged them to let me marry Daniel. They agreed even though he was eight years older. He had a good job and his own apartment. I felt safe when I was with him.

He wasn't Lucas, but Lucas was gone. I didn't know how to reach him or tell him about the baby. Daniel loved me and promised to take care of Cecelia and me." Rose returned the look her daughter leveled at her.

"Cecelia, Dan was not your blood father, but he loved you very much. He came home from the war and couldn't have children because of what happened to him. I was fortunate to have a man that loved my daughter and me."

Cece remained by her mother. "Did you ever tell my—" Her face twisted into an expression of disdain, "my real father about me?"

Rose shook her head, but Matt remembered the newspapers at Lucas's house. He remembered Rose's name underlined and a clipping of her daughter winning some award and another when Cece married.

"How did you get here from Clarksburg?" Matt asked.

Rose turned her head as if she had forgotten there were others in the room. "Daniel had money. He took a job as an engineer for the Tennessee Valley Authority. He traveled for them, working on projects. He was gone for long periods. Since he just needed a base to work from, I moved us back to Millerton." Her eyes went back to Cece. "Honey, do you hate me?"

Cece shook her head. "No, but why did it take you this long to tell me? Were you ever going to tell me?"

"I wrote you a letter about all this, and it's with the lawyer. You'll get it when I die. This young man needed some answers that no one in town would give to him. My mother told me once that Katherine Sullivan was a hussy and that she enticed all the men in town to pay attention to her. When her husband died, she couldn't feed her family anymore and wanted to get rid of the boys. Mom said the town took her children away."

"You don't know what she did?" Selma leaned forward on her chair. Matt appreciated how she reached out to Rose and spoke with kindness when Matt wanted to yell and shout.

"Matt and I saw a fire at the house. Did that happen before or after they took the boys?"

Rose frowned again, "There was a story going around that Mrs. Sullivan burned her house down. Lucas told Joseph that he rescued all his toys from the house before the folks of Millerton came and tried to take things from it. He said the sheriff stood there and said if anything went missing from the Sullivan house, he would tear their houses apart looking for them and haul them off to jail."

"So no one knows where my grandmother went or what happened to her.

Did they kill her?" Matt whispered.

"No one would have killed her," Rose responded.

"You don't know that," Matt retorted. "I'm sorry, but you weren't there. If they didn't tell you where they took her, and no one would talk about it, it almost sounds like the townspeople took her out and killed her." Matt stood and motioned for Selma to follow.

"Thank you for telling us about Lucas and my father. My uncle took my father to live with one of my aunts. Joseph lived and worked in Columbus until he met my mother and got married." Matt took a few steps towards the door.

Rose relaxed against the pillows. Izzy replaced the air mask.

As Cecelia walked them to the door, Selma asked her, "Are you going to contact Matt's uncle and tell him what you know?"

"I don't know. What good would it do now after all these years? I have my own family and life now. Lucas has never been here in town, and from what my mother has said, I don't think he would want anything to do with anyone in Millerton anyway."

Matt nodded, but he wrote his uncle's number down on a page in his pocket notebook, tore it out, and handed it to her. "If you choose to contact him at some point."

Matt's phone rang, waking him up from his nap. He fumbled for it, almost knocking it off the nightstand before wrapping his fingers around it. He pressed the green button.

"Hello." His voice sounded rough from sleep.

"Now, what's going on?" It took a moment for Matt to recognize the voice of Henry's manager, Kenneth Mullins.

"I hear you've been beaten up and are in the hospital. Why don't you go home where you belong and stop all this nonsense?" Something in the man's voice sounded feverish, almost desperate.

"When Henry tells me what happened on the day his mother left them, I'll go home." Matt could tell he was on speakerphone by the sound of movement and papers rustled in the background.

"He doesn't know anything. He told you what he knew." Kenneth growled.

"When Henry found Lucas, they had to have talked." Matt sighed, tired of the back-and-forth.

Henry spoke up from the background. "I'm running for President. The opposition wants to know all about my past. None of this is good for my campaign, Matthew."

"Nice to hear from you, Uncle Henry. Maybe the media will jog some people's memories because I'm not making much headway. I am not giving up. The media is just a step behind me." Matt picked up the local paper Mrs. Millard had left on the nightstand and scanned it. He read the story on the front page but below the fold aloud. "'The nephew of Senator Henry Sullivan was in the hospital due to an altercation that left him with black eyes and cracked bruised ribs.'" He stopped reading. "This is going to end up all over the news, Uncle. You're just going to have to deal with it. If you aren't willing to talk, I guess this conversation is over."

Matt heard some muffled speaking as Kenneth and Henry argued over what was the better course to take.

"Let me talk to Henry. Alone." Matt grit his teeth as he hears an adamant discussion and the slamming of a door.

"I'm sorry about what happened. I don't mean to be evasive," Henry offered, his voice now speaking directly into the line.

"Henry, I spoke with Rose McClure. Do you remember her?"

There was a slight pause. "I remember a family named McClure. I think I went to school with a couple of the boys. Why?"

"Rose McClure told me Katherine had a reputation of being—" He paused and tried to find the words to reveal what he'd learned. "That she was a little loose with her favors, maybe a tease?"

Henry's voice blasted into Matt's ear. "My mother was not a loose woman!" After a moment, a calmer Henry spoke, but he spoke through clenched teeth. "I won't have anything besmirch my mother's name."

"I'm not saying she was. I'm saying this is what I heard. It might be a perception handed down."

"Matt, your grandmother was a beautiful woman in her day. She was a great cook, and she sold her baked goods to pay for our food. She was also a great seamstress. The ladies in town hired her to sew their dresses." There was a sigh on the other end, but Matt didn't interrupt. "There may have been some jealousy there from the women in town, but I don't see that it would be the cause of my mother leaving us."

"Rose mentioned something else. Katherine might have tried to give you all away because she couldn't take care of you anymore. Is it possible she allowed the town's people to care for you because she couldn't?" Matt offered gently.

"No." Henry's voice was vehement. "I don't remember what was said or why or anything else. I remember being torn from her arms and held by men. She begged them not to take us away and said they were wrong. I could see her crying as the sheriff and others held her arms and handcuffed her. Then I was taken away in a car. I never saw her again or anyone from my family until Lucas contacted me in college."

"Thank you, Uncle Henry. If that's all you know, then I won't bother you again. If I find out any other news, I'll call you."

There was a long pause and then a deep sigh from the other end of the phone. "Thank you." Henry disconnected the call.

Matt mulled everything he learned. What part was genuine, and what part was perception?

A knock on the door interrupted Matt's thoughts, and Selma called his name. He pulled himself out of bed; his clothing rumpled after sleeping in them. Selma entered in with a tray of food.

"Who was on the phone?" she asked.

Matt smiled at the comfortable feeling the question induced.

"Back to bed with you," she said, shooing him in that direction. Matt chuckled as he retreated before her mothering.

Once he was back in bed, Selma slid the tray onto his lap. Matt smiled at the soup, sandwich, and side of applesauce. Picking up the cup, he sipped the soup while Selma sat in anticipation.

"Henry was on the phone," Matt answered at length. "He said he remembers forcibly taken away from his mother while she cried and told the people not to take her children. He also remembers the sheriff handcuffing his mother and forcing her into his car." He took another sip of soup.

"That kind of puts another twist to the situation. If the Sheriff took her children from her, then the story as a loose woman wouldn't fit with the story that she tried to kill her children. If that were true, she wouldn't have cried like your uncle Henry said." Selma fished the ever-present notebook from her bag and found a blank page.

Matt watched as Selma's pen scratched across the page at light speed. This woman amazed him. She was a strong, protective, and aggressive woman. He felt pride and respect welling in his chest along with something else that affected his body lower more than his heart. She fit him like two pieces of a puzzle. He hoped she felt the same way. On the one hand, he wanted to speak out and tell her how he felt, but on the other, he worried his quest only challenged her and that she didn't see him in the same way.

CHAPTER 23

MILLERTON, WV

September 1947

KATHERINE STOOD AT THE EDGE OF THE ROAD and watched as the hearse pulled into the driveway, stirring the dust into swirls. Her boys, dressed in their Sunday best, stood in a line beside her. With them were Thomas and Emma, who had traveled from Columbus with the girls wearing their hats and gloves firmly in place.

Ben and Carrie Lundgren stood next to her, waiting for Monty to bring the coffin. She would never have made it through the last months without their support, and now she needed it more than ever. Ben had stepped in to mentor the boys, teaching them the things Samuel would have done had he been there. Now Samuel was gone. She pressed the white lace-edged hanky to her trembling lips.

As the hearse passed, Katherine glanced past the dust toward the road. No one followed the vehicle. Not one family or a single person from town came to the funeral. A pain stabbed at her, and she swallowed the lump that threatened to rise in her throat. Rejection by the townspeople was complete.

In a line, they followed the hearse around the house to the backyard. Lucas stood next to Ben with Henry and Joseph solemnly waiting for Monty to open the back of the hearse.

"I don't think the rollers will make it through the grass." Monty stood back and scratched his head.

Ben said quietly, "Why don't you drive the hearse across the grass to the site?" He pointed to the mound of dirt visible between the trees.

Monty nodded and climbed back into the driver's seat, maneuvering the hearse to the grave.

The heat of the sun raised perspiration on Katherine's neck, and she lifted the heavy braid she had woven her hair into that morning and hoped for a cool breeze. The navy dress she wore trapped the heat against her body as she walked to stand beside her family. The netting on the matching hat didn't move. No wind eased the oppression in the air or her heart.

Monty stood back near his vehicle, waiting for them to perform the burial.

Ben spoke to him. "Monty, don't feel you have to stay. We understand."

"I have to. Sam was a good man and always went out of his way to help the missus and me. Color didn't matter to him. The missus sent along with some food for you." He nodded his nappy black-and-gray-haired head. Monty adjusted his dark cotton suit and starched white shirt, folding his hands in front of his waist, and waited.

Ben turned to Katherine, who nodded. He opened the Bible and unfolded a paper. "Being asked to say words on this occasion is an honor and a solemn responsibility. I have chosen some words from the Good Book. We all know what a wonderful man and father Samuel were, so we don't need to reiterate his accomplishments." Ben went on to read the passage he had chosen.

"'But I would not have you to be ignorant, brother, concerning them which are asleep, that ye sorrow not, even as others which have no hope. For if we believe that Jesus died and rose again, even so, them also which sleep in Jesus, will God bring with him.'"

Then the boys spoke of their love, and each told their favorite memory of their father. Emma read from a letter Martha mailed to her and spoke of her love for her father. Thomas kept his arm around her, and his girls stood close, holding onto her as she wept.

Ben went on to recite; "The Lord is my shepherd—" The rest chimed into the end. Then he began, "Our Father, who art—"

When the prayer ended, each took a handful of dirt and threw it on the lowered coffin. Katherine stepped forward and tossed in her clump of dirt, wincing at the sound of it hitting the wood. She also threw the two roses from the bush next to the back porch. Then, she noticed the sides and bottom of the grave lined with a mixture of cement. Next to it, boards covered with more cement lay ready to be put on top. She looked at Ben then Lucas in curiosity.

"The boys wanted to make sure animals didn't dig him up, or his grave disturbed," Ben explained. Katherine saw the expectation in their faces. She gave a weak smile of approval and nodded.

Emma hugged her mother, and Thomas pressed an envelope into her hand. "Don't open it now. Wait until tonight." He bent and kissed her cheek.

The drive back to Columbus was long, and they needed to get on the road. Katherine watched as the car disappeared down the road. She felt as if her soul dried up and lay in the same dust. Emma, Thomas, and the girls arrived early the previous morning, and the visit had been too short.

Cassie looped her arm through Katherine's, distracting her from her thoughts. "Come. Monty is waiting, as well as the boys." Katherine allowed Cassie to lead her into the house.

Monty waited for her in the kitchen and pointed to the basket on the counter. "Ma'am, this is from my missus and me. You can bring the basket back anytime you come to town next." He touched his hat and backed out the door when she thanked him. She heard the sound of the hearse as it drove away.

Cassie took a sniff. "Smells like Sunday chicken to me." She sniffed again and added, "If I'm not mistaken, there might be some pumpkin and maybe pecan pie."

Katherine let her take the booty from the basket and set it out on the table. No matter how good it smelled, she wasn't hungry. She wanted to crawl into bed and never get up again.

She must've been staring at the bedroom doorway because Cassie said, in a soft but firm voice, "You can't do that. You have three boys to tend. There'll be plenty of time for bawlin' and feelin' sorry for yourself when the work is over."

Katherine jerked at Cassie's harsh admonition but said nothing.

"I'll get Emma's basket from the cooler. Why don't we see what that girl cooked? She's almost as good a cook as you."

The comment brought a brief smile to Katherine's lips.

Cassie followed Katherine and the boys as they brought the last of the food into the dining room and set it on the table. The menfolk stood in the doorway.

Cassie motioned for them in. "Everyone sit while I bring the tea. You, too, Katherine. Sit." They did, in silence.

Ben asked the blessing over the food, and they ate. No one felt much like eating, but the sound of knives and forks scraping across the plates followed in a rhythm. After the quiet dinner, Ben excused himself. "I'll go take care of the grave."

"I'll help." Lucas stood, followed by the two younger boys. Katherine nodded, and it was quiet again.

Cassie helped Katherine clear the table and put the food away. They had almost finished when a knock at the door interrupted them.

"I'll get it." Katherine dried her hands on her apron.

Beau stood on the porch, dressed in his uniform. Katherine didn't open the door but spoke from her side. "What can I do for you, Sheriff?"

"Can I come in?"

Katherine stepped out onto the porch and motioned for him to sit. She sat across the small table from him.

"I'm sorry for your loss. Sam was a good man, and he sure didn't deserve to die so young. If there's anything I can do to help out, let me know."

Katherine bent her head in acknowledgment.

"There are some changes in town we're having a meeting. We're not rebuilding the post office. All mail will be delivered and picked up from Connersville; you'll have to allow extra time when mailing in your bills." He had his hat in his hand and ran his fingers around and around the inside edge.

"So, what's the town meeting for?" Katherine was glad to have some anger to replace the feelings of loss.

"It's just a formality. I wanted to let the citizens of Millerton know about the post office closing." He stared at the twirling hat in his hands.

"Thank you for informing me of the meeting. You'll forgive me if I don't attend. One can only take so much rejection and fault finding." Katherine did not hide the sarcasm.

"Katherine, I'm sorry. The townspeople can be cruel, but they are goodhearted."

Katherine stood quickly and stared down at him until he rose also. "I think you'd better leave unless you have something important to say. I have never done anything to the people of Millerton to deserve the treatment I've received. When you speak to at the meeting, I suggest that you might tell those people they need to change their attitude, especially that man—. It seems going to church isn't doing anything."

"Katherine! That's enough. Mike is suffering. He's resigned his pastorship to be a lay pastor under Pastor Bob. Have some compassion." Beau reached out his hand to her, but Katherine took two steps away.

"Compassion? You ask me to have compassion?" She balled her fists at her sides. "I've been helpful, supportive, brought food to the sick and needy, and when I needed something from them, they turn on me." Tears ran down her cheeks, and Beau's hand went to her, but she slapped it away. "Go back and tell those women they can find someone else to sew their clothes, and I'm taking my baked goods to Connersville on the mail truck. Good day, Sheriff." She glared at him while the tears fell unheeded.

He nodded and turned but then stopped and looked back at her. "Katherine." He paused, gathering the right words. "You frighten the women."

"Frighten? What are you talking about? I don't scare them." She held her ground, though her expression shifted from furious to confuse.

"Maybe that isn't the right word. You're beautiful, you sew better than anyone in the county, you cook better than any woman, and the blue ribbons you won at the fair proved it. None of the women in Millerton can compete with you."

"I've heard all that falderal. Who asked them to? Who decided that I cook better than they do?" Her hands returned to her waist, and she pushed her chin and chest out.

Cassie stepped from inside the house. "What the sheriff is trying to say, Katherine, as delicately as he can, is that the women of Millerton are green-faced with envy. You're better than they are." She smiled at Katherine's snorted response.

"Pushaw! That's a bunch of hogwash."

"No, it isn't." Cassie smiled sadly.

Katherine looked from one to the other. "Why? I cook, I clean, and I bake like every other woman. I'm nothing special." She waved her hand in a dismissive gesture.

Beau cleared his throat, but Cassie let the screen door close behind her as she moved to stand between Beau and Katherine.

"Katherine, I've tried to tell you this before, but you ignored what I said. Now that the sheriff is trying to say the same thing, you might listen this time. The women are jealous because their men are vocal about how they feel about you. I've overheard women when you aren't around talking about how their husbands wish they would dress more like you, cook like you, clean their house like you, and have sex like you."

"What? They don't say that! The last part—" Katherine held up her hands, disclaiming that. "I heard that before."

Cassie looked at Beau, and he just gave a weak grin and shrugged. "It's more of a guess than any personal knowledge. Sam never said anything, but he did tell Ben the men in town seemed to hold you to a different yardstick than other women."

"That's not fair. You go right back and tell everyone so." She made a sweeping motion with her hands to Beau, who took a step down off the porch.

"Nothin' I say will change their minds," he told her. "You attacked the reverend, and they know that. Someone saw you fleeing out of town right after it happened. Now you know I hold none of that against you."

She railed at him. "You're the sheriff! They'll believe you!"

He shook his head sadly. "They won't. They've made up their minds, and nothing will change them. I'm sorry." He nodded to the two women and left, his car churning dust as Katherine mulled over his words.

"Cassie, what is wrong with these women? Why would they even allow their men to say or think things like that?" Her voice was pleading for understanding.

"I know it isn't fair. Once women get something in their minds, it's tough to change it. The nicer you are, the more they feel guilty for thinking bad thoughts. Then their husbands make these ridiculous comments, and it starts all over."

"So there's nothing I can do." Katherine's expression turned to tears. Her situation got the better of her emotions.

Cassie put her arms around Katherine and hugged her. She led her friend to her bedroom and helped the tired woman to bed.

CHAPTER 24

MILLERTON, WV

December 1947–March 1948

KATHERINE WORKED HARD TO PUT FOOD ON the table and pay the bills with the pittance the foundry collected from Sam's coworkers in the following months. Katherine was surprised to receive the card and money when Sam's foreman stopped by to deliver it. The sentiment was something Katherine had a little experience from anyone in Millerton.

Ben and Cassie helped her apply for Social Security benefits Cassie had heard about, and Katherine gave the papers to Cassie to mail when they went into Clarksburg.

On that same day, as she was sitting in the kitchen trying to figure out where to pinch the next pennies, Katherine remembered the envelope Thomas had pressed on her after the funeral. It took her a few minutes of digging around in the bedroom to find it, but when she did, she had to hold back tears as she remembered that day. She opened it to see three hundred dollars in ten and twenties. Katherine cried all over again, hugging the money to her chest and thanking God for her children.

With frugal spending, the money lasted another three months while she waited for some notice from the government that she would get money to support her and the boys. Cassie called the Social Security Department of West Virginia, but they claimed they couldn't find her paperwork.

Frustrated, Cassie and Katherine filled out the forms again. This time, Katherine sent the letter registered. Her fear overshadowed the frustration. What was going to happen if the money didn't come through?

The money from Thomas and Emma was gone. She made enough with what she sold in Connersville to keep the bills paid, but they were falling behind. Soon, the utilities would be cut off. They had the wood stove and the fireplace for warmth and cooking, but she couldn't sew without electricity. Not that she had anything to sew for a while now.

The town's women had cut any ties with her after what had happened with the reverend. No matter how hard it was, Katherine couldn't make herself feel bad for having defended herself. No amount of rudeness from the town ladies would make her think otherwise.

In desperation, Katherine wrote to her daughter. Martha sent her an apology, but she and David were saving for a house of their own and couldn't afford to send anything to help her mother and siblings. Katherine smiled at the letter in a sad little way. Martha always had thought of her own needs first. She didn't fault her oldest for not helping but knew more was at stake: there were the boys.

After delivering pies and a cake to Robert, Katherine left Barker's, paying what she could on her bills. She thought the weather was beautiful that day, at least, as she looked upward and carried her meager purchases to the buggy. The thought didn't last. Beau called her name as he approached her from behind the market. "I want to talk to you. Can you meet me at Flat Rock?"

He reached out to help her with her bag, but Katherine pulled it out of his reach. Beau sighed and shook his head but didn't press the matter.

"Beau, I'm sorry about Cynthia's passing, but what would you want to talk to me for?" She continued to walk toward the buggy, and the horse whinnied at her approach.

"I have something I want to talk to you about, and I don't want the whole town breathing down my neck wondering what."

Katherine shook her head and pulled herself into the buggy seat. She didn't answer when she picked up the reins and kept her eyes firmly straight ahead.

"Meet me at Flat Rock," he ordered and turned to walk away, vanishing again behind the store.

Katherine turned the buggy toward home and ignored him. When she reached the lane that led to Flat Rock, she paused and turned the buggy down the lane toward the creek after a moment of thought. Flat Rock was just that: a large, flat rock that hung over the creek. In the summer, families brought a picnic and ate on the rock while the children played in the water. At one time, she remembered hearing, Indians run buffalo over the horseshoe cliff above the area and skinned them there, letting the blood run into the creek.

Katherine remained in her buggy when Beau arrived. Beau paced his head down and his hands behind his back, but he stopped in front of Katherine.

"Katherine, I know times are tough. I know this is too soon after both your Sam and my Cynthia have passed, but if we combine our households, it would be easier on both of us. I can take care of you and the boys."

Katherine looked at the large man. Beau hadn't seemed to grieve over the death of Cynthia. Not that she had shown her grief for Sam in public, either, but he was there every time she came to town since his wife's death. Just as before, he helped her with her groceries or whatever she brought to Barker's.

Ben mentioned Beau's attentive attitude once. "Doesn't he think you're strong enough to carry your own groceries?" Ben joked.

"He's worried I'll stir up trouble. Maybe snag someone's husband and haul them around back. Or maybe entice those men to buy pies and cakes." The hard edge to her voice had kept any comment from Ben inside.

Now, here at Flat Rock, the sheriff asked her a question.

Katherine figured being honest was the best. "I loved Sam. I do not need another husband."

"I respect that. What I'm thinking is more of a joining of family and economics. I need someone to cook, clean, and take care of my place; you need a stable home for you and the boys. You'd have security for them until they're on their own. I think us being together would be the best."

Katherine eyed him and then spoke her mind. "Beau, you are asking me to marry you?"

The sheriff looked away. He kicked his toe in the dirt, then said, "Not married. More like a housekeeper with benefits."

When the words sunk into Katherine's brain and she realized what he'd said. She spat on the ground at his feet. "How dare you! How dare you even speak those words!" She snapped the reins to get the horse moving.

He pulled on the harness to keep the horse where she was. The horse reared her head and tried to break his hold, but Beau held on tight.

"Katie, there'll come a day that you might have to take that offer. It isn't getting any easier since the war's over. I know times are hard for you."

Katherine let the words roll over her. "Give me one reason why you wouldn't marry me?" She narrowed her eyes down at his.

He stared at his hand holding the leather strap, then looked up at her. "Cynthia's grandparents left her money with the stipulation that if she died, it would stop unless there were children. Later, when she found out she was ill, she amended her will to read that the inheritance would go to charity if I got married again. I can afford to pay you but not marry you."

Katherine almost felt sorry for him. "You're in quite a pickle, then." She slapped the reins and braced for the jerk when the horse pulled on the reins.

She wouldn't, and she couldn't think of anything that would have her stoop that low. Katherine had prayed for a miracle, but she was pretty sure that had not been a plan sent from God. The breeze dried her tears as the mare galloped down the highway to home.

Katherine stood in the kitchen with the cupboard opened. There were three jars of canned corn, six green beans, a few more jars of beets, and some canned meat. It wouldn't be enough food to last them through March, and she knew it. Over the last few weeks, Katherine sold or traded almost everything out of her kitchen to try and make ends meet, and it wasn't working. She dropped her head on her chest, her arms hung on the handles as if she was being crucified.

"Mother, are we going to die? Are we going to starve to death?"

Katherine slammed the doors shut on the cupboard and whirled to face her second youngest son. "Oh, honey, of course not. We have vegetables from the garden in the cellar. I can make green tomato pie. You like those." She tried to work a smile to her tight lips. "Do you want to help me make potato soup?"

Henry made a face. "Again? Isn't there something else? We had that last week."

Katherine felt a pain in her stomach. "I'll see if there's something else I can put together. Why don't you go ask Lucas if he can find one of those wild hens running around, and we'll have chicken and dumplings?"

Henry thrust his fist in the air and ran out the back door, letting it slam behind him.

Lucas didn't find a hen that night, but he came home with some rabbits a couple of nights later. Everyone was happy not to have potatoes again for a few days.

A week later, Cassie ran up the back porch steps and waved a note. The boys had long stopped going over for lessons. Katherine couldn't afford school, and as bad as things were, it probably didn't matter. Three weeks had come and gone with no news from the Social Security office.

Not until Cassie spoke. "Katherine, there's news. Here's your mail. You got a letter, the same as the rest of the town. Read it."

"Stop waving it so I can read it." She snatched the letter from Cassie and looked at the return address. It wasn't from the Social Security Office; it was from the U.S. Department of Agriculture. "Could this be something about Lucas? Maybe he won one of those free schooling ships."

Cassie chuckled. "You mean a scholarship. No, this isn't about that. I think it's something else that many people in this area received."

Katherine picked up the knife on the counter and slit the flap. This flap stuck tight, not like the ones she had opened when she had picked up the mail from Shirley.

The letter stated a truck would come to their area due to a surplus of food processed. The letter instructed the recipient to be the letter and receive a box of food supplies for their family.

Katherine looked up at Cassie with wide, hopeful eyes. "I can't look a gift horse in the mouth. I could use the food, but I could use a little cash, too. The bills, you know."

Cassie nodded. "This is something you won't have to use the credit on." She hugged the thin frame of her friend. Katherine made sure the boys had enough to eat while she made do with leftovers if there were any.

As it happened that morning, Cassie didn't get her ration card for gas, so that she couldn't take Katherine to town. Lucas brought the buggy around to Katherine, and she left for town.

She dressed in her Sunday best dress. The weather was cool, and she wrapped her wool coat tight around her bony body. She handled the reins with her suede gloves.

A crowd milled in the square, waiting for the government truck as she arrived in town. Katherine didn't get out of the buggy. There was no reason to go into the store as there was no money. She took her towel-wrapped tin bottle and poured hot water into a cup. She couldn't afford coffee or tea, but she brought the hot water to warm her while she waited.

The clock on the city hall tower chimed one, and everyone turned to look down the road that would bring the truck into the town. A half an hour went by, and then another, and another. When the clock chimed three, people became restless and angry at the delay and the possibility the whole town had been duped.

Then a cry went out that the trucks were on their way. Everyone moved to line the sidewalks along the square.

CHAPTER 25

MILLERTON, WV

August–September 2000

THE CUTS AND BRUISING ON MATT'S FACE FADED from yellow to his normal, tan skin.

Lavon and his boys were seen around town a little worse for wear. The whole lot of them stayed well away from Matt and Selma, which was just fine with them.

Evening found the pair sitting on the inn porch, watching the world goes by when Matt reached out his hand. "Come and walk with me."

She sighed and rose to follow him.

"What was that for?" He turned her to face him. The sun had set over the mountains, and they hadn't put on the lights that would attract the insects.

"I just want to be with you and not share you with anyone." Selma didn't look at him when she said it, but her posture was nervous and uncertain.

Matt turned to Selma to face him. He dipped his head and explored her lips in a slow, warm dance. She responded with pressure, her body leaning into his, her hands at his waist. Matt's lips parted her and deepened the kiss. What he had held back all these years, and especially over the past weeks that he spent with Selma, poured through him. His hands pulled her closer, and he turned his head to fit her into the kiss.

Their embrace lasted for what seemed like hours until Matt broke the connection and leaned his forehead against hers. Both of them were panting for air and smiling at each other in the dark.

"We got past that issue. I take it you don't hate me," Matt teased.

"You think?" She gave him a peck on the lips. "Matt, I love the way you handled Rose, Cece, and Izzy. I think there's more to you, and I'd love the opportunity to find that out."

"I think we can manage that." He leaned in to capture her lips a second time and lengthen the kiss.

They didn't go for a walk but stood in the shadows of the porch. Communication came in short sentences punctuated with kisses, and neither wanted to part.

With Selma's help, Matt contacted other families in Millerton, interviewing some that came forward, but they had no new information to give. Matt and Cece talked after her mother's big reveal, and she asked Matt not to tell Lucas about her. If at some time she felt comfortable, she would contact him herself. Matt agreed. He didn't see any reason to step into the middle of this situation. He had enough on his plate.

After several days with no new information, Matt couldn't justify staying. That and he had classes to teach. He promised Selma he'd call her with any information he received, and she promised the same. Neither of them wanted him to leave, but they arranged to have her visit him in Columbus soon.

At home, Lucas h rad been released from the hospital and into Matt's care. Lucas' house still wasn't prepared for him to move home.

Lucas shuffled into Matt's house, sat in Joseph's recliner with the remote, and was happy to have Matt wait on him. Matt tried to get his uncle to talk about the day Grandma Katherine had vanished and shared a little of what he found out. He even told him about getting beat up.

After hearing what had happened, Lucas sat up abruptly in his chair. "Whaddu call that sheriff?"

"His name is Lavon Shelton." Matt looked up from the newspaper he was reading.

"Any relation to Beau Shelton?" Lucas's eyes bored into Matt's.

"Yep, his nephew."

"Figures. What happened after that? I get the impression you aren't scared of him."

"Now that you mention it, there was a little comeuppance for the good sheriff and his boys. It seems that Selma has relations up the hill." Matt watched his uncle stiffen. "They made themselves known to the sheriff, and the Sheriff and his deputies looked a little like me when I saw them the next time."

Uncle Lucas gave a dry chuckle that turned into an even dryer laugh. "You're right. Those hill folk know just how to handle a man like that." The laughter stopped, and Uncle Lucas looked away. "You don't seem to know much about those folks. Did you go up the hill?"

"No." Matt held the paper open. His eyes didn't focus on the print but waited for this conversation to progress.

"Their life isn't easy, and most of the time, it's a choice to stay there," Lucas explained, nostalgic.

"You've been up the hill?"

"Oh, yes. I learned a few things from them I didn't know. They were good to me." Lucas stopped speaking and stared into space.

"You didn't stay?" Matt prompted.

Uncle Lucas looked at his nephew with raised bushy eyebrows. "Are you kidding me, Son? I gagged the first time I went inside their homes. They don't bathe. They eat pretty well, but I didn't want that life."

"You didn't take to the incest?" Matt breathed, testing the water.

Lucas swung his head. "No, I didn't."

Matt laughed.

The phone rang and interrupted the conversation. "Hello," Matt spoke into the phone.

"Matthew Sullivan?"

"Yes, this is he."

"I'm Anna, a friend of Rita's, the nurse at the hospital where you stayed. She called me and asked me to see what I could find out about a family member you're researching. I found a Katherine Sullivan in our records."

"You did?" Matt dropped the paper he held and walked out of the room for privacy. "What did you find? Where was she buried?"

"Buried? Honey, she's alive."

Matt whooped. "Yes! Oh! Sorry, I didn't mean to break your eardrum." There was a laugh at the other end of the line. "You didn't.

Katherine Sullivan has been in a home for twenty-five years. When the former home closed, Katherine transferred to our facility." She gave Matt the name and phone number of the rest home where she lived.

"You're going to need some paperwork to prove who you are. Katherine has not had any family ever come to visit or have contact with her, so they'll want to verify who you are."

"That's going to be a little difficult. I have a family Bible. I hope that will be enough." He said goodbye, disconnected the call and hit the speed dial for Selma's number.

Selma answered, "This is Selma."

"I found her!" He wanted to yell, but he didn't want his Uncle Lucas to know until he was sure it was the right woman. Quick steps carried Matt down the hall to the front door and out onto the porch. "I just got a call from Rita's friend, Anna. She found Katherine. She's alive!"

He smiled at her shout of joy over the phone. When she calmed down a little, she asked, "When do we get to meet her?"

The smile on Matt's face remained. She said we as if the two of them were more than just— whatever they were.

"I have to bring proof of our relationship. I'm going to drive over there first to see what I'll need to provide to see her." The silence on the other end reflected her disappointment. "I don't want you to drive up here for nothing. We still aren't sure if she's the Katherine Sullivan that I'm related to." He heard her sigh.

"You're right." The words came out in a sigh. "Call me as soon as you find anything."

Matt went back into the living room, where he left his uncle. Lucas looked up from his TV program. "Who was that?"

Matt had a quick flash of his father sitting in the same chair, asking the same question in the same tone.

"Selma. Are you my father, now?" Matt smiled to let Uncle Lucas know there was no malice in his question.

"Do you need one?" Uncle Lucas shot back.

The question stumped Matt for a moment. His father was gone. They had a good relationship, but his father had a hard time relating to his children after they were grown. When they were children, he'd been a wonderful father. Once Matt and his siblings were adults and needed guidance with choices of college or life, his father took a back seat. He let Betty take that place while he retreated to his office or the attic. Was he ashamed of his lack of education or background?

"Would you know how to be a good father?" Matt returned softly, thinking of Cecelia.

"I think so, though I never got that chance." His answer caused Matt to frown. Did he know about Cecilia? Was there some way he might have found out he was a father?

"You helped to raise your brothers," Matt offered.

"Just your father. Henry went with someone else. Joseph… Well, he needed more guidin'. I thought it would be better if he went to live with Thomas and Emma. They had girls, and Thomas was glad to have a boy to raise. He did a good job with Joseph. The boy had a good work ethic, and he did a good job with ya'll." He turned his eyes back at the TV. "I'd be proud of you, your brother, and your sister if I was your pa."

Matt had a warm feeling that started at the pit of his gut and spread up to his heart. Despite all the stress and dealing with his uncle's packrat issues, he loved Uncle Lucas. When he was younger, he spent summers on the farm with Lucas, having fun with the animals, learning how to survive the outdoors, and shooting a gun.

"Uncle Lucas, I don't know if I've ever said this to you, but I love you. We've had our differences, but I looked forward to spending summers at your house growing up. You talked to me like an adult, even when I wasn't one. I want you to know I appreciate all you taught me." Matt didn't look at his uncle. He was dealing with emotions of his own.

"You're welcome, Son. I loved those summers, too. I know you want to help me, and I'm stubborn. I'm glad for what you did even though I haven't seen the house since you, Sam, and the boy clean it up."

Matt plowed right in. "What is it that you're opposed to in me finding my grandmother? You've fought me on it since the beginning, but you won't tell me why."

Uncle Lucas didn't answer, so Matt continued, "I've been looking for information about what happened to her. What are you going to feel if I do find her and she's alive? Or dead?"

This time he looked across the semi-darkness of the room to his uncle.

There was an expression of pain and sorrow, but he still didn't answer.

Matt continued. "I don't want you to hate me for looking for her, but I want to know why a whole town hated her and why they won't talk about her. Why didn't she try to find you and your brothers and sisters? I don't believe a mother would walk away from her children and not look back. Do you think your mother did that?" Matt waited, watching his uncle's expression.

Uncle Lucas dropped his head in his hands. The only sound in the room was the TV host asking questions and the beep of the contestant's answers.

"The town didn't appreciate the woman that was my mother. She didn't deserve the way they treated her. I don't think she would've done what they said."

"What did they say she did?"

Uncle Lucas pursed his lips. "That's old news. We don't need to go there. If you need to find her, then go ahead and knock yourself out, but I don't want to talk about it anymore." He pressed the volume to drown out any further conversation.

Matt sat for a while longer to make sure his uncle didn't think he was leaving mad. He yawned and stretched and excused himself. His uncle waved him away.

In the office, Matt looked up the mileage to Morganville, West Virginia. It was about a three-hour drive. If he left early in the morning, he could be back home late or stay the night.

Upstairs, he packed a bag just in case. His briefcase held the family Bible and all the notes he and Selma had compiled. He was going to go without calling first. Sometimes, it's hard to say no when they find you drove all the way there.

It didn't work out for Matt to leave the next day. A thunderstorm blew in, and tornado warnings kept everyone inside. Matt had to cool his heels around the house and his uncle.

He moved things to the back of the attic to the clear space near the door. From under a table covered with a sheet, he found a trunk. It wasn't big or heavy. He pulled in into the light and lifted the lid.

Inside were blankets, toys, and school books with composition and lessons. Matt sat on the floor and read.

These were lessons from his father and Uncle Henry's days in school. A stack of vocabulary and spelling lists. Book reports with his Uncle Henry's name on them.

His father's reports were outlined with few details. In the margins were pencil drawings of scenes in the story. Some were flowers and trees. They were so detailed Matt checked the name inside the notebook again to make sure. The writing was clear: Joseph Sullivan. His father was talented. How had he not known that about his father?

At the bottom of the trunk, he found a tray of whittled animals. Matt frowned and stood. He swung his flashlight around the room until it stopped where he remembered seeing another trunk, where he'd seen a couple of wooden animals lying on top of a blanket. He found the chest and opened the lid.

Under the blanket, more wooden carvings lay nestled in the newspaper. Matt found himself admiring the details by inspecting the carvings, turning them over in his hands to catch every nuance of the pieces. He picked up other packages in the trunk and peeled the old newspaper off to reveal a few more figurines. He checked the newspaper dates and discovered the years his father had packed the pieces.

In the lid of the trunk, bands held two leather pouches. Matt pulled them from their protection and opened the leather strap. Burned into the leather were the initials J.D.S. for Joseph Daniel Sullivan. Inside he found carving tools. Reverently, he held the pouch and the tray of carvings as he made his way down to the living room.

Uncle Lucas shouted at the TV as if some game show required his interference.

"Uncle Lucas." There was no response, "Uncle Lucas!" Matt raised his voice over the din of the announcer. "Turn off the TV!" When Lucas didn't respond, Matt yanked the remote from his hand and hit the mute button.

"Hey! What's the matter with you?" His eyes were wild as he frowned and searched Matt's face for some explanation. Matt laid the pouch and the newspaper-wrapped carvings on his uncle's lap.

There was a long silence, and then Lucas looked up at Matt. "Where'd you find this?"

"In a trunk in the attic. Did you know? Dad did this?" Even though he was sure it was his father's carving tools, he wanted confirmation.

Uncle Lucas ignored the leather pouch and picked up the wad of newspaper, and unwrapped the carving. He held the bear, standing with its paws out as if clawing something. Its mouth wide open with teeth bared. Matt watched his uncle's reaction.

"He improved." Uncle Lucas set the first carving down and picked up the next one from the tray on his lap. Gnarled fingers smoothed the form of a bunny with its ears laid back and sitting on its haunches. Its nose pointed in the air, as if sniffing, while its paws held a lettuce leaf. Matt smiled despite his curiosity.

"When did he learn to do this?" Matt asked.

"I suspect your father did them when he needed to relax or to keep busy. He learned to carve from our father. Dad's side job at the furniture factory was to carve designs into the frames of some of the pieces. He saw Joseph had artistic talent and showed him how to do it. The two would sit around in the evening and whittle. You remember that flute you got when you were little?" Lucas looked from the figure to Matt.

Matt thought for a moment. A picture of opening a birthday gift of a flute came to his mind. He remembered blowing it until his mother demanded he go outside or put it away. He also recalled his father and mother had words about the flute. Matt put it away and later forgot about it. "I don't know where it went. I think I put it away when my mother complained. I don't remember ever playing with it again."

Uncle Lucas looked at the carvings. "You found these carvings hidden in a trunk." Matt nodded.

The older man stared down at the carvings. Matt saw his uncle's eyes water. "What?" Matt asked.

"Your father's talent was never appreciated. Your mother thought his whittling a waste of time. She never saw it as a release of stress or, possibly, a means of income. He was talented, and he hid it." He stroked the carvings with reverence.

Matt and Lucas pulled the truck from the attic to the main floor. The two unwrapped the pieces and set them out on the table. There were seventy-six carvings of animals. Like the two he had previously discovered, several animals stood in an aggressive stance. Others were cute and cuddly. Matt wondered if there was a market for them. Some he would keep; he would gift some to his siblings and their children if they wanted them, and he'd look for an outlet for their sale.

After spending the rainy day reminiscing about his father with Lucas, Matt retired to bed. As he listened to the rain on the roof, he sighed, his head swimming with memory and thoughts of what could have been.

The following morning, Matt rose early. The sun poured in through the windows, and outside, the roads were dry. The bright, clear skies lifted his spirits, and Matt whistled as he collected his overnight bag and briefcase by the door.

"Where are you off to?" Uncle Lucas looked up from his cup of coffee.

"I'm heading out to follow up a lead on Grandma Katherine. I plan on being home tonight, but if I'm not, I'll call you. There's food in the fridge." Matt slung the backpack over his shoulder.

"Fine, just leave me to starve," Uncle Lucas grumbled.

"If you get bored, call Sam or Kathy. I'm sure one of them will come over and babysit you." Matt kept his voice friendly.

"Hrumph!" was all he heard as he left the house with a smile on his face.

CHAPTER 26

MORGANVILLE, WV

September 2000

AT THE FRONT DESK OF THE COUNTY REST Home, Matt leaned on the counter and spoke to the receptionist. "I need to find out about a woman you have living here. Who can I talk to?"

The young woman picked up the receiver and spoke into the phone. After a brief conversation, she hung up. "Someone will be with you shortly, sir."

A few minutes later, a woman came toward him, her brown hair wrapped in a knot at the back of her head. She wore high heels, a tight navy pinstripe skirt, and a matching jacket barely buttoned under her breasts. A lacy camisole stretched across her bust.

She smiled at him and held out a hand in a limp touch to greet him. "Hello, I'm Chelsea Wilson, the manager here."

"Matt Sullivan." He took her hand and released it immediately, "Can we talk somewhere private?"

"Sure, come with me."

She led him to her office and motioned for him to sit while she walked around the desk. "I usually have a coffee break about now. Would you join me?"

Matt nodded, and she placed a call to add a cup and extra sweets to the plate. She sat down and smiled again.

"Now, what can I do for you?" she asked.

"I have information that you have a Katherine Sullivan living here. She would be in her nineties and have had no family visitors." He waited for her answer.

"Yes, we do have a Katherine Sullivan here, and indeed, she is in her nineties." What is your interest in her?"

"I believe she's my long-lost grandmother."

Matthew opened the notebook and leaned across the desk, showing her the census list with Sam and Katherine and the list of the children. Then he showed her his birth certificate that Joseph Daniel Sullivan was his father.

"Do you have any concrete evidence that the woman we have here is this Katherine Sullivan?" Chelsea pressed.

"If I did, I would've been here years ago. I didn't know anything about my grandmother until a couple of months ago."

She gave him a hard look. "You never questioned where your grandparents were?"

"I asked and got the answer, 'They're gone.' I assumed they were dead. I didn't think about stuff like that until my father died and my uncle got sick. Then I began to wonder about my family history. My grandfather died of tuberculosis; my mother and father both died of cancer. I couldn't find a death record for my grandmother and wondered what happened to her." He looked down at the notebook. "She lived in Millerton, West Virginia, and left there in 1948. I heard that she'd been sent to a sanatorium, and then when that place closed, she may have been sent here." He sat back in the chair.

They were interrupted when a young man brought in a tray with a coffee urn, two cups and saucers, and a plate of rolls and sweetbreads with butter pats. Chelsea poured the coffee and passed Matt the plate of sweets. She pressed a button and asked to have Katherine Sullivan's file brought to her when she finished. It arrived before Matt had consumed a danish.

After Chelsea read through the file, she laid it on her desk, not allowing Matt to see inside it. "Mr. Sullivan, it seems everything you told me is true. However, that could be public knowledge, and I have no idea if you are who you say you are. We're careful to protect those who are with us who can't protect themselves." She took a sip from her cup and peered over the rim at him.

"Then do you want a blood test taken? I would be more than happy to provide a DNA sample for you to compare to Katherine's." His voice had gone from amiable to terse.

"That's something I have to talk to her doctor about and to our legal department." She looked at her watch. "This isn't something that we can get to the bottom of today. Can you come back in a couple of days?"

"I can stay a day longer, but I need to be back home for Monday. However, if all the information I gave you matches Katherine Sullivan's file, then at least I say there's a pretty good chance she is my grandmother. Can I see her?"

"I'm sorry, but she's been ill. I can't let you talk to her until I clear your connection to her and her doctor allows her visitors."

Matt started to stand. "All the more reason for me to see her. If she's terminal, then she would want to know her family found her and love her."

"I understand. I'll talk to Ms. Katherine's doctor and see what she says is safe." Chelsea stood and walked around the desk to meet him, her hand positioned so that he had no choice but to walk with her to the door. "Give your phone number to my assistant, and someone will call you."

He passed through the doorway then turned. "Oh, I want my paperwork back." He brushed by her and took his folder, and tucked it under his arm. "I'll wait for your call tomorrow." He walked to the lobby and stopped at the desk of the woman he'd spoken to earlier to leave his phone number.

After booking a hotel room in town, he called his uncle to tell him he would be spending the night away from home and then called Selma. He relayed to her what Chelsea told him.

"Maybe this is the one time you should use your connection to your Uncle Henry." She laughed.

"I don't think so. I just searched the Internet to see if the doctors for the County Home were listed, but they aren't. I think I'll call over there and ask for the name of a doctor there."

"I don't think that'll work." She was silent for a while. "Sorry, I don't know what to do. Just wait to see what happens tomorrow. If you don't hear from anything by noon, go over there and sign in. Then walk down a hall and ask one of the staff what her room is. Tell them you were lost as you thought her room was 166."

Matt laughed. "That's a good idea. I'll try that. You're becoming a bit devious."

"It's rubbed off being around you." She teased.

Matt told her about the carvings he'd found and what his uncle said about them.

"Selma, I feel bad. All those years, he must've made his carvings in the attic and left them there where no one could see them. I'm getting a feeling that my mother and father weren't as in love as I always thought they were. Now that I think about it, I never saw them kiss, nor do I remember them ever showing any affection to each other.

As a boy, I never thought of it. As a young man, my life was too busy with college and then teaching. We were at the folks' home every Sunday for dinner until Kathy and Sam got married. Then the Sunday dinners were once a month. We talked and then left. I have a sick feeling that none of us has that affectionate gene. I'm going to talk to both my siblings. If they don't show affection to their spouses, they'll end up like Mom and Dad." Matt stopped talking. "Are you still there?"

Selma spoke. "You're amazing. I see in you a man who will work at his marriage to make sure his wife is happy, and in turn, you'll be happy." There was a pause, and she added, "Just the kind of man a woman would love to have."

"Including you?" he slipped in the gap then regretted it.

"Yes, including me." A pregnant pause followed the comment.

"Good." Matt let the comment pass.

They talked for a little longer and hung up. Matt lay on the bed, feeling better after talking to Selma. She wasn't afraid to tell him what she thought and add to his ideas. He daydreamed for a moment about coming home to her at night, sharing the cooking and cleaning, fighting, then making up. The making up might be more fun than all the other stuff.

The following day, Matt checked his phone every few minutes. At a restaurant near the rest home, he questioned some of the patrons.

"Do you have any friends or relatives in the County Home?" Matt asked the group sitting near him.

"I do. I have an aunt there. She likes it, and they are good to her." A white-haired woman spoke up.

"My parents were there. They lost their farm, and their health issues mandated they have total care. I have not had any problems with them. I have heard others who didn't get the same care for their loved ones." The man seated next to him added. "Were you thinking of putting your family member in the home?"

"I'm considering it." Matt took a drink from his cup to stall any further answer or questions.

One of the men at the counter turned around and called to a woman in a booth. "Hey, Shelly."

The woman got up and said goodbye to her booth mates and came to the counter.

"This young man is looking to put his relative at the County. Do you think you can take him for a little tour off the record? He wants to know what it's like and not the PR version."

Shelly looked at him and smiled. "Sure. I'm one of the occupational therapists. I'm on my way there right now, and I have a little time before my first appointment."

Matt slid off the stool and put a bill on the counter for the server. "I'm right behind you. Do you need a ride, or did you drive?"

"I could use a ride. I rode over here with my friends."

He showed Shelly where he'd parked his car, and then followed her directions to a side street and a back entrance of the rest home.

They went in the back door after she pressed a series of buttons on the security pad. Matt saw the notice that they were under surveillance. "So there's good security here?"

She laughed. "No, there isn't any. They bought the service for six months but didn't hook up any cameras. They let the service lapse but never removed the signs."

Shelly moved down the hall told him to wait while she put her things in her locker. The staff passed him, but none asked what he was doing there. When Shelly emerged dressed for work, he followed her down the hall to the main rooms. She talked about her job, and the food served, the activities, and the Home's housekeeping.

"Who are your favorite residents?" Matt asked. She named a few, but none were Katherine.

"Any idea who the oldest residents might be?" he slipped into the conversation.

"Oh, that would be Miss Katherine. She's in her nineties, and she's been here for years." Her expression turned serious. She smoothed her dark blond hair back to its clip. "It's sad. She doesn't have any family. She mentioned her sons and daughters, but none of them or their kids ever visited. We always give her a bang-up birthday party. If she makes it for another few weeks, we'll celebrate her ninety-seventh birthday."

"Can I peek in on her?" he whispered.

"I don't know. Katherine might be sleeping and hasn't been well."

They walked down a hall. Shelly stopped in front of a door and looked in the small window. "You can look through here." She stepped aside.

Matt took a deep breath and looked through the glass. The woman lying on the bed looked nothing like the wedding picture he'd found in the back of the Bible. Long, wavy white hair framed her face in stark contrast to the short, tight curls most women in the home wore. He could tell she was tall as her feet poked the sheets at the bottom of the bed, and her head almost reached the head rail.

His father was six feet tall, and his uncle was about the same height. He knew his aunts weren't that tall, but they also weren't short by any means. His height was something he had always taken for granted, used it to an advantage with the girls, but now he felt a particular pride as he looked at his grandmother. It was something she gave him.

As he looked for some facial resemblance to his family, her eyes opened. She felt someone watching her. Her pale eyes stared at the door and looked straight at him. Katherine's eyes widened and her hand went to her mouth. Her other hand reached for him. He looked at Shelly.

"She reached out to me. She saw me in the window." He moved aside and let her look through the window.

Shelly opened the door a few inches. "Miss Katherine, how are you feeling? Better? Good. What?" She moved into the room, and Matt stood at the doorway. Katherine looked past Shelly at Matt.

"Joseph," she called to him.

"No, I think his name is Matt." She turned to Matt, and her eyes widened as she looked past him.

"What's going on here?" a voice demanded behind him. Matt has pushed aside as a woman in a uniform came in.

"Miss Katherine is not to be disturbed. She hasn't been well and needs her rest." She turned to confront Matt and Shelly.

"Sorry," Matt said before Shelly could. "I was looking for the exit, and this woman was helping me. She noticed the woman calling out and stepped in to see if she could help her."

The nurse jabbed a finger down the hallway. "The exit is that way and two lefts to the front door." Matt nodded and winked at Shelly before retracing their steps and slipping out of the building.

Having never received a call from Chelsea, Matt called her from the parking lot. "I'm sorry, she isn't available."

"Oh, that's too bad. Ms. Chelsea is getting me Katherine Sullivan's doctor's name. Do you know who it is?" Matt kept his voice positive and friendly.

"Oh, of course, Sir. That's Doctor Sweeney. She isn't in today. Do you want her service number? They'll get a message to her."

"Yes, that would be helpful." He pulled the pen from his folder and wrote the doctor's name and number on the cover. After a long time considering it, Matt decided to stay one more night at the hotel and see Katherine again the following day. He called the school and told them he thought he might be coming down with something, and they went about setting up a substitute.

That afternoon, Matt relaxed in his room and waited for his grandmother's doctor to call. When the phone rang, he forced himself not to answer on the first ring and took several steadying breaths to try and soothe his excitement.

"Hello."

"What are you doing, boy? When are you comin' home?" Uncle Lucas's voice was gruff and a little worried. Kathy and Sam agreed to check in on him while Matt was gone, so he wasn't concerned about Uncle Lucas getting food.

He spoke low and slow. "Uncle Lucas, I found your mother."

"You did what? Did you found my mother? Where's she buried?" Lucas's voice was a little shaky.

"She isn't dead. In fact, she's going to have a birthday in a few days. The home here is going to have a big party for her."

"Did you talk to her?"

"No, but she saw me. She called me Joseph. I didn't think I looked that much like my dad."

"You have his face." Lucas coughed into the receiver.

"Uncle Lucas, are you okay? Have you been taking your medicine?" He could hear the heavy, uneven breaths.

"Lucas!" He heard the phone drop on the floor.

He hung up, dialed 911. After being transferred to Columbus 911, they dispatched an ambulance to his house. He told them where they could find a house key. He then called Sam and told him what happened to Lucas. He said he'd call Kathy and not to worry.

Matt paced the floor. He thought of Selma and called her. He explained what happened to Lucas as well as what happened at the County home.

"You covered that pretty fast. I bet Shelly was thankful. So you did see your grandmother? What's she like?" Selma's voice rose with excitement.

Matt described Katherine to Selma. "She isn't what I thought as I only have her wedding picture. Selma, she saw me and called me by my father's name."

"That's a good sign. I'd say it's a good possibility that she's your grandmother. What are you going to do now?"

"Wait, I guess. I have to find out what happened to Uncle Lucas. I'd better hang up and call home."

He dialed his house number and waited as it rang and went to his voice mail. He phoned back, and this time, someone answered it.

"Hello?"

"This is Matt Sullivan. I called about my uncle. How is he?"

The phone call transferred to someone else, and a different voice came on the phone. "Mr. Sullivan, it was good that you called us. His breathing and his heartbeat are irregular. We're taking him to the hospital. You can come and see him. I don't think he's in critical condition, but we're taking him in for observation anyway."

"I'm three hours away, but I'll be there tomorrow. My sister and brother should be there any minute."

"Yes, they're here." His brother took over the conversation and answered all his concerns.

Matt relaxed. It felt good to have his siblings there to take control of the situation and rang off. His hands shook a little as he put his phone on the table beside the bed.

With all the excitement, he couldn't sleep. He went downstairs to an all-night diner and had soup and a sandwich. Back in his hotel room, time passed as he stared at the ceiling.

Sometime after midnight, Matt dozed off. When he woke, the sun shone through the window. Matt covered his eyes as they adjusted and fumbled for the blinds. He'd slept in his clothes, and after he ran the toothbrush through his mouth, he was on his way back to Columbus.

CHAPTER 27

COLUMBUS, OH

MATT LEFT THE COLUMBUS HOSPITAL AFTER he made sure his uncle was in stable condition. It was a relapse due to stress, the doctors had said. He would need to keep calm until his heart healed more. Matthew watched the fragile older man in bed for a time but decided he wouldn't put off seeing his grandmother sit with his uncle.

When Matt got home, he listened to a message from Kenneth Mullins to call him right away.

Matt called the number, and Kenneth answered. When Matt identified himself, Kenneth passed the phone to Henry.

"What's wrong with Lucas?" Henry barked into the phone.

"He had a relapse. He's fine and will be home in a few days. He just needs some quiet time."

"What caused it? I thought he was fine. The doctor said he was eating regularly and gaining weight; that's why he was released to you." Henry's voice teetered on the edge of accusation.

"You have the doctor calling you with updates?" Matt asked as he hung his keys on the hook and his jacket in the closet, the phone tucked to his ear.

"Yes. Lucas is my brother. I've been keeping track of him for years. He gave me his savings to invest for him, and with my help, he made enough to pay off that farm from the old couple and bury them in a nice plot when the time came."

"I'm glad he had you to invest for him." Matt was frowning. Uncle Lucas had been at his house for some time, and he had been footing all the bills. Not that Uncle Lucas ate a lot, but Lucas never offered to help out in any way. Matt had been under the impression he lived on his social security checks.

There was that money he found, now stashed away safely in the office safe. He still had to deal with that problem. Neither uncle knew anything about it.

"What got him all fired up that he ended up in the hospital?" The voice was firm and authoritative, one of the things that made him a good politician.

Matt let the bomb drop matter-of-factly. "It was my fault. I called to check on him and told him I found his mother."

"You what?" Henry's voice a rapier in his ear. "I said I found your mother."

"How? I looked for her for years and never got anywhere with anyone in that town."

"I didn't get the information from anyone in the town. I was fortunate to be in the right place at the right time. Katherine will be ninety-seven years old soon." Matt picked up a blanket left in a ball on the floor. He folded it and set it on the recliner his uncle had made his own.

As he waited for Henry's reply, Matt shook his head at the pile of cups, plates, and trash on the end table next to his uncle's chair.

"Where is she?" Henry's voice was breathless.

"She's been ill. I'm not telling you until I talk to her doctor and find out her health. Then I'll let you know where she is."

There was some conversation between his uncle and someone else in the room. After a moment, Henry returned to the phone. "Where were you when Lucas had his episode last night?"

"What makes you think I wasn't here?" Matt countered.

There was a pause, and then Henry answered, "Never mind. I'll find out where she is."

"You couldn't find her for thirty years or more." The phone went dead.

Matt dialed the doctor's number. This time, a live voice answered.

"Doctor Sweeny's office."

"This is Matt Sullivan. I'm Katherine Sullivan's grandson. Could I speak with Doctor Sweeny about my grandmother's health situation? I need to know when I can visit her." Matt kept his voice confident.

"Doctor Sweeny is on rounds right now. I can leave her a message to call you." The woman was young and friendly. She didn't ask any questions about his authority to see Katherine.

"I left a message yesterday, and she didn't call me back," Matt countered.

"I'm sorry, that was my fault. I wrote the message down and left it on the doctor's desk; she didn't come back to her office and went straight to the hospital this morning." The woman's voice was apologetic.

"When will she be available to speak with, or when can you get a message to her with my phone number?" Matt dumped the trash he collected from around his uncle's chair into the garbage bin.

"I left her your number this morning on her cell phone's voice mail. In an hour, she will be finished with her rounds. I can't say for sure, but I've never known her to ignore a phone message."

"Thanks. I'll wait for her call."

Matt set the phone on its base and began pacing. He wanted to drive back to Morganville to see Katherine right then and there, but he was forced to wait. Again.

Trying to occupy himself, Matt went to his office and looked through paperwork to ensure he had everything he needed to prove his relationship with his grandmother. Nervous fingers smoothed the stained birth certificate with his father's name's tiny footprints in the corner. The file held all the credentials he'd found of his and his uncle.

An hour later, his phone rang.

"Hello." "Mr. Sullivan?"

"Yes, I'm Matt Sullivan.

"This is Doctor Jessica Sweeney. You left a message for me to call you." Her voice was rough, almost as if she were a smoker.

"Doctor, I've just recently discovered that I'm the grandson of Katherine Sullivan, your patient. I'd like to know if it's possible to visit her."

"Who is Joseph?" the woman asked. "That's my father."

"Could he have visited her recently?" The question was almost dismissive.

"Not in the physical. My father passed away a couple of years ago. Why do you ask?"

"I was with her this morning, and she asked to see Joseph and claimed he was in the window. I'm worried about her mental state.

Now that you say there is such a person, I wonder if she might have seen his spirit." The doctor's tone gave Matt hope.

Matt didn't want to reveal that he was the one she might have seen. Instead, he rubbed his damp palm on his pant leg. Adrenalin rushed through his veins. "Is she well enough for visitors?"

"Yes, I think so. She had the flu, but she's better now. I think she'd like to see you. You may not know, but her birthday is this Saturday. If you can come this week and stay for her party, I know she would love it." Now her voice was animated, then became serious. "You do have proof of your relationship?"

"I have census copies listing Katherine and her family. I also have the birth and death certificates of her children. My birth certificate—"

"That's enough for me. When can you see Katherine?"

"Would tomorrow be too soon? I can leave tonight and drive over and be there early in the morning." He hated to ask for a substitute this early in the school year, but there were more important things than teaching kids who were getting used to being back in school.

There was a laugh from the other end of the phone. "The staff gets the patients up early for breakfast, but most of them go right back to sleep for a few hours. I'd say if you come about ten-thirty, she'll be ready for visitors."

"Great. I'll be there at ten-thirty. Thank you, Doctor."

"I'll see you tomorrow." There was a pause. "If you don't mind, could you tell me why you're just now coming to see her after all these years?"

"I didn't know about her. I've spent the last two months looking for her." His voice became a little desperate. "I don't know what happened to tear my family apart, but I'm hoping to meet her and discover the story."

"I see. I hope I'm there to see this reunion. You have my cell phone number.

Call me when you get there."

Matt called his school asking for a family emergency leave, then called Henry's phone number.

Kenneth answered. "What do you want, Matthew?"

"I need to speak to my uncle." Matt kept his voice firm and a bit forceful.

"Sorry, but he's in a meeting. I'll tell him you called."

This man irritated him. Every time he spoke to Kenneth Mullins, something in the pit of his stomach rebelled, and that something was a certainty that the man had something to do with Tim's death. "Tell him I have some important information regarding his mother."

"Right. Look, young man, this is not the time to have this information go public. We're close to getting what we need for the presidency. We don't need this nonsense to interfere with the process."

"What does this have anything to do with votes?" Matt raised his fist in the air even though Kenneth couldn't see him. "This is about family, and I know Uncle Henry—"

"Matthew, we don't want anything to cause questions in the voters' minds," Kenneth snapped. "We've had enough close calls during this campaign. I think you should stop calling."

"What does Henry finding his mother have to do with votes?" Matt repeated, anger welling in his gut. He heard a snort of disgust.

"Henry is educated, comfortable in high society, and a class act. If people found his parents were no good Hillbillys and might even come from an incestuous family it would not be good for his image." Kenneth must have been walking as he seemed to be breathing hard.

Matt ground his teeth and spoke. "Just so you know, when I do talk to my uncle, and I tell him what you said, I don't believe he's going to be happy." Matt wished his cell phone was an old-fashioned receiver for a moment as he hit the disconnect button. It would have been much more satisfying to slam a phone down. After taking a few calming breaths, he called the hospital and asked to be transferred to his Uncle Lucas's room.

"How are you feeling today?" Matt asked his Uncle.

"Much better. The doctor says I can go home tomorrow." Uncle Lucas's voice sounded as strong as ever.

"I won't be here when you come to the house. I'll call Kathy and Sam to meet your transportation and get you settled in."

"Where're you going?" Lucas demanded.

"I'm going to see my grandmother." Matt put his briefcase on the floor next to the jamb of the office door.

"You found her, and you're sure it's her?" Now Uncle Lucas's voice softened and became almost childlike.

"Yes, I saw her before I left to come home to you. She saw me in the window and called out, thinking I was my father. I talked to her doctor and got permission to visit her. I'll be leaving in an hour or so. I'll be staying over the weekend as they're having a birthday party for her on Saturday afternoon."

"Call me when you talk to her. Tell me everything she says." His uncle's tone worried Matt. It was pleading, almost afraid.

Hearing the change in Lucas's voice reinforced the importance of his search and this meeting. Everything he'd gone through, everything he'd seen and heard was validated at that moment as Lucas all but begged.

"I'll call you after I talk to her, Uncle Lucas." Matt hung up the phone, his mind spinning with activity. Did he dare ask his uncle to come with him? What would it do to his heart? He didn't want the older man dying before he was strong enough to meet his mother. No, he decided, he had to be confident, and he had to make sure Lucas was well enough to make the trip.

Matt moved the overnight bag and briefcase into the car and drove out of town. Driving down the interstate, Matt dialed Selma's number. She answered his call before the first ring ended. "Matt?"

"It's me. Do you want to come with me to meet my grandmother tomorrow morning?"

"Of course I want to meet her. I'll leave right away and meet you there. It should take a few hours to drive to Morganville. I'm hoping you could get me a room at the same hotel where you're staying. Matt."

"That's a yes, I take it." A smile spread across Matt's lips.

"Thank you for inviting me. It means a lot to be included." Selma's whispered voice tickled his ear.

"You've been there the whole journey; you should be there at the end." He smiled. "See you soon."

The smile stayed on his lips as he drove the freeway toward his grandmother. The truth was in the details, and what he said to Selma had come from the heart. He couldn't wait to share the next great moments with her.

CHAPTER 28

MORGANVILLE, WV

September, 2000

ON SATURDAY MORNING, MATT MET SELMA in the hallway of the hotel. They kissed, and Matt put his arm around her waist as they went downstairs for breakfast.

"What do you think the story behind her leaving her family will be?"

"I don't know. I'm interested in finding Katherine's side of what happened all those years ago." Matt glanced at his watch. "It's nine-thirty. Why don't we see what's going on and if we can see her early."

As Matt drove down the street toward the County Homebuilding, he saw a commotion ahead. The vehicles filled the street. Matt inched their way toward the building. Media vans parked up and down the road in front of the entrance. Their large dishes faced the sky. Reporters milled around the entrance, and a stand of microphones graced a sitting area next to the steps leading to the front door of the County Home.

Matt turned down a side street and gritted his teeth in frustration.

"What's going on there?" Selma turned her head to watch the insanity.

"The media must've found out about Grandma Katherine." He cursed and followed the route Shelly had shown him, bringing them to the back service parking lot.

It was deserted other than a few vehicles presumably belonging to the staff. Matt grabbed his case, and together, he and Selma ran to the service entrance. A guard standing at the door waved them to leave.

"I'm here to see Dr. Jessica Sweeney," Matt called out. "I didn't want to risk taking the front entrance with the circus out there." The door didn't open, and the security guard stepped out of sight.

"What do we do now?" Selma pressed her face to the window.

"Thank Shelly." Matt typed the code Shelly had used into the pad next to the door and heard the click. With a smile plastered on his face, Matt grabbed the door and pulled it open.

The man, who had been at the door, stared at them in surprise and suspicion. "How did you know the code?"

"I told you I was here to see the doctor." Matt didn't wait for an answer and took Selma's hand, all but jogging down the hall.

Matt remembered the turns to Katherine's room to avoid the crowd of doctors, nurses, and elderly folk cluttering the hallways. After a few narrow misses with wheelchairs and linen carts, he stopped so quickly that Selma crashed into his back.

"What in the—" Matt yelped as he stared down the hall. Two women, one with a white lab coat and the other dressed in a designer suit, watched two familiar men, Henry and Lucas, march toward Matt and Selma.

Chelsea, the manager, tried to keep up in her spike heels and tight skirt, sputtering apologies, and excuses. The doctor stood between Matt and his uncle with her back to him. Still holding Selma's hand, Matt stepped into a clear area and waited for the two.

"Matthew." Henry nodded to him as they came to a stop by Katherine's door and Dr. Sweeney.

"Sir, I'm Doctor Jessica Sweeney. This is quite an honor. I had no idea you were related to our Katherine." She smiled at him.

Matt looked at the other man standing next to the candidate for President of the United States. If he hadn't been so angry at Henry, he would have burst out laughing. He was surprised his uncle would appear with his brother dressed as he was.

Uncle Lucas wore seersucker slacks, a plaid shirt, and a striped tie, none of which matched. How in the world did Uncle Henry allow Uncle Lucas out of the house dressed like that? If the TV cameras camped outside got a look at him, Henry's reputation was going to go into a tailspin.

Matt turned to the doctor. "I'm Matt Sullivan." He held out his hand.

She shook it and smiled. "We spoke on the phone yesterday."

"I can't believe this happened so quickly. I just met you yesterday, and now you're here. Katherine knows she's going to have visitors and is anxious to see you," the doctor said with a brilliant smile on her weathered face.

Chelsea moved to open the door; Henry stepped forward and touched her arm. "Ma'am, if you don't mind, I would appreciate this meeting to be private. The doctor said Katherine was ready for visitors. I think it would be less stressful for her if we go in."

Chelsea stood still, her hand on the door. Her lips pursed for a moment, and frustration blossomed on her face. Matt could see the stark hunger for the attention being the privilege would have netted her from the reporters outside. There was nothing she could do to force the issue. The woman nodded and stepped aside, her eyes narrowing at Selma to see if the other woman would be admitted.

Matt let go of Selma's hand. "Sorry. Stay on watch."

Despite the brief disappointment in Selma's eyes, she nodded and kissed Matt's cheek. "Sure, I'll keep an eye on her," she whispered.

When he followed his uncles into the room, Selma moved to stand in front of the window.

Matt stood near the door as there was only one chair next to the older woman's bed.

Katherine's freshly washed and dried white hair lay in soft waves, gathered in a neat tail behind her head. Around her shoulders lay a dingy gray bed jacket with the lace missing on most of the collar. A granny square afghan covered her lap and most of the lower part of the bed.

The woman's bright eyes inspected Henry's face first. When she was satisfied, her gaze moved to Lucas. He flinched and looked away; his Adam's apple bobbed as he swallowed repeatedly.

Katherine's expression softened and Matt saw the glimmer of tears on her cheeks. When her eyes moved to Matt, they narrowed.

"You were the one I saw in the window. You left without speaking to me," she accused.

Matt moved forward to stand by her side. "I'm Matthew Sullivan, Joseph's oldest son. I'm sorry I couldn't talk to you. I had to sneak in to find you. I got caught and had to leave."

"How did you find me after all these years? Why did it take so long?" She blinked back the moisture that had gathered.

"My father passed away two years ago. I found the family Bible and the letters you and Sam wrote to each other. Lucas had them. I decided to find out anything I could about you." He turned his eyes to his uncles, who remained silent.

"How did you find me?" She reached out to him with a hand that was more bone than skin. Matt wrapped her fingers in his and held them.

"It was an accident. I was in the hospital and met a woman named Rita. She talked to a friend who worked at the other place where you were." He hesitated to give it a name.

She filled in the unspoken word. "The asylum."

"Yes. I came to see if you were my grandmother, Katherine Sullivan. When you spoke my father's name, I knew."

"You didn't come back." It was more a question than an accusation.

"I had to drive back to Columbus to make sure Uncle Lucas was okay. He had quite a shock when I told him. As you can see, he's all right now."

Henry and Lucas remained silent, but their expressions showed a mixture of joy, shame, and nervousness.

"I have a question. One that I think we all want to know the answer to." Matt took a breath and looked at his uncles, who didn't argue.

"You want to know what happened to me all those years ago." She looked at each of them.

"You don't have to talk about it if you don't want to, Mother," Henry said after clearing his throat.

Matt glared at his uncles for a moment before turning back to the older woman. "If you don't mind telling it, I want to know why you were taken where no one could find you."

Katherine smiled and patted his hand. "Young people are so impatient." She looked at Lucas and motioned for him to sit beside her in the vacant chair across from Matt.

Lucas's eyes filled with tears. At first, he didn't move, but she gave him a long look, and he sagged in the seat.

"Ma," he choked. She held out her hand to him, and he took it in both of his. Then, as if someone sucked all the air out of him, he leaned over and began to sob. Lucas' body shook with the force of his sorrow.

"Oh, my Lucas, enough. It wasn't that bad." She let go of Matt's hand and reached over to pat Lucas's bent head. "It started with the women and men of Millerton."

She leaned back into the pillows. Her hand still clasped in Uncle Lucas's. "On the day we all met at the square to wait for the government trucks that would bring us our surplus boxes, it came to a head. I stayed in the wagon then went to the square where everyone else stood. Not one of them came to talk to me. I smiled and tried to speak to them, but everyone walked away.

"The truck was hours late, and everyone was restless and mad as hornets.

The women began making rude remarks to me, and someone yelled to Sheriff Beau that maybe I was a witch and responsible for the fires.

"The men tried to shut them up, but that only made it worse. The sheriff tried to stop them and send them home, but the women weren't having it." Her voice shook as if it were happening at the moment.

Matt leaned over to her. "Are you sure you want to continue? We can wait a moment."

"Matty boy." She grinned at him as if she had known him for all his life. It gave him a warm feeling somewhere around his heart. "I've had years to think and stew over this. At last, I can share this with someone who will understand." She patted his hand then continued.

"One of the boys came running into town, yelling the truck was on its way. Everyone lined the sidewalk as it parked near the square. You can imagine my shock when I saw my three boys in the front seat with the driver."

Henry choked, and Matt saw his eyes widen as the words burst forth. "The fire. Joseph and I ran into the house to try to put it out. The flames were up to the ceiling. I grabbed the blanket off the couch, and Joseph grabbed his toys. I sent Joseph to go to the road to flag down anyone there to come and help."

"Where was Lucas?" Matt asked.

Lucas raised his head. "Pumping water into buckets for Henry to throw on the fire. All of a sudden, a man broke one of the windows and threw me the hose, and I sprayed water until it was out."

"I wonder how the fire started?" Katherine asked no one in particular.

There was a long silence. Lucas' sobbing filled the silence. "It was my fault, my fault. I did it," he cried.

"Your fault?" Henry frowned at his brother's broken sobs. "I was outside. I came in to get something and saw the fire. What happened?"

"Upstairs. I heard you yell and came down," he mumbled. "Why did you say it was your fault?" Katherine broke in.

Lucas looked up at his brother then his mother. "I started a fire. I was the one who set the fires. I loved to start fires. I tried to be careful to keep them small, but sometimes, it just didn't work, and they got away from me."

"You set the fire at Ollie and Camila's house?" Katherine asked.

He nodded.

"The post office?" This time, her voice was low and soft.

Lucas nodded again.

Katherine tilted her head back and closed her eyes.

After a moment, Lucas reached out to her. "I'm sorry, Ma. I hated it when those men said bad things about you. I hated it when the women treated you like nothing. I got mad when I heard that the Post Mistress read your mail and passing your letters around to everyone. I didn't even think about it being wrong. I just wanted to get back at her for what she did to you."

The tears flowed, and Matt looked around to find a box of tissues. When he saw one, he offered it to Lucas, then squeezed the bony shoulder and remained by his side.

"You started all those fires? What were you thinking? You set our house on fire. You—" Henry looked like he might explode: his voice raised, his fists balled at his side as he leaned toward his brother. Matt moved to stand between them, ready to defend his Uncle Lucas if he had to.

"That's enough, Henry," Katherine snapped.

Henry shut his mouth and walked in a small circle, muttering to himself as he tried to let off steam. Matt was somewhere between surprised and amused to see the effect his mother still had on his uncle.

"Lucas, did you start the fire in the house on purpose?" Katherine reached out to touch her son's head. His forehead rested on the edge of the bed.

"Yes and no. I started the fire in the fireplace to burn some papers and boxes. I don't know how it set the rug on fire. I thought I put it out when I went upstairs." His voice sounded muffled.

"Did you stop the fire?" Matt interjected softly. This time, Henry answered, "Yes. The trucker used the hose to put out the fire. We tried to do it ourselves, but the wall and the ceiling up to the bedroom were gone."

"The whole floor's gone. That fire would've had to have been pretty big to put out with a simple garden hose. What happened to the bed? The dressers? When I was there, it was empty," Matt said, looking at his uncles in confusion.

"You were at the homestead?" Katherine looked at Matt for confirmation.

"Yes. Selma and I drove to the house. We wanted to find where Grandpa was buried and to see if there were any clues to where you went."

"I never went back. That wasn't allowed." Her face showed a deep, old sorrow.

"Grandma Katherine, what happened in town when the truck got there?" Matt needed to hear the end of the story, to know how she had vanished and why.

Henry sat on the edge of the bed next to Lucas and sighed, patting his brother's back. The door to the room opened, and Selma came in with two folding chairs. Matt turned and opened one for Henry, leaning the other against the wall. He didn't want to sit right now; he had too much going on in his head.

Selma whispered, "It's a zoo out front." Matt nodded to her, thanking her for the chairs before she slipped back out of the room.

With a sense of urgency, Matt turned to his grandmother. "Can you tell us what happened when the truck arrived in town?"

Katherine held the hands of her sons as she spoke. "The truck stopped, the boys spilled out of the cab and came running to me. They were dirty and covered with soot. Joseph hugged me and cried. You, Henry, hugged me and cried that you were sorry you couldn't save the house." She smiled. "You said the house was all burned up. Lucas stood there and said, "It wasn't burned up, just the living room and the girl's bedroom.""

Lucas nodded, still not looking up. "I was hugging the boys and talking to them as Sheriff Beau spoke to the driver. I looked up to see some of the men standing close, listening to what was said. I waited for them to stop talking and to start handing out the boxes. I wanted to thank the drivers for saving my boys. Then Sheriff Beau came to me and told me that he needed to talk about the fire.

"All of a sudden, the Mayor's wife started yelling, 'She started the fire!' Then the rest of the women picked up on it. They said awful things about how I tried to kill my boys to start over somewhere else and how I had a lover somewhere. It made me so sick. I could see the hate in their eyes." Katherine was stiff. Her hands left her sons to ball the quilt in her bony fists.

Matt recalled the people in the diner where he and Selma had eaten as his grandmother spoke. He could believe the ancestors of some of those people could very well have been the ones who had accused his grandmother of trying to kill his uncles.

"They kept yelling until Beau came to me and yanked the boys from my arms. He told me that he needed to calm the crowd, so he sent the boys away to be safe until he could check out everyone's story. They tried to take Lucas, but he fought them. Lucas, where did you go?" Katherine turned her eyes to her eldest son and reached out to touch his face.

"To the hills." He looked up at his mother. "You went to my family?" She frowned at him.

"No, I went to the shed I'd built up in the hills. I stayed there while I took stuff from the house there so no one would steal it."

"You have all my things?" Katherine's voice sounded hopeful.

"Not everything. I have most of the dishes, tablecloths, and some of your clothes. When people showed up to ransack the house, I put a note for the sheriff under his door, and he told everyone to stay away."

Henry spoke up. "I tried to go back, Mother, but they were holding us and hauling us away. Someone picked up Joseph and carried him off like a pig. They sent me off to the Garlands' house, where I was locked in a room. I tried to run away, but they caught me every time. It got so bad; they tied me to the bed at night. It was a rough few months. I cried for you and my brothers."

Henry looked at the window. "The Garlands were good to me. They had no other children and gave me lots of toys. A tutor came to teach me for a while, and then I went to a school. When I turned nineteen, I went to college." He looked at his mother, and, to Matt's surprise, the man blushed. "Now I'm a candidate for President of the United States."

"I'm proud of you, Son. I thought you must be my Henry when I watched the news."

Henry reached across Lucas and gently squeezed his mother's arm. "I went back to Millerton years ago, looking for you," Henry continued. "When I started asking questions, Sheriff Lavon found me and told me to leave. He told me my mother had left town and no one knew where she was. I blew him off and continued to ask anyone I saw, but I found out he was right. None of the people I stopped would even look at me.

"At the house, I found a few things left that I took. When I got back to the campus, I called the police and asked them what to do. They said to hire a detective." He ended with a tone of resignation. Henry brushed the leg of his pant leg to remove some invisible speck.

"Did you?" Matt asked his uncle. He looked beyond the sports jacket, custom-made shirt, and perfectly pressed pants for the first time to see the lost little boy wanting to find his mother.

"Years later, but he found nothing."

Matt stood and walked over to the window. The view outside showed an enclosed courtyard with a few trees, some benches, and several flower beds. People crowded other windows, and a few lingered in the yard with long lenses on their cameras, clicking away.

CHAPTER 29

MORGANVILLE, WV

MATT CLOSED THE CURTAINS TO KEEP THEIR privacy, and the room went dark. He flicked the lights on as he returned to his chair. Everyone in the room fell silent for what seemed like an eternity, all lost in their thoughts.

"Where were we?" he asked, breaking the stillness in the room.

Henry shook himself and picked up where he left off. "After I finished college and started working on Wall Street, I hired another detective." He made a snorting noise. "That was a waste of money. He ran into the same roadblock I did. In three months, he could find nothing about where you were. I was sure if you had left us—and what I had been told all my life was accurate—you had to work, but he never found any record of it.

Unless you were a lady of the night or married to some rich guy, I thought there had to be something. There wasn't. Not even a death certificate. I gave up."

"You were always my golden boy. Smart as a whip and always thinking up things and trying to make life easier. Remember how you got water from the creek to the garden? It worked great until the creek dried up." They laughed a little, and Katherine smiled at him like an indulgent mother.

"I don't have any pictures of Dad or you. Lucas had them, I guess," Henry accused.

Matt bit a grin back. He thought, *at least they acted like brothers.*

Matt reached into his messenger bag and pulled out the family Bible. Turning to the back, he pulled out the wedding photo he found and handed it to Henry.

Henry pulled a pair of glasses from his front pocket and put them on. He looked up and frowned at Matt. "Where did you get this?"

"I found the Bible on Dad's desk." He looked at Katherine. "What happened to you after they took the boys away?"

His grandmother folded her hands on the quilt and turned to him. "The women and some men were still screaming at me, accusing me of starting the fire to kill my children. Sheriff Beau stood in front of me, but I saw some women pick up rocks. Beau pushed me into his car and drove across the square to the jailhouse. The women and men taunted me as we went, saying that was where I belonged, and I would never see the light of day again." Katherine's voice shook, and she steadied her hands against the afghan on her lap.

"Beau told me that I had a choice. If I moved in with him, he would get the boys back, but if I didn't, he couldn't stop whatever the town wanted to do to press charges against me. I didn't want to make that choice right away, so he locked me in jail." The woman sighed, looking at once frail and sad, weary of the years weighing heavily on her thin shoulders.

Lucas reached over to take her hands in his. "I tried to get you out." Katherine looked surprised at his words. "I tried to get in the jail to break you out, but Beau had deputies inside and outside the whole time you were there. They almost caught me, so I had to go back to the shed and hide. When I came back to town, you were gone." The last part of the sentence showed his despair.

"Lucas, you couldn't have done anything. I refused Beau's offer. Even if he'd asked me to marry him, having to live in that town would've been cruel to you boys and the death of me.

"The judge arrived from the county seat to hear what everybody had to say about me. They told the judge I started the fire, that I tried to send my boys to other farms, and then I would go out of town for days at a time. I don't remember all that was said, but the judge said I had not committed a crime.

"Then Mr. Beacon's wife whispered to her husband. He asked the judge, 'Isn't it true if a person cannot care for themselves or their children that the state will care for them?'

"They got their way. The judge sent me to an insane asylum, and that's where I've been for all these years. I wrote letters to Cassie and Ben, but they never answered. I'm not sure the letters were ever sent.

"I tried to be friends with nurses to pass me information about my boys and my friends. They wouldn't do it. When new directors arrived, I tried to get my status changed, but it never happened. It wasn't a bad life. I got three meals, clothes, and I got to see movies and sew. I even got to make some of my favorite cakes and pies, but I couldn't leave the grounds."

Matt couldn't stop the tears that welled in his eyes as he thought about how that must have felt. She hadn't deserved that.

Katherine wiped the tears from her own eyes. "When they closed that place down, I thought they might release me. I had a long meeting with the director, but I couldn't provide anyone to take me in and give me a home. I didn't know if any of my children were alive or if they even knew me."

Matt stood and walked to the door, running his hand through his hair. "If we had just known where you were, if you were alive or not, we could've done something."

"It isn't worth looking back. I look to the future. I've had a good life. Not as good as it could've been, I wasn't abused in any way. I had many freedoms since I wasn't insane, and I learned a lot. I know sign language, and I can speak Spanish pretty well." Katherine drew herself up and stuck her nose in the air before breaking into laughter. It was infectious, and soon everyone in the room joined in on her merriment.

Henry stood up. "I have to concentrate on my campaign, but I'm putting Matt here in charge of taking care of you for now. My lawyers will see to it that you get whatever you need.

"I'm sure the media is going to have a feeding frenzy about all this. I hope you won't talk to them until after the election. We have a month and a half to D-Day. I trust the rest of you to keep the story to a minimum. That means you, Lucas."

The older man nodded. "I haven't talked to them yet, and I don't figure on that changin'."

Henry walked over and touched Katherine's shoulder. "I have to go. As soon as Matt can find a home in Columbus, we'll get you moved. I have a meeting. I'll have Kenneth make sure no reporters bother you. I also need to have him prepare a press release for me." He checked his watch then looked at the woman in the bed.

"Mother." Henry stuck both his hands in his pockets like a small boy. Matt suppressed a smile. His Uncle Henry, the man who had the confidence to run the most powerful country in the world, was at a loss for words.

Katherine reached out both hands to him, and Henry went to her and kissed her cheek.

"I'm glad Matthew found you. I promise you I will never allow our family to be apart again." Henry looked at his brother. "Wipe your nose, Lucas. Sit up." At his firm words, Lucas sat up and smoothed his tie with shaky hands before scrubbing his face with a wadded tissue.

Henry turned to Matt. "Matt, I've been handling Lucas's affairs, but the man has no clothes! I almost left him home when he walked out looking like that."

Uncle Lucas started to speak up to defend himself at those words, but Henry frowned at him. Lucas glared at his brother.

"Boys…" Katherine's tone was a warning. Lucas laid his hand on her arm. "Sorry, Ma."

"Yes, I'm sorry," Henry added. "Matt, you will buy Lucas some nice clothes. I don't want to go to dinner with—this." He swept his hand from Lucas's head to toe. "When I win this election, I want my family beside me, dressed nice." Henry pulled out his wallet and handed Matt some folded bills. "Let me know if there's more needed."

"I'll take care of it, Uncle Henry. Don't worry about anything." Matt put the bills into his pocket without looking at them.

Henry nodded and waved before heading out the door. Selma took that chance to peek in. Matt saw her looking around the door frame and motioned her to enter.

"Grandma Katherine, this is Selma Greeley. She lives in Millerton and helped me find you." He held Selma's hand and smiled at her.

Katherine smiled back at the young woman with knowing eyes. "I'm happy to meet you, young lady. Greeley? Do you have any relations in the Hills area?"

Selma stepped to Katherine's side and answered, "Yes, Ma'am. They're just across Tanner's Holler. You might have known my aunts, Gemma and Ginny? They're twins."

"Yes, I do." Katherine closed her eyes and stayed quiet, and then she opened her eyes and looked at Selma. "They had red hair." Selma nodded and looked at Matt with a twinkle in her eye.

"You'll probably be seeing more of her as we're dating." Matt offered. Selma just smiled at him and squeezed his fingers.

"I look forward to talking to you about what's happening on the mountain," Katherine said, and Selma nodded and stepped away from the bed.

Lucas sat still, his hands laced on his lap. "Ma, how come I couldn't find you? I looked all over. After the night I went to try and get you out of jail, you were gone."

Katherine turned her eyes to him. "Lucas, you may have started the fire that burned our house, but there is no way you were responsible for what happened later. The anger towards me was there already. When you showed up and told me about the fire, it was just the opportunity to hurt me. They wanted me out, and accusing me of starting the fire to kill you all was just a convenient story."

Tears flowed down wrinkled cheeks on both mother and son, and Lucas buried his head in the hand he held. His words muffled until Katherine stroked his gray hair. "I can't hear you."

"I should've spoken up. I should've told the sheriff I started the fire, but I was afraid he would figure out I started the other fires." His sobs filled the room. "I was afraid he would put me in jail forever. I didn't know they'd take you from us."

"I can't tell you what might have happened or how things might have changed. It happened, and we have to deal with it."

Matt opened his mouth to speak, and then stopped. What did he call her? He'd referred to her as Katherine for so long that he didn't relate to the fact she was his grandmother. He cleared his throat a couple of times, trying to dislodge the lump that rose. "Ah… Can I call you Grandma?"

Katherine looked at him. "I'm so proud of you. I tried to find my children. One of the nurses even went to Millerton, but no one would tell her where they were. She was told to leave town and not to bother people with that memory, that it was sad what I had done to my children."

"Don't you have to pass some test that proves you're insane to be committed?" Selma asked. She stood behind Matt in the chair Henry had vacated.

"I always suspected the mayor and some of the other people in Millerton had paid off the judge to forge papers to have me committed. My guess is someone continued to pay to keep me there and isolated. None of my letters were mailed. One of the nurses told me they had orders to bring all my mail to the director. I stopped writing." She lay back against the pillows. She took a big breath and let it out.

"Are you tired? Do you need to rest?" Matt leaned forward, his hand on her arm.

"A little, but this has been a wonderful day. I have my family back. There is so much I want to know. Where are the girls and their families?"

Matt answered her question. "I'm sorry, but Aunt Emma, Aunt Martha, and their spouses have passed. My father, Joseph, and my mother, Betty, are also deceased."

A tear slid out of the corner of her eye and disappeared into her hairline. "It's a sad thing to outlive your children," Katherine whispered.

Matt kept his hand on his grandmother's arm. "I know. I miss them, too.

I'm sorry. We'll contact my cousins and have them meet you."

The door opened, and Dr. Sweeney stepped in. "I think Miss Katherine needs to rest now. Today has been a big day for her. She needs to eat, and I want to check her over. You can come back tomorrow."

Matt leaned over and kissed his grandmother's cheek. "We'll see you tomorrow morning. I'll leave my phone number with the nurses at the desk if you need anything."

She patted his arm and smiled at Lucas as he also kissed his mother. "Lucas, don't fret about this all night," she ordered. He nodded and stepped back to stand near the door.

The four of them stood in the hall as nurses and staff walked by and stared at them. Out of the corner of his eye, he spotted one of the staff taking photos with a small camera he thought he was hiding.

Matt turned his back to the man, took Selma's and Lucas's arms, and hurried down the back hall toward his car.

At the door to the parking lot, Matt peeked outside. Other than the few cars that had been there when they had arrived, no one seemed to have discovered this back door. Relief flooded Matt as he pushed the door open and motioned to the others.

"Let's get out of here. I'm sure someone called by now and told the reporters we're in the back."

The three of them ran straight to his car. Just as they reached it, a woman and man carrying a camera popped up from behind a van near them and approached them at a run.

"Get in the car!" Matt ordered his companions as he fumbled with his keys to unlock the doors. They were almost in the car when the pair reached him. The woman shoved a microphone toward him.

"Matthew Sullivan! Can you tell us why your uncle was at this rest home? Who did you visit?" The woman fired questions at him as he started to get in the car.

"No comment." Matt slammed the door and started the car.

The reporter stood beside the car window while the cameraman focused this lens on Matt and the others. Outside, he could hear her muffled voice still asking questions. "How are you related to the Senator?"

Matt turned away to look behind him as he put the car into reverse and backed away, leaving them standing in the lot.

"I can just see the news tonight," Selma said. She held her fist up to her mouth like a microphone and spoke like a reporter. "We're on location at the County Rest Home where Senator Sullivan and an unknown man entered to visit someone there. We were there when Matthew Sullivan and the unknown man and woman left by the back door. Matthew refused to comment. We'll see if we can get any of the staff to speak to us to see who they visited here and why."

Lucas didn't laugh, but Matt smiled a little.

"What are they going to say when they find out who we are?" Selma added. "A lot, I'm afraid. From now on, you don't answer the door here or at my house," Matt ordered Lucas. "This is only going to get worse until after the election. There will be a media tornado, and we'll be at the center of it." He gave Selma an apologetic smile.

The news vans lined with reporters assembled on the front steps to the rest home at the corner. Matt turned away from them and kept an eye on the rearview mirror to see if anyone followed. He was sure he was in the clear until he noticed a car following at a distance.

"Uncle Lucas, you got your seatbelt on?"

"Yes."

"Selma?"

She nodded. "Yes."

"Then hold on. We have to lose this tail."

Matt turned the car down an alley. He didn't know his way around this small town, and there was no way he could keep the media out of his life from now on, but he could for at least for tonight. Matt turned down one street then another until he lost the tail and pulled into another hotel with private parking.

"Stay here." Matt jumped out. Inside, he looked around and was glad to see the lobby empty of patrons. A maid ran a vacuum across the geometrically patterned carpet. The manager who booked his rooms promised their clients would have privacy, but Matt paid cash to ensure no one could pull up his credit history.

After booking their rooms, Matt returned to the car and drove into the private parking area, finding a spot in the middle not visible from either opening to the street. Matt kept an eye for slow-driving cars while Selma and Lucas carried their things inside.

The security door closed behind them, and Matt sighed in relief, sagging against it for a moment before following his uncle and Selma up the stairs. In Lucas's room, Matt upended the brown bag and frowned at its contents. Inside, he discovered three left shoes, a pair of torn underwear, and a single sock with more holes than material.

When Matt looked at Lucas, the older man shrugged. "I had to pack light."

"We're going shopping."

He walked to the connecting door and knocked. Selma opened her side. "I'm taking Lucas shopping." Matt pointed to the small pile of "clothing" on the bed, and Selma grimaced.

Matt shook his head, "I'll find a shop we can get in and out of as fast as possible."

Selma smiled at Lucas. "It might be easier to measure his waist and inseam. It will give you an idea where to go instead of having him try everything on."

"How am I going to get that?"

"You can get a measuring tape at a department store."

"Come on. I have no idea what to get or how to do that."

Selma chuckled and grabbed her purse, locking the connecting door, and waited for the two men. Lucas protested loudly, but Matt knew his heart wasn't in it.

After a bit of wandering, the group found a department store and bought Lucas jeans that fit correctly, pullover shirts, several buttoned shirts, boots, loafers, socks, and underwear. Finally, Matt took him to a barber and got Lucas a haircut, much to his disagreement.

After a brief discussion, Selma helped Matt and Lucas buy birthday gifts for Katherine's party tomorrow: a bed jacket and a matching nightgown with slippers of the same color. Matt had no idea what size his grandmother wore, but they guessed anyway.

"I'll bet she has big feet. She could almost wear my shoes when I was a teenager." His lips rose in a pleasant memory, and then disappeared just as quick.

The following day, Lucas joined Selma and Matt for breakfast looked as if he might be the brother of a Senator running for the President of the United States.

Selma whispered loud enough for Lucas to hear, "Who is the handsome man at our table? Do we know him?"

"Oh, come on," Uncle Lucas grumbled and picked up the menu, hiding his red face behind it.

Matt bought the local paper and looked for the latest news on the previous day's event. The front page showed Matt, Selma, and Lucas getting in their car. The camera had caught them as they all looked up at the same time.

"We look pretty good." Matt's sarcasm leaked out. "Good thing we went shopping yesterday."

Breakfast at the hotel passed without conversation, and they left for the rest home a little over an hour later. Matt wasn't surprised to see news vehicles displaying every network he'd ever heard of and several he hadn't in front of the Home.

Matt drove to the back entrance, where more media personnel waited.

"It's no surprise they found our secret entrance." Matt sneered.

Matt drove past the lot and pulled to the curb before turning to the other two. "We don't have a choice. We're going to have to face them. Uncle Lucas put your hat on."

Selma reached over to squeeze his arm. "We have to do it. I say we just go for it. If we walk fast, stay confident, and say nothing, it'll be fine."

Despite the media frenzy outside, Matt felt good. He had someone supporting him and wanted to be with him. They were going to visit his grandmother, his grandmother.

"Maybe we should've bought uniforms," Matt offered as they pulled past the reporters and camera crews to the lot entrance. He could hear them as they clicked every second or so.

Someone had lined the entrance with barricades, and the same security guard stood in the opening.

Matt pulled to the opening, and the guard stopped him. Matt rolled down his window facing the guard. The man recognized Matt and waved them through.

The media pressed close to the car yelled, "It's the kid. He's the nephew of Candidate Henry Sullivan!" Others joined the rush for the car, but the security guard held them back.

When the three got out of the car, reporters yelled questions at them as they hurried inside. Matt let the little group inside, relieved to discover that the code to the back door hadn't changed.

Once they arrived in the main sitting area, they found it decorated with streamers and balloons printed with Happy Birthday. A banner announced, "Happy Birthday, Katherine!" and her age of ninety-seven. At Katherine's door, a uniformed guard stood on duty to forestall intrusions.

"We're Katherine's family," Matt informed the guard, but he didn't move. "What's the problem here?"

"None, sir, but no one is allowed in unless pre-authorized." The officer stood, his feet spread, and arms crossed, and barred the door.

"We're her family," Matt explained. "Do you have authorization?" The guard repeated.

"Come on, who do you think we are?" Matt's voice rose, and Dr. Sweeney came rushing down the hall.

"How did you get in here?" The doctor's voice was more curious than angry as she stopped several feet away. Director Chelsea followed right behind her, fixing her hair.

Matt used his best teacher voice. "It doesn't matter. I want to see my grandmother."

Dr. Sweeney nodded. "Of course, of course." She waved the guard aside.

The guard moved to admit them, and Chelsea glared at the doctor but said nothing as they moved into Katherine's room.

Katherine sat in a chair next to her bed. Her hair combed, wearing a light blue blouse and matching skirt. She had a black sweater thrown over her shoulders and buttoned at the top. Her serious expression changed to one of joy at the three as they entered.

"Happy Birthday, Grandmother." Matt kissed her cheek. He then moved aside and let Lucas greet her.

The door opened behind them, and Henry entered the room with a broad smile on his face. "Happy Birthday, Mother." He crossed the room, kissed her cheek before placing a large, brightly-colored bag on the table next to her.

Lucas presented his mother with the presents they had bought during their shopping trip the day before. "I thought you might want to wear something new to the party." He grinned at her like a kid wanting his mother's approval.

Katherine smiled and opened the present. "Oh, how thoughtful, Lucas.

They're lovely. And so soft, too!"

Uncle Henry put his gift on the bed next. Katherine smiled as she unwrapped the red knee-length colored skirt and matching blouse.

"How'd you know my size?"

Uncle Henry wiggled his eyebrows, a massive grin splitting his usually somber feature. "I have my sources." They all laughed.

The group stepped out into the hallway while the nurse helped Katherine change into her new outfit, and when she emerged wearing the new bed jacket over the blouse, no one said a thing.

EPILOGUE

ENRY INVITED LUCAS, MATT, AND SELMA TO the hotel the evening of the election. They excused themselves and chose to spend the evening with Katherine. When the votes were tallied, Henry didn't win. Henry spoke with Katherine and promised to visit with his wife as soon as the media attention died down.

It wasn't long after the election when Matt saw a news brief that Kenneth Mullins was taken into custody for his possible involvement in the death of a young freelance writer. The Columbus Police refused to comment.

"Uncle Henry, what's going on with Kenneth?" Matt asked when he spoke with Henry.

"You've seen the news; I take it."

"I can't help it; they have him in the Columbus jail. Did he honestly have something to do with Tim's murder?"

"I have no idea. I didn't know the young man or have any contact with him."

"If that's the truth, Uncle, I'd stick to it. I feel bad that Tim died after helping me. I hope they catch his killer."

"Me, too." Henry's answer was short and clipped.

Kenneth was found guilty of conspiring to murder Tim Pelton. Kenneth had treated one too many of his employees with disrespect, and they turned him in.

Lucas sold his house to the developer and moved to a retirement center. Matt went to his apartment and cleaned out anything his uncle seemed to accumulate. Lucas grumbled, but not too much. The staff kept his apartment clean and tidy.

A few months after the election, Matthew Sullivan asked Selma Greely to marry him on February fourteenth. She said yes, according to the local engagement page.

They married six months later in a small chapel outside of Millerton. It was a family affair to Katherine's delight, including her relatives and Selma's from the Hills.

Henry arranged for Katherine to move to a facility near Matt and Lucas. Her other grandchildren and great-grandchildren came to visit.

Lucas visited her almost every day. Her grandchildren and great-grandchildren, as well as some great-great-grandchildren, had their pictures with her. A national television station anchor interviewed her.

"I will not talk about what happened on that day. It's enough that I know it, and my family knows what happened. The people of Millerton, West Virginia, will have to deal with their conscience on their own. I don't hold grudges. I have my family, and I'm happy." Katherine responded to the reporter's question.

The new anchors respected her wish and spoke very little about the actual incident and more about what happened to people who were committed without cause.

Matt researched any bank robberies or any private robbery of large sums of money. None of the serial numbers he had matched numbers of known thefts.

The following summer Selma told the family that Rose passed away. A month later, Lucas received a letter requesting permission for Cecelia to visit him. He agreed but told Matt he wondered what she wanted.

"Just listen with an open mind, Uncle," Matt advised him.